Scotland Reformed:

The Reformation
in Angus and the Mearns

Scotland Reformed:

The Reformation
in Angus and the Mearns

FRANK D. BARDGETT

JOHN DONALD PUBLISHERS LTD
EDINBURGH

ISBN 0 85976 261 0

Distribution in the United States of America and Canada by
Humanities Press Inc., Atlantic Highlands, NJ 07716, USA.

Phototypeset by Beecee Typesetting Services
Printed in Great Britain by Bell & Bain Ltd., Glasgow

Acknowledgements

I owe a considerable debt of gratitude to the Rev. Professor A.C. Cheyne, former Principal of New College, for giving me the initial encouragement to set aside three years for post-graduate research — a decision that I have never regretted. Apart from academic satisfaction, hunting down sources for the thesis which preceded this book brought with it new friends and Christian fellowship. The families who acted as my hosts during research trips or for more extended periods provided so much more than bed and board. That the work was ever concluded at all owed a great deal to, in Edinburgh, Jean and Alick Lothian and Kathleen and John Barclay; in Dundee, to Kathleen and Iain Phillips; in Manchester, to Mary and Bob Watson; in Glasgow, to Mary and Douglas Wiseman. Hospitality, support and encouragement were unstintingly provided by my parents, Mr and Mrs S. Bardgett, and my parents-in-law, Dr and Mrs J.B. Barclay. Permission to view and use various private archives was much appreciated and is given detailed acknowledgement in the Bibliography; however, I must record my gratitude to the Rt. Hon. the Earl of Southesk for his hospitality at Kinnaird Castle and to Professor Gordon Donaldson for giving me access to his record-card collections. The scholarship and friendship of members of the Scottish History Departments of the Universities of Edinburgh and Glasgow in welcoming a convert from a Divinity Faculty was exemplary — as was, especially, the committed and challenging example of Dr Michael Lynch. The interest and encouragement of Mr John Middleton and Mrs Joan Morris greatly assisted the task of composition. I must thank my wife, Alison, for preventing me from making many errors and for cartographic and other advice offered; and must also apologise to her for providing her, somewhat unexpectedly, with an education-by-extension in both Church History and post-graduate Scottish History. Finally, I wish to thank the Hope Trust for assisting with the costs of publication.

Frank Bardgett
Strathy Manse, January 1989.

Contents

Abbreviations

ADCP
Acts of the Lords of Council in Public Affairs, 1501-1554, ed. R.K. Hannay (Edinburgh 1932)

APL
Arbroath Public Library

APS
Acts of the Parliaments of Scotland, ed. T. Thomson and C. Innes: 12 vols. (Edinburgh 1814-75)

AUL
Aberdeen University Library

Brechin tests; also Edin. tests. and St.A. tests.
Ms registers of Brechin, Edinburgh and St Andrews testaments, SRO

BUK
Acts and Proceedings of the General Assembly of the Kirk of Scotland, ed. T. Thomson (Bannatyne and Maitland Clubs, 1839-45)

Calderwood, *History*
History of the Church of Scotland by Mr David Calderwood (Wodrow Society 1842-9)

CSP(F)
Calendar of State Papers Foreign (various series)

CSP(S)
Calendar of the State Papers relating to Scotland and Mary Queen of Scots, 1547-1603, i (1547-1563), ed. Joseph Bain (Edinburgh 1898) and subsequent volumes

Diurnal
A Diurnal of Remarkable Occurrents that have passed within the country of Scotland, since the death of King James the Fourth till the year 1575 (Bannatyne and Maitland Clubs 1833)

ER
The Exchequer Rolls of Scotland, xvi (1529-36), ed. George Powell McNeill (Edinburgh 1897) and subsequent volumes

IR
Innes Review

JEH
Journal of Ecclesiastical History

JRL
The John Rylands University Library of Manchester

Knox's History
John Knox's History of the Reformation in Scotland, ed. W.C. Dicksinson
(Edinburgh 1949)

Knox, Works
The Works of John Knox, ed. D. Laing (Edinburgh 1846-64)

L&P Henry VIII
Letters and Papers, foreign and domestic of the reign of Henry VIII, ed. J.S. Brewer
and others (London 1864-1932)

LHT
Accounts of the Lord High Treasurer of Scotland, eds. T. Dickson and Sir J. Balfour
Paul (1877-1916)

MTH
Montrose Town House, Montrose

NLS
National Library of Scotland, Edinburgh

NRA(S)
National Register of Archives (Scotland)

NRH
New Register House, Edinburgh

PRO
Public Record Office, London

RCRB
Records of the Convention of the Royal Burghs of Scotland, 1295-1597 (Edinburgh
1866)

REB
Registrum Episcopatus Brechinensis, ed. J.I. Chalmers (2 vols. Aberdeen 1856)

RFVA
Draft calendars of materials in the Vatican archives: held at Glasgow University's
department of Scottish History, derived from Ross Fund materials.

These include: ASPA   Acta Sancti Paenitentiarae Apostolicae
                 Reg.Lat.   Registra Lateranensa
                 Reg.Sup.   Registra Supplicationum
                 Reg.Vat.   Registra Vaticana
                 SRR   Sacra Romana Rota

RMS
Register of the Great Seal of Scotland: Registrum Magni Sigilli Regum Scotorum, 1513-1546, ed. James Balfour Paul and J.M. Thomson (Edinburgh 1883) and subsequent volumes

RPC
The Register of the Privy Council of Scotland, i, ed. J.H. Burton (Edinburgh 1877) and subsequent volumes

RSCHS
Records of the Scottish Church History Society

RSS
Register of the Privy Seal of Scotland: Registrum Secreti Sigilli Regum Scotorum, ii (1529-42), ed. D.H. Fleming (Edinburgh 1921) and subsequent volumes

StAUL
St Andrews University Library

SFBC
Year-book of the Society of Friends of Brechin Cathedral

SHR
Scottish Historical Review

SHS
Scottish History Society

SRO
Scottish Record Office, Edinburgh

SRS
Scottish Record Society

STS
Scottish Text Society

WRH
West Register House, Edinburgh

Conventions

1. Place-names are given (where possible) in the form in which they occur on the Ordnance Survey *Landranger series* maps, sheets 44, 45, 53 and 54. John Ainslie's 1 inch to 1 mile *Map of the county of Forfar* (Edinburgh 1794) has also been consulted at the NLS map room, Edinburgh.
2. Personal names have been, reluctantly, modernised in the interests of standardisation. The 'Lichtoun' lairds of 'Ullishaven' thus become the Leightons of Usan. 'Symmer' is used rather than 'Somer' or 'Summer' for the ancient house of Balzeordie. 'Gardyne' demonstrates the laird of that ilk; otherwise, 'Garden' is used.
3. In transcribing documents from manuscripts, contractions have been expanded, with additional characters placed in [square brackets]. '&' has been rendered 'and'; 'y' is used for the sixteenth-century character called thorn and 'z' for yogh. Names are normally capitalised, and punctuation introduced where this seems obvious. Original usage of 'w', 'v' and 'u' has not been altered. In numerals, 'j' has been transcribed as 'i'. G.G. Simpson, *Scottish Handwriting, 1150-1650* (Aberdeen 1983) has been of great assistance.
4. Documents cited from printed works are given as printed and may not, therefore, adhere to the conventions above.
5. In the interests of clarity and authenticity dates which occur within the overlap between the old and new calendars are given as, for example, 'January 1559/60'. This form serves to preserve the text of the original while acknowledging our present methods of counting time.
6. The currency used was expressed as merks, pounds, shillings and pence and is cited as Scots and not English.

    1 merk = 13s. 4d.
    12 d. = 1 s.
    20 s. = £ 1 Scots.

    For an up-to-date guide to Scottish currency, weights and measures, see: *The Concise Scots Dictionary*, ed. M. Robinson (Aberdeen 1985), pp. 817-9. This work has also been consulted for the spelling of occasional Scots words used in the text.
7. 'Sir' is used to denote a knight; 'sir' for a catholic priest.
8. This book is based on an Edinburgh University Ph.D. thesis (1987), 'Faith, families and factions: the Scottish Reformation in Angus and the Mearns', by the author. References in the notes to various appendices, refer to the second volume of the thesis, which is available at Edinburgh. It was not possible to include the appendices in this printed edition.

CHAPTER 1

Angus and the Mearns in the Early Sixteenth Century

The romantic and dramatic aspects of the Scottish reformation of religion — the stories of Mary, queen of Scots and of John Knox — are well known. Yet an answer to perhaps the most significant question regarding the Scottish Reformation has yet to be found. Many nations were affected by the religious reformation of the sixteenth century: but it took root and survived in comparatively few. In Scotland, the reformed kirk gained for itself a lasting role in the history of the nation. Why was this? What was it that ensured the endurance of the new — and radical — faith? Reformed Scotland — the Scotland of the General Assembly of the Kirk, of parochial kirk sessions, of the metrical psalms — this Scotland was born in the years of the mid-sixteenth century, and, despite opposition from the Stuart monarchs (and despite its own frequent failings), the infant survived. Explanations for this success are to be sought, not in chance nor simply in the providence of God, but by studying the growing relationship between the characteristics of the new kirk and those of more general Scottish society. This book provides a limited and, to some extent, a preliminary search for these explanations. One region of Scotland has been studied in depth for a period of thirty years before, and thirty years after, the Reformation Parliament of 1560. The region chosen was one of the first areas of Scotland to be 'infected' by the Protestant heresy; its lairds were central to the Reformation crisis. This study of the success of Scotland Reformed concentrates on the shires of Angus and the Mearns: Forfarshire and Kincardineshire.

To the modern motorist, Angus and the Mearns can appear to be no more than the areas to be traversed between the Dundee bypass and Aberdeen. To the holidaymaker, the woods and glens of the Braes of Angus are less well known than Royal Deeside, over the hills. Even one of its own historians has described the ancient cathedral city of Brechin as 'quiet and unobtrusive', enjoying only a 'little place' in the general history of Scotland.[1] Perceptions of these districts between the Tay and the Dee were different in the fifteenth and sixteenth centuries. To at least one Englishman, control of southern Angus was a key to the control of Scotland during the wars of the mid-sixteenth century. Nationally significant battles were fought near Brechin in 1453 and 1570.[2] Yet the lairdly families that

1

comprised society in these two shires were on the whole from the smaller Scottish kin-groups. Perhaps because of this, the more politically ambitious sought power by seeking office in the royal household or as officers of the state: their success during the sixteenth century marked a change in the structure of national affairs.[3] The unsettled politics of the minorities of both Queen Mary and King James VI gave much scope for certain of the gentry of Angus and the Mearns.

In the religious turmoil of Mary's reign, 'the gentlemen of Angus and Mearns' were credited by John Knox with a leading role in the crisis of May 1559 that led to the Reformation in Scotland. His account of the events leading to the key parliament of 1560 has several references to these protestant gentlemen, sometimes described as the 'professors', sometimes as 'the Congregation of Angus and Mearns'. It was they who, by their threat of armed support for their preachers, first challenged the queen regent, Mary of Guise, in the field. During the confrontation at Cupar Muir these gentlemen, aided by others from Fife, 'kept themselves close in knot, nigh to the number of a thousand spears'.[4] Who were these 'gentlemen'? How deep was their commitment to the protestant Reformation? How did it come that an area listed amongst those most fervent for the Reform in the 1550s can be described as part of the religiously conservative north of Scotland by the 1580s?[5] One objective of this study is to seek answers to these questions and to the issues underlying them: what were the causes of the Reformation of religion, and what was its effect on the society of the sheriffdoms of Angus and the Mearns?

Use of the very words 'religion' and 'society', however, raises issues both of definition and of substance: issues increasingly addressed in the context of the Scottish Reformation.[6] For 'society' refers to a total community: to the complete nexus of all the groups, families and institutions of a given area. The church as an institution must, therefore, be an integral part of a given society. Moreover it is difficult to conceive a society whose individual members — whether churchmen or not — were not influenced in some degree by religious faith. Sixteenth-century Europe has been described as profoundly religious.[7] The values and teaching of the Christian faith were interwoven with daily life from morality to economic theory, from constitutional thought to principles of causation, in a way foreign to the twentieth-century mind.[8] It is to be expected, therefore, not only that the new elements of religious thought would have their impact on the traditional structures of society but that the other sectors of Scottish life and thought would also exercise their influence over the kirk. In seeking the causes of the success of the Reformation in Angus and the Mearns, it must be asked how far the doctrinal and institutional changes of the protestant reformation were related to political and other developments in these particular shires of Scotland. Was it only religion that bound together these lairds of 'The Congregation'? Were these religious upheavals the product of a static or a turbulant society? Before examination of the years immediately preceding the Reformation Crisis in Scotland, it is worth exploring the social and political setting of Angus and the Mearns in which the new doctrines were to take root.

In discussion of the society of these lands between the Grampians and the east coast, it must not be forgotten that Angus and the Mearns were separate counties. Each was a distinct sheriffdom: that of Angus, based on the royal burgh of Forfar, and that of the Mearns, on Kincardine. Somewhat smaller than its southern neighbour, most of the Mearns was separated from Aberdeenshire by the Dee and from Angus by the North Esk. In simple distance closer to Aberdeen than Dundee, the core of the Mearns — the triangle of lands formed by Dunnottar, Inverbervie and Fettercairn — lay nevertheless largely south of the Mounth. Cut off by the forests of Durris and Fetteresso and by the Red Moss from Deeside, the society of the Mearns looked rather to Montrose and Brechin, though the greater families of the earls Marischal and the Douglas lairds of Glenbervie did also have extensive northern interests.

The fact that both Angus and Mearns, though small in overall area, can be divided into separate geographical sectors that were yet united in a single economy, demonstrates something of the complexity and intricacy of their society. Politically, too, the pattern of kin-groups and landholding was labyrinthine. It cannot be said that any single magnate or clan was dominant. In the Mearns, although the chief house of the Keith earls Marischal was at Dunnottar and the earl was sheriff of Kincardineshire, Keith lairds were few in number. Besides, the spread of their lands throughout Scotland seems to have diluted their local influence so that the lesser lairds of Douglas of Glenbervie, Arbuthnott of that ilk, the Strathauchin/Strachan and Wishart families, and the Straitons of that ilk/of Lauriston retained considerable independence. Barclay of Mathers, in the south of the county, was the deputy-sheriff.[9]

In Angus, too, the social tradition was one of long-established minor families. The important barony of Dun, on the Angus-Mearns border between Brechin and Montrose, was held by the Erskines of Dun. South of Brechin lay lands of the Carnegies of Kinnaird; south of Montrose, those of the Woods of Bonnyton and Craig, the Melvilles of Dysart and Baldovie, and Leighton of Ullishaven/Usan. East of Forfar were the Guthries of that ilk and the Gardynes of that ilk, with their kin throughout the county. In south-eastern Angus there were branches of the Strachan family: at

Monifieth, the Durhams of Grange were tenants-in-chief, with the Maules of Panmure as their neighbours. Less independent than these, though still long-established, were Auchinleck of that ilk, Monorgund of that ilk and Symmer of Balzeordie — of which family, according to A.J. Warden, all the chiefs between 1531 and 1643 enjoyed the common first name of George.[10] None of these families, with the exception of Erskine of Dun, can be said to be part of a kin-group with significant septs outside Angus or the Mearns.

Even at the higher levels of Angus society, it was local names that predominated. Holding the hereditary office of constable of Dundee and the baronies of Dudhope and Dundee was a Scrymgeour; the provost of Dundee, apart from a few exceptional years throughout the period of the Reformation, was a Haliburton. The Lyon family held the baronies of Glamis, Tannadice and Baikie and were Lords of Glamis. The kin of Lord Gray, sheriff of Forfarshire, proliferated throughout Angus from Fowlis on the Perthshire border. Only along the Braes of Angus were there substantial united holdings of land controlled by the same kin sufficient to give their chief a national importance. The Lords Ogilvy of Airlie and others of their name (descendants of the lesser family of Ogilvy of that ilk in the Glen of Ogilvy), together with the Lindsay earls of Crawford based at Finhaven/Finavon, controlled the entire length of Strathmore from Alyth to Edzell. Both these magnates had kin outside Angus and Perthshire — the Ogilvies of Findlater, and the Lords Lindsay of the Byres. Significant omissions from these lists of land holders are the national names of Stewart, Douglas or Campbell: only single members of these power-groups can be found in Angus and the Mearns.[11]

This intricate, localised society was a small one in twentieth-century terms. A contemporary estimate calculated the population of Arbroath, one of the fifteen or so richest burghs of Scotland, to be no more than some two hundred households.[12] It is thought that Dundee itself can have had no more than 5000 to 6000 inhabitants in 1560.[13] Gordon Donaldson suggests that the sixteenth-century population of Scotland was around 700,000: an average of 700 men, women and children a parish or 150 households.[14] In such a society, personal relationships could be close and well-known. The birth, 'geir' and status of each was known and defined. The importance of family in Scotland in this period is emphasised in modern writing: it took on further significance in the small lairdly families of Angus and Mearns. Thus Margaret Haliburton, wife of Thomas Maule of Panmure and daughter of George Haliburton of Pitcur, was said by commissary Maule, in his seventeenth-century account of his family, to have

delytit mikil to talk of auld histories, knewe the heale genealogie of hir father's hous, as also of her mothers . . . .

Her father-in-law, too, Sir Robert Maule of Panmure, was said to be[15] '. . . expert in countine of genealogies . . .' Evidence of the same passion among the families of the Mearns can be found in the details recorded in the 'Genealogie of the barons in the Mearns of late memory deschending lineally unto the year of God 1578', whose original is in the Barclay-Allardice muniments.[16] Continuity of line of descent from father to son — often with the same Christian name — in the same lands, was appreciated both as a key to understanding personal identity and as indicative of the continuity of society with the values of the past. Social rights, duties and status — even dress as defined by the sumptuary laws — were inherited together with land and name.

The observing and witnessing of legality and due form were socially important neighbourly and family responsibilities that served to protect and enhance ties between man and land, and lord and man. The institutions of church and state could also serve to tie potentially rival families into one integrated and stable society. Feudal duties owed to the crown included attendance at sheriff courts for service on juries. These could be for a criminal assize: but more usually were for finding on question of fact. Juries were empanelled to investigate boundary disputes, to discover liability for dues, to attest lawful inheritance during the process of infefting an heir.[17] When in 1530 the instrument recording John Erskine of Dun's assythment for his killing of sir William Froster was drawn up, witnesses subscribing the deed included William Fullerton of Ardoch and George Erskine of Whitefield — a leading friend, and a cadet of the house of Dun.[18] When in 1541 David earl of Crawford gave John Erskine of Dun sasine in an annual rent from the customs of Montrose and Aberdeen as part of a marriage settlement, the witnesses to the precept were David Lindsay of Edzell, fiar of the earldom, and Andrew Lundy of Benholm, an ally of Dun.[19] The more important the issue, the higher was the status of the witnesses required. Hence during his dispute with Sir Thomas Erskine of Brechin over the lands of Downie, the eighth earl of Crawford petitioned the Lords of Council that the issue, which concerned his inheritance, should not be settled by a common jury.[20] Whether gathered for the public occasions of jury service, sheriff court and wappenshaw, or for witnessing a private charter or instrument, men of status in the counties expected to exercise corporate and communal responsibilities and were well accustomed to each other's company. The nexus of land, name, kin and their associated myths and genealogies was a potent factor for stability in the social networks of Angus and Mearns.

Economically, Angus was a crossroads where both north-south and east-west routes met. Close to the heart of the ancient Kingdom of Alba, part of

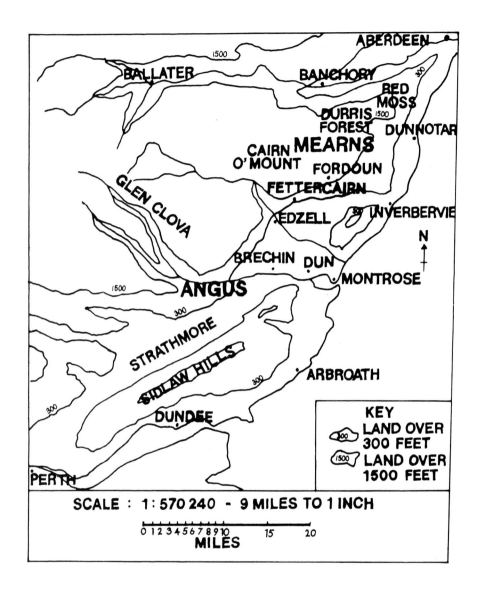

SCALE : 1 : 570 240 - 9 MILES TO 1 INCH

MILES

non-Gaelic Scotland from the fourteenth century, Angus connected the northern agrarian lowland counties of Aberdeenshire, Buchan, Moray and Nairn to the southern lowlands of Fife and the Lothians.[21] An ancient trading route crossed the Dee at Banchory, reached Fettercairn via the Cairn o' Mount, and continued on to Edzell and Brechin. Less obvious to the modern motorist was the route from Ballater that led over the hills from the north-west via Glen Muick and Glen Clova down the South Esk. Cattle from the Highlands were driven down these roads from the west and north to the fair of St Palladius at Fordoun and the great Trinity Fair at Brechin in increasing numbers as the sixteenth century progressed.[22] Situated at the point where these routes merged and were restricted by the waters of the basin of Montrose to the east and the proximity of the highlands behind Edzell, Brechin's castle controlled the movement of trade and troops between north and south — and hence was the site of conflicts between earls of Huntly and southern magnates in both 1452 and 1570.

Trading routes across the ocean to Europe were also important to the Scottish economy of the sixteenth century. Grain and timber were imported from the Baltic to supplement dearth at home; luxury cargoes of wines and clothes from France were balanced by increasing exports of coal, salt, hides and wool. After Edinburgh, Dundee and Aberdeen were the wealthiest burghs of Scotland for most of the century. Dr I.F. Grant's classic study of the economic development of Scotland before 1603 emphasised how much exporting in this period was of simple rural produce: of rough woollen cloth, of sheepskins and cattle-hide. The accounts of the royal customs levied on exports from Dundee and Montrose feature these items, with the addition of salmon and herring from the fishings off the North and South Esk as a speciality of Montrose.[23] The prosperity of Dundee was closely connected, therefore, with its rural hinterland whence came both the necessities of life and goods for trading. The coastal fringe of Angus and the valley of Strathmore were suitable for growing barley and oats — some land was even capable of a wheat harvest. The less fertile Sidlaws and the Grampian foothills were grazed by cattle and sheep. Angus, and in particular Dundee, was therefore a trading centre between east and west: lairds seeking timber for building, or French silks, or sugar, oil or wine, looked to Dundee's merchants to supply their needs.[24]

Many, therefore, were the factors that made for continuity and stability in the society of Angus and Mearns in the early sixteenth century. Economic interdependence integrated rural hinterland with the royal burghs of the coast; and provided links with the wider communities of Scotland, Britain and Europe. Geography and localism interacted to produce a kin-group community distinct from Scotland as a whole, families bound together in

intricate relationships of lordship, clientage and marriage. The services of
the mediaeval church and the institutions of shire government; the handing
on of name and land from generation to generation — these institutions and
ideals linked the gentry families of the two counties. The central political
ideals of Scotland were also held in common: these being a belief in the
commonweal, the 'auld libertie, privileges and fredomes in all estatis as it
hes bene in all tymes bigane'. Ultimate responsibility for the maintenance of
these freedoms was entrusted to the king, as the fount of justice, the
defender of the nation and the apex of a feudal structure of land-tenure.[25] If
local life in the counties was experienced as communal, it was so only within
the context of an independent national community led, ruled and
symbolised by its hereditary judge and prince.

Although society in Angus and the Mearns maintained strongly-held
traditional values, so that it can be described as deeply conservative, yet in
the early sixteenth century it was subject to considerable forces working for
change. These were in part economic. Those who sought to lead society
were expected to demonstrate their status in many tangible ways — all of
which required wealth.[26] Symbols of power ranged from the household men
who made up a magnate's retinue, the foreign clothes he himself wore or
purchased for his wife, to the major expenditure required to build or
modernise his tower-house or castle. Even middle-ranking families could be
involved in this increasingly ostentatious expenditure.[27] The magnate status
of the earldom of Crawford required considerable expense to maintain a
proper dignity and superiority over these lesser families.

Some indication of the luxury items acquiring currency during the
sixteenth century can be found in the Crawford muniments. When Dame
Katherine Campbell, dowager countess of Crawford, made her will in 1578
at the end of a career that began with marriage to the master of Ogilvy
before 1539, she left to James Lord Ogilvy, her eldest son, a silver basin, a
gilded silver cup and cover, and a bed valance in gold cloth with taffeta and
silk. David Lindsay of Edzell, her eldest son by the ninth earl of Crawford,
was left similar gifts of a silver basin, a gilded silver cup from Paris, her
'greatest chenzie of gold' and a bed pand in green, embroidered with black
velvet and white silk, curtained with green Spanish taffeta. Other legacies
included, for her daughters, gowns in black velvet and damask, ornamental
gold bracelets and necklaces.[28] Earlier in the century, when the Ogilvies
sacked Finavon Castle on the succession of the ninth earl of Crawford, the
summons of spulzie listed the goods seized by the raiders. Apart from 1,100
sheep, 120 oxen and nineteen horses, Crawford lost the furnishing for
twenty-four beds, the silver, silk, velvet, satin and damask furnishings of the
chapel, a hundred barrels, tuns and puncheons — presumably full of wines:

twenty-four pieces of artillery, two great iron yetts, a hundred spears, and over 1000 assorted trees — valuable for their fruit, and for timber of birch and ash. He also claimed for the destruction of sixteen great windows of glass in oaken casements and for twelve double doors of oak.[29]

Provision and maintenance of such imported and expensive items required considerable supplies of cash for the payment of merchants and craftsmen. With the heightened level of expectation in living standards in the early sixteenth century came a growth of a cash economy alongside the traditional calculation of revenues in kind. This was facilitated by two practices: the feuing and the wadsetting of land. Feuing of crown land became increasingly common from the reign of James IV and encouraged a wider use of the practice, which involved the granting of a hereditary right of tenancy for an initial lump sum and fixed annual payments.[30] In effect, the grantor lost possession of lands so feued in exchange for an increased cash income — provided the latter was not eroded by inflation.

When combined with an agreement that the lands sold or feued might revert to their original owner on payment or repayment by him of a large sum, the sale or feu operated as a wadset or mortgage: the grantor obtaining a cash loan on the security of a hereditary right in land. The financial pressure on the eighth earl of Crawford is shown by charters whereby he sold lands to his close kinsman David Lindsay of Edzell in exchange for sums paid to enable him to redeem them from others.[31] As ninth earl of Crawford, Lindsay of Edzell was himself to spend much effort attempting to regain lands lost by the earldom since the death of the duke of Montrose.[32] A magnate such as the earl of Crawford, however, had vast resources and credit on which to draw: a lesser laird who by ill-judgment or mismanagement fell into debt could be driven from his lands. John Ramsay of Canterland was forced in 1541 to grant Sir Thomas Erskine of Brechin his barony of Canterland in exchange for the smaller property of Logie-next-Cowie.[33] Similarly, David Lindsay of the Haugh of Finavon, having granted his lands of the Haugh to the dowager countess of Crawford to release a horning due to a debt, found himself excluded from return when Dame Katherine granted the lands to her son Walter and denied that she had conceded Lindsay conditions for reversion.[34] Such loss of patrimonial lands was the ultimate disaster of the sixteenth century. Faced with financial and social pressures, active hostility and a particular crisis, the minor landholder confronted catastrophe. Feuing, whether by magnates or the crown, tended to lessen traditional loyalties: to slacken the bonds that held society together. Wadsetting similarly divided baronies and increased the likelihood that a man of any substance would hold lands from several, perhaps politically opposed, superiors. Economic developments were a decided threat to the values of traditional society.

In early sixteenth-century Angus, by far the greatest disruptions of land-ownership were caused by the crown. During his reign, James V, recently described as 'probably the most unpleasant of all the Stewarts',[35] forfeited all the tenants of the Douglas regality of Kirriemuir and the entire lordship of Glamis. In addition, the legitimate heir of the earldom of Crawford was bypassed in favour of the junior house of Edzell. The king also exploited to his advantage a disputed succession in the lordship of Gray. The combined effect of these intrusions into the regular process of inheritance in such a conservative society must have been considerable — the crown thus successfully asserting its power over both the major earldoms of Angus and both the leading lords of parliament — one of whom (Lord Gray) was the sheriff-principal. That the lordship of Glamis was not added to the lordship of the Isles as the permanent forfeitures of the five reigns James III to James VI[36] was no fault of James V: the life of the heir was saved only by the king's death. Both the Angus and the Glamis forfeitures were in fact reversed: in the course of time — though not without cost — the legitimate superiors, their heirs and their tenants recovered their lands from the crown or its assignees.

Of all James V's interventions with Angus property-rights, that with the longest-lasting results was the alteration of the line of inheritance of the earldom of Crawford. Since the death of David, duke of Montrose and fifth earl of Crawford in 1495, the earldom had been in decline.[37] His heir had been unable to claim the dukedom: and instead, William, third Lord Graham, had been advanced to the earldom of Montrose in 1503. John, sixth earl of Crawford, having sold the sheriffdom of Aberdeen,[38] was among those slain at Flodden: his heir, Alexander, died only four years later in 1517. David, eighth earl, suffered the revocation of his and his father's instruments of sasine by parliament and his estates were subjected to nonentries since the death of the duke of Montrose. In consequence, he was forced to sell and wadset lands. Seventeen such charters are recorded in the Register of the Great Seal: William Wood of Bonnyton was the main beneficiary.[39] Sir Thomas Erskine of Brechin, having had a gift of the nonentries payable by Crawford on the lands of Downie, used the gift to have the lands apprized to him for nonpayment. He did not seek, however, to invoke the full vigour of law and was content to settle with the earl by charters of excambion.[40]

To these troubles of the eighth earl was added the increasingly reckless behaviour of his heir, Alexander, master of Crawford. Perhaps in misguided attempts to restore the fortunes and vigour of the earldom, the master extorted by force heavy dues from his tenants in Glenesk, Menmuir, Tannadice and Fern. Exceeding his rights as lord of Glenesk, he attacked and seized his father's 'room' of Dalbog. The earl appealed to the crown for protection, and a settlement (1526) was reached under the arbitration of the archbishop of St Andrews. When this broke down, the master was tried at Dundee, 16 February 1530/31, before the Court of Justiciary under Sir John Campbell of Lundie, justice-depute. Charges against the master included violent assault against, and wrongful imprisonment of, his own father. Further accusations included similar attacks on Lindsay of Edzell, including 'hamesucken' committed at Edzell itself, in company with others including one 'evill Sandy'. Alexander Lindsday, called in Angus historiography 'The Wicked Master', having been found guilty of these offences, was forced in 1537 to surrender his lands and rights as heir of Crawford in favour of Lindsay of Edzell, and was dead within the year.[41] On the death of the eighth earl, David Lindsay of Edzell was granted sasine in the entire earldom.[42]

This apparently simple tale of the 'Absalom of his century', one who 'exceeded all his compeers in prodigality, recklessness and crime',[43] by no means ended with the 'Wicked Master' obtaining his just deserts at the hands of a 'sutor of Dundee'.[44] By his wife Jean Sinclair, the master had had a son, David Lindsay, to whom the then childless ninth earl surrendered back the fee of the earldom on condition that the young man bound himself to serve the earl, to accept his advice and not to alienate land without his consent.[45] In the transactions preceding Edzell's infeftment, the ninth earl had already obtained a grant of the superiority of his own lands of Edzell in fee with others in Glenesk from the eighth earl during his life and thereafter from the crown as a free barony.[46] He further advanced the fortunes of his own house, by retaining the superiorities of the baronies of Glenesk, Fern and Newdosk in his own hands when the future tenth earl — the 'wicked master's' son — was infeft as fiar of Crawford. At the time, the new master was forced to accept these conditions as part of the contracts surrounding his marriage to Cardinal Beaton's daughter,[47] but later he was to complain that Edzell had thus secured for himself revenues of up to 600 merks a year 'quhilkis ar better nor ye haif of ye said Erldome'.[48] Considerable legal actions took place between the earl and the master, each at different times having the other excommunicated for breach of promise. The ninth earl died in 1558, having spent his last months in ward in Edinburgh Castle at the instance of the master for nonfulfilment of supposed promises to deliver the reversions of the earldom. Only in 1570 did the tenth earl finally come to terms with the loss of superiority of the Edzell lands in the contract by which the then David Lindsay of Edzell married his daughter Helen without tocher (dowry).[49]

Nor were these disputes between the leading branches of the Lindsays without result in Angus at large. Immediately on the succession of the ninth earl, the cause of the apparently dispossessed son of the 'wicked master' was taken up by James Lord Ogilvy of Airlie — after Crawford, the most powerful magnate of Angus. Supported by William Wood of Bonnyton, Thomas Leighton of Usan, George Arrat of that ilk, David Garden of the Leys and others, the Ogilvies and the master's son besieged Finavon Castle, finally seizing its contents after an action lasting 'two days or thereabouts'.[50] While the earl delayed at court securing the royal letters necessary to evict the trespassers, his own lands of Glenesk bore the brunt of a continued campaign as they were harried by 'sax hundreth persones fut and horse' on 15 October 1543.[51] Various suits by the tenants concerned and the curate of Finavon against the raiders continued well into the 1550s. Despite the attempts of Dame Katherine Campbell, countess of Crawford, her sons by the ninth earl attempted to reopen their inherited case for damages against the Ogilvies in the late 1570s.[52] The immediate problems of county-wide violence seem to have been solved by the arbitration of friends. James Lord Ogilvy for the master and John Erskine of Dun for the earl agreed to meet with up to a dozen followers each, 'for stanchin rowbry' and 'dressing of al materis'. As James Lord Ogilvy was Cardinal Beaton's closest associate in Angus, the marriage of the master of Crawford to the cardinal's daughter and the splendid dowry paid over to the earl in consequence should also be viewed as part of the settlement for the 'spulzie of Finhaven'.[53] The ninth earl was in need of funds, not only because of the spulzie and the mortgaged state of the earldom he had obtained: King James had infeft him as earl of Crawford only on condition that he should resign back to the Crown or pay a fine of 100,000 merks. Governor Arran added to the earl's problems of 1543 by attempting to enforce the obligation.[54]

The demand by James V for such a huge sum from David Lindsay of Edzell makes it clear that much of the blame for the violence, legal strife and for divisions still festering into the 1570s should be laid at the door of the king's own malevolence and acquisitiveness. It is also possible that competition between James's chief secretary (Sir Thomas Erskine) and his comptroller (Wood of Craig, a brother of Bonnyton) played a part. David Lindsay of Edzell had been one of the secretary's friends from the early 1530s; after the death of James V, Erskine attempted to keep from Arran the documentation necessary to prove the extent of Crawford's obligations to the Crown.[55] It had been the comptroller, Wood of Craig, who had benefited from the Glamis forfeiture, while Erskine had obtained lands from the earldom at Downie. Certainly, the Woods and their allies took the opposite side to the house of Edzell in 1543, while Erskine of Dun acted as arbiter for the ninth earl.

It is in fact possible to distinguish two separate factions in Angus and the Mearns in this period: those associated with the houses of Dun and Edzell on one hand, and those with Cardinal Beaton and the house of Airlie on the other. When both Sir Thomas of Brechin and David Beaton were sent abroad as ambassadors during the negotiations for James's marriages, their friends, clients and servants received royal protection from adverse legal suits or judgments while their 'lord' was absent. There is considerable correspondence between the sides at the spulzie of Finavon, and the earlier lists of the mid-1530s.[56] Sir Thomas and the cardinal were, of course, associated with the same national policies as trusted servants of the same king. Nevertheless their power-bases were very different:[57] and, at least in 1543, their clients could come to blows. It is a remarkable consequence of James V's patronage of lesser men from the shires that one can suspect the former Mr Thomas Erskine of Haltoun and David Wood of Craig of Inchbrayock as the powers at court representing the opposing interests of the two Angus magnates, the earl of Crawford and James Lord Ogilvy of Airlie.

The composition of these lairdly factions of Angus and the Mearns serves to warn us that powerful loyalties existed in the sixteenth century beyond that of kin. Rivalry could exist between the major branches of a clan: in this case, between the earls of Crawford and the Lindsays of Edzell. In the previous century, Thomas Ogilvy had fought with the earl of Crawford against his brother Alexander Ogilvy of Inverquharity at the battle of Arbroath, being rewarded with a grant of Clova from Crawford and Cortachy from James III.[58] John Ogilvy of Inverquharity found his own loyalties torn in the period of the Reformation between his chief, Ogilvy of Airlie, and his duties to the earl of Angus as bailie of the regality of Kirriemuir. Inverquharity did not appear as a principal in the spulzie of Finavon: nor did he receive a protection with the abbot of Arbroath. James Ogilvy of Cookston's support for the abbot was based on more than sheer kin-loyalty to Airlie: otherwise known as Ogilvy of Balfour, in 1539/40 he had a grant of Balfour in the barony of Kingoldrum from the regality of Arbroath. He held the post of chamberlain to the abbey of Arbroath.[59] Also among the participants in the spulzie holding lands from Beaton were the Gardens of Leys, elder and younger, whose grants had been confirmed in 1542. They, too, had had protections as friends of Beaton in the 1530s. These ties to the cardinal cut across their ties to Gardyne of that ilk, a member of Sir Thomas Erskine's connection.

The twin factors of marriages and grants of lands seem to have cemented or created relationships between those connected to David Beaton. Beaton's own long-established mistress, Marion, was a daughter of the house of Airlie. She was infeft by him in the barony of Melgund: their son David inherited from her, having failed to secure a permanent hold on the Glamis barony of Baikie.[60] As well as Ogilvy of Cookston/Balfour, David Wood of Craig had grants of church lands from the cardinal/archbishop.[61] William Wood of Bonnyton, on the other hand, was married to an Ogilvy: all three Woods of Bonnyton, Craig and Balbegno could be described as 'near kinsmen' of Ogilvy on the strength of this marriage.[62] Further, the strong ties of the Grahams of Fintry and Claverhouse with David Beaton seem to be based on Fintry's marriage to Katherine Beaton. David Ogilvy of that ilk was to be curator for David Graham, Fintry's heir.[63] Marriage in the sixteenth century was not primarily a bond of love, but a contract entered into by the deliberate will of both families bearing in mind their own political aims: the grant of a daughter was somewhat similar to a grant of land and sprang from the same motives. The element of choice was crucial to these connections between men. Indeed, it is important to note that Angus lairds of this period, faced with the often conflicting bonds of kin, marriage, jurisdictions and land-tenure, had a much wider area of freedom than is generally realised in deciding which connection had a priority claim upon them.[64] The greater their scope for choice became, the more urgent was the problem of loyalty, which was also a question of identity — to which family or grouping did the individual belong?

James V's policy of reliance on minor lairds had a marked impact on the society of Angus and the Mearns. His employment of such men as Erskine of Haltoun, Wood of Craig and Wishart of Pittarrow — respectively his secretary, comptroller and treasurer — combined with his avaricious pursuit of advantage against such as lords Glamis and Gray and the earls of Crawford thoroughly to disrupt the society of Forfarshire in the 1530s and 1540s. As a direct result of royal policy during these decades, there was very considerable dislocation in the normal patterns of inheritance. (The Mearns was rather more fortunate.) These problems reached their climax with the violence of the spulzie of Finavon, and seem to have encouraged the existence of factions among the lairds of the shire. Royal patronage gave power and its symbols — jurisdictions and lands — into the hands of lesser men while the magnates were stripped of office and even disinherited by means of dubious or nonexistent legality. Yet it was to the crown that traditional society looked for justice and for the protection of hereditary rights. By mid-century, the forces of change — both political and economic — were directly attacking those that made for stability in Angus: traditional attachment to crown and kin, the importance of hereditary landed tenure. In consequence, basic questions of loyalty, security and identity were asked of those who supported one or other of the factions. These questions were both political and religious. The English wars were to add a further complication to the question of identity. For those sufficiently bold, the rise of heresy and the coming of the Reformation was to offer one solution to the dilemma of belonging — the myth of a revived and purified nation bound together in a single congregation under God. Most apparently considered that maintaining their own estates in such troubled times was a sufficient aspiration.

NOTES

1. D.B. Thoms, 'The Cathedral Kirk of Brechin', *SFBC* xi (1958), p.13.
2. For the Englishman, (2 Mar. 1547/8): *CSP(S)*, i 203. For 1453, between James II's supporter the earl of Huntly and the earl of Crawford, an ally of the Douglases: see, David Hume, *History of the House and Race of Douglas and Angus* (London 1820), i 292-3. For 1570, page 134 below.
3. Jenny Wormald, *Court, Kirk and Community* (London 1981), p. 33.
4. *John Knox's History of the Reformation in Scotland,* ed. W. Croft Dickinson (Edinburgh 1949), i pp. 160, 172-3, 178, 181.
5. *Wodrow Society Miscellany* (Edinburgh 1844), i p. 54; Gordon Donaldson, *Scottish Church History* (Edinburgh 1985), pp. 191-6.
6. Alan D. Gilbert, *The Making of post-Christian Britain* (London 1980) helpfully introduces the general issues of the place of religion in society: pp.2-40.
7. Owen Chadwick, *The Reformation* (London 1972), p.22.
8. Ian B. Cowan, *The Scottish Reformation* (London 1982), Ch. 1.
9. *REB* ii no.ccccix: an inquest-jury held 4 March 1554/5 under William, earl Marischal and David Barclay of Mathers his deputy gives a fair picture of the major lairds of the county on the eve of the Reformation. They are listed as: Archibald Douglas of Glenbervie, Robert Arbuthnott of that ilk, John Wishart of Pittarrow, John Strachan of Thornton, George Straiton of that ilk, David Wood of Craig, David Barclay of Mathers, Robert Graham of Morphie, John Strachan of Monboddo, Walter Bisset fiar of Easter Kinneff, Andrew Stewart of Logie Cowie, Robert Melville of Harvieston, William Hay of Ury, Alexander Bannerman of Elsick, David Strachan in Wemysmanton, John Middleton in Kilhill and Robert Keith in Barnhill.
10. A.J. Warden, *Angus or Forfarshire* (Dundee 1884), iii, p.360.
11. The Stewart Lords of Innermeath owned Redcastle on the Angus coast: the Stewart/ Douglas earls of Buchan had their seat at Auchterhouse but held few lands in Angus. The regality of Kirriemuir belonged to the Douglas earls of Angus — but the only Douglas laird in either shire was Glenbervie in the Mearns. Campbell of Lundie was the only one of his name in the region.
12. Arthur Boece, clerk of Brechin, giving witness during a consistorial process, October 1517: the inhabitants were husbandmen, craftsmen and a few merchants. *The Letters of James Vth,* ed. D. Hay (Edinburgh 1954), p.54; *RCB 1295-1597*, pp.514, 518.
13. T.M. Devine and S.G.E. Lythe, "The economy of Scotland under James VI — a revision article", *SHR* 1 (1971), p.95.
14. Gordon Donaldson, *Scottish Church History*, p.220.
15. SRO, Dalhousie mss. GD 45.26.53 pp.69, 64.
16. *The Third Spalding Club Miscellany* (Aberdeen 1940), ii p.213f.
17. See, for example, the jury of the Mearns given above, n.9. Also *REB* ii no.cxxii, 25 May 1535, records an inquiry by the sheriff court of Forfar into holdings "past memory of man" and encroachment on the common of Brechin.

18. *Spalding Club Miscellany* (Aberdeen 1849), iv p.26. *(Spald. Misc.* hereafter.*)*
19. *Spald. Misc.,* iv p.38.
20. 30 Sept. 1533; WRH, Inventory of Scottish muniments at Haigh, NRA(S) 0237 box B. (Cited as Haigh Inventory hereafter.)
21. *Dundee and District,* ed. S.J. Jones (The British Association 1968), pp.152, 154-5.
22. A.R.B. Haldane, *The Drove Roads of Scotland* (Edinburgh 1960), pp.123-134.
23. T.M. Devine and S.G.E. Lythe, 'The economy of Scotland', p.91f; also *ER* vols. xvi-xxi (1529-1588).
24. This paragraph owes much to discussion in I.F. Grant, *The social and economic development of Scotland before 1603* (Edinburgh 1930), p.305f: p.353 for a table comparing the relative importance of the burghs. Also, *ER* xviii pp.47, 51 etc. See map 1.1, which illustrates these paragraphs.
25. R.A. Mason, 'Kingship and Commonweal: political thought and ideology in Reformation Scotland' (Edinburgh Ph.D. 1983), Ch. 6 *passim;* p.192 for the extract from APS. See also R.A. Mason, 'Covenant and Commonweal: the language of politics in Reformation Scotland', in *Church, Politics and Society: Scotland 1408-1929,* ed. Norman Macdougall (Edinburgh 1983), pp.108-9. (Cited as *Church, Politics and Society* hereafter.)
26. Jennifer M. Brown, 'Introduction' to *Scottish Society in the Fifteenth Century,* p.7: also Geoffrey Stell, 'Architecture: the changing needs of society', *ibid.,* pp.181-3.
27. D. MacGibbon and T. Ross, *The castellated and domestic architecture of Scotland from the 12th to the 18th centuries* (Edinburgh 1887). Vol. ii contains, for example, the sixteenth century castles of Balbegno, Allardice and Muchalls in the Mearns; Brackie, Glamis, Claypotts, Fintry, Ethie and Gardyne in Angus.
28. Glenis A. Matheson and F. Taylor, *Handlist of personal papers from the muniments of the earl of Crawford and Balcarres* (Manchester 1976), 3.1.14-17. Cited hereafter as 'Craw. mss.' with code numbers if in the *Handlist* and box numbers for other mss. at the JRL.
29. WRH, The Haigh Inventory, i pp.71-2.
30. S.G.E. Lythe, 'Economic Life', in *Scottish Society in the Fifteenth Century,* ed. Brown (London 1977), p.68.
31. *RMS* iii 1910, 1951: charters dated 28 Nov. 1538 and 15 Jan. 1538/9.
32. Lord Lindsay, *Lives of the Lindsays* (London 1849), i p.201.
33. *RMS* iii 2347.
34. *RSS* iv 2897, 12 Dec. 1554: gift of escheat of Lindsay of the Haugh. WRH, The Haigh inventory, ii p.76, 2 Apr. 1555, for Dame Katherine's infeftment in the Haugh and its associated office of keeper of Finavon castle: then ibid., 8 Jun. 1558, suspension at instance of David earl of Crawford and Dame Katherine of a reversion of the lands of Haugh; ibid., p.79, 12 Jun. 1559, charge for removing against Lindsay of Haugh at instance of Dame Katherine and ibid., p.82, 14 Feb. 1561/2, summons at her instance against Lindsay of the Haugh for violent and masterful withholding and occupation from her of her liferent in the Haugh. Finally, ibid., p.86, 5 July 1564, executions on decreet of removing against Lindsay of Haugh and ibid., i, p.100 for Walter Lindsay's infeftment (s.d.).
35. J. Wormald, *Court, Kirk and Community,* p.12.
36. J. Wormald, *Court, Kirk and Community,* p.29.
37. *Scots Peerage,* iii, p.23.
38. *ADCP,* p.478: to Errol, under 600 merk reversion. Huntly bought these rights 3 Feb. 1538/9 from Crawford for 1,400 merks and was granted the sheriffdom of 3 Mar. 1540/41: *RMS,* iii 2296. In 1595, the eleventh earl attempted to regain the sheriffdom by payment of the £550 Scots agreed in a settlement of 28 Sept. 1532: WRH, The Haigh Inventory, i 108: JRL, The Craw. mss. box C.
39. *RMS,* iii 1056, 1055, 1248, 1252 and the Haigh Inventory i 57, 58 for Wood's charters. *RMS* iii 617 (a double confirmation), 1249, 1250, 1334, 1465, 1525, 1645, 1835, 1936, 2020, 2888 for the others. J. Wormald, *Court, Kirk and Community* pp.10, 11 for discussion of increasingly stringent application of feudal law by the crown.

40. WRH, The Haigh Inventory, i 53-54; JRL, Craw. mss. box B; also, *RMS,* iii 1336, 1942. Erskine gained Newbiggin, Muirdrum and a third of Dunsyn in Downie together with Bractullo in Inverarity while restoring the Mains of Downie and half of Carlungie.

41. WRH, The Haigh Inventory, i pp.69-70, 80; Lord Lindsay, *Lives of the Lindsays,* i 194-7. J. Low, *Edzell Castle: past and present* (Montrose 1900), pp.36-38.

42. *RMS,* iii 3231, 2 May 1546.

43. J. Low, *Edzell Castle,* p.36 citing Lord Lindsay.

44. JRL, The Craw. mss. 81.1.11, Edzell family genealogy of 1623. Ibid., 81.1.8: another Edzell late sixteenth-century genealogy calls Alexander Lindsay 'ye evil maister'.

45. WRH, The Haigh Inventory, ii 45: JRL, Craw. mss. box E, 9 Aug. 1546.

46. *RMS,* ii 1951.

47. WRH, Inventory of Kinfauns Muniments NRA(S) 0369, i 4, for the marriage contract by which Edzell was obliged to put David Lindsay into the fee of the earldom. Also, the Craw. mss. 81.1.5: 'Thairefter David erle of Crauford laird of Edzell agreit w[i]t David maister of Crauford oy to David erle of Carauford fayther to the evill maister of Crauford and mareit the cardinellis dochter q[uhi]lk wes restorit to the haill erledom of Craufurd except the landis of Glenesk Ferne and Newdosk q[uhi]lk war resevant to the lands of Edzell'.

48. WRH, The Haigh Inventory, i 100: JRL, Craw. ms. box C.

49. WRH, The Haigh Inventory i 92-5; ii 53, 64-5, 69. The warding was originally for Dunbarton Castle, but Mary of Guise transported the order on account of the earl's illness, the castle being 'a cald ruinous place'. JRL, The Craw. mss. 1.1.13. The contract of marriage of 1570 lists the previous contracts attempting to solve the disputes as 10 April 1546 (the Beaton marriage); 15 April 1546 (the master's bond to the earl), and 16 March 1555/6 (which led to the warding mentioned above). Ibid., i 99: The Craw. mss. box C.

50. WRH, The Haigh Inventory, i 88: royal letters charging those listed to desist under pain of treason from the siege — 4 Oct. 1543. Ibid., i 72-3, summons of spulzie listing the goods taken (see n.27 above), 15 Oct. 1543. Ibid., i 88: letters of the Council ordering the Ogilvies to surrender Finavon to the earl, 15 Oct. 1543. JRL, The Craw. mss. boxes C and B.

51. WRH, The Haigh Inventory, i 93, ii 63: JRL, Craw. mss. boxes C, E.

52. Dame Katherine, first married to the Master of Ogilvy and hence mother of James, later Lord Ogilvy, married secondly David, ninth earl of Crawford, and was mother also of his heirs in Edzell. Thus being in the invidious position of parent to both sides of the feud, she attempted in her will to make her legacies conditional on a termination of legal actions — but without success. JRL, The Craw. mss. box 3.1.18, 'the eik of my lady Craufurd testament subscrivit w[i]t hir hand', 10 Aug. 1578.

53. WRH, The Haigh Inventory, ii 52. Lord James Ogilvy, see n.56 below.

54. *Spald. Misc.* ii 197-9.

55. *ADCP* p.420: *Spald. Misc.,* ii 197-9.

56. *ADCP* p.420 lists the Erskine connection on 13 March 1533/4. The long list includes the following lairds from Angus and Mearns: John Erskine of Dun, George Arrat of that ilk, Alexander Fullerton of Kinnaber, Alexander Fullerton portioner of Craigo, Robert Graham of Morphie, Alexander Lyall of Balmaledie, David Barclay of Mathers, Andrew Lundie of Benholm, David Falconer of Haulkerton, John Wishart of Pittarrow, Mr Alexander Strachan of Thornton, John Lamby of Dunkenny, David Lindsay of Edzell, James Crawmond of Aldbar, David Stirling of Braikie, Alexander Durham of Grange, Thomas Leighton of Usan, George Symmer of Balzeordie, James Fenton of Ogil, Robert Arbuthnott of that ilk, Robert Carnegy of Kinnaird, Robert Auchinleck of that ilk, James Durham in Ardestie, Patrick Gardyne of that ilk. Of these, only Leighton of Usan and Arrat of that ilk supported the postulant master of Crawford — and Arrat seems to have suffered in consequence. Protections for the clients of David Beaton, abbot of Arbroath, are listed in *RSS,* ii 1508 (16 Feb. 1532/3), 2166 (31 Aug. 1536), 2307 (10 July 1537) and 4117 (13 July 1541). The following lairds of Angus and Mearns (apart from Beaton's own kin) occur in one or more of these protections: James Lord Ogilvy of Airlie, James Ogilvie of Cookston, William Graham

of Fintry, John Graham of Claverhouse, Robert Maule of Panmure, Alexander Ouchterlony of Kellie, David Ogilvy of that ilk, David Garden of Leys, Henry Fithe in Boysack. Of these, Airlie, Cookston, Leys and Boysack were principals in the spulzie. The remaining principals, the Woods, could not, of course, obtain protections from Beaton, as they were already 'protected' as royal servants. They are clearly supporters of Beaton, however. Craig held his lands and others from Beaton as archbishop of St Andrews: *RMS,* iii 2741; also, Vatican archives, ASPA, vols. 91, 101, 103 for papal confirmations of these feu charters.

57. Beaton was from Fife: as the above lists indicate, his following in Angus and Mearns was much restricted before 1543. His kin in the counties were the Beatons of Westhall and Melgund. Erskine increased his influence in Angus and the Mearns by obtaining the fee of the royal Lordship of Brechin and Navar, including Brechin Castle, 4 Feb. 1533/4; and had assorted other gains erected as the barony of Easter Brechin, 8 Aug. 1537: *RMS,* iii 1148, 1345, 1700. Erskine lost office on James's death, thus giving an opening to his enemies. Margaret Sanderson, 'Kin, freindis and servandis' (of Beaton) in: *The medieval church of St Andrews* (Glasgow 1976), ed. D. McRoberts.

58. Sir J. Ramsay of Bamff, 'Ogilvys of Auchterhouse, Ogilvys of Airlie, Ogilvys of Inverquharity, Ogilvys of Clova', *The Genealogist* xxxv, (1919), pp.162f. Ogilvy of Clova also held Alyth from the earldom of Crawford. *RMS,* iii 693.

59. *RSS,* ii 3423 and RFVA ASPA vol. 103 for royal and papal confirmations of the feu-charter. Warden, *Angus or Forfar,* iv 248 for his witnessing a charter as chamberlain.

60. *RMS,* iii 1931, 3108, 3150; M.H.B. Sanderson, *Cardinal of Scotland: David Beaton* (Edinburgh 1986), Ch. 3 on Marion Ogilvy.

61. See n.56 above.

62. *RMS,* iii 782, 783: *CSP(S),* i 533 — report of 28 Aug. 1559.

63. *RMS,* iii 2604.

64. Jennifer Brown, 'Bonds of Manrent of Scotland before 1603' (Glasgow Ph.D. 1977), pp.163f. suggests that marriage was the least binding of bonds — and hence probably undervalues it.

CHAPTER 2

Faith, Heresy and War

The history of the church in Angus and the Mearns during the mid-sixteenth century can be viewed as a history of faith nurtured within the church in conflict with the institutions of the church. Lairds and others by 1540 no longer looked to their parish clergy for spiritual guidance: they actively sought out either friars, or their own selected chaplains. Others resented their loss of control over matters that touched them deeply — the salvation of themselves and their kin; and, less worthily, the payment of teinds to men others had nominated. During the reign of James V, a mood of anti-clericalism was encouraged; with his death came an opportunity for dissent to turn into protestantism. By 1550, a combination of political and religious events had exposed the majority of the lairdly families of Angus and the Mearns to the virus of heresy.

By the sixteenth century the parish had enjoyed a long history as a basic institution for the provision of Christian ministry. It was to their local clergy that parishioners were taught to look for the sacraments that marked out the important stages of life; the local festivals of the church regulated the passage of the year. Yet by mid-century a variety of factors had combined to weaken the parish ministry, the foundation institution of the western church. The root of this cancer has been traced to the system of appropriation, whereby the revenues allocated for the maintenance both of the parish church itself and of its clergy were annexed and diverted to other uses: to cathedral buildings and staff, to monasteries and other convents, to universities or other such non-parochial ecclesiastical institutions. It has been calculated that there was no other European country in which this annexation of revenues from the parishes was as developed as in Scotland.[1] Such diverse evils as the dilapidation of buildings and the rapacity of the lower clergy have been deduced as consequences of the system of appropriation.[2]

If appropriation of the teinds was a well-established institutional abuse, further problems were caused by the system of presentations purchased or secured at Rome — a system of benefit to the Papacy and those who served as legal agents, but one often used to frustrate local interests and patrons.[3] The church also suffered from patrons presenting clerics who had no intention of serving their cures in person. These abuses of non-residence and pluralism have, of course, been long known to historians and, indeed, were acknowledged and discussed in sixteenth-century Scotland itself.[4] What is important is to recognise just how far the parochial institutions had been corrupted by the alienation of stipends from their proper use. For some decades before the Reformation, many — probably the majority — of benefices still unappropriated were competed for and secured by men whose prime interests were political or personal and who had neither training, desire nor intention to serve as priests within their parishes. The ancient institution of a ministry supported by teinds and dues from the priest's own parishioners had, after centuries of decline, reached its nadir, and had become a hindrance rather than a support to the faith it purported to serve.[5]

For much of the sixteenth century John Hepburn was bishop of Brechin.[6] Provided in 1516 to the see, Hepburn would prove to be a conservative member of the Scottish episcopate. Equating opposition to tradition-sanctioned abuses with heresy, he unavailingly sought to arrest friar William Arth after the latter's sermons at Dundee. The burgesses of Dundee also challenged his authority when they shielded friar Alexander Dick, a refugee from Aberdeen; George Wishart, however, fled from Montrose when the bishop objected to his activities as the burgh's schoolmaster. Another heretic with connections at Montrose was forcibly rescued from the bishop's own cells in Brechin, and Hepburn had to appeal to the Privy Council to support his authority.[7] This consistent support of the traditional practices of the church made Hepburn a natural colleague of cardinal David Beaton: he had already attended the trial and execution of Mr Patrick Hamilton in 1528. It was entirely consistent with his conservatism that he should also have refused to pay his share of the royal 'contribution' of 1546. John Hepburn was a traditional cleric in another sense too: no fewer than four of his sons were legitimated in 1542/3, one of whom was to become the first protestant minister of Brechin.[8] While Hepburn was bishop of Brechin he remained a barrier against reform of the institutions of the church from within: his diehard opposition to change in the long run helped to drive those seeking spiritual renewal to seek it outside of the Roman church.

To fill the place of the neglected and under-financed parish ministry, the wealthy faithful supplied their own chaplains or patronised their local friaries.[9] The less well-off found funds further to endow existing altars.[10] It is in connection with the friars and the non-parochial priests that evidence of continuing catholic faith is best to be found. In the linked practices of endowing masses for the dead and the employment of private chaplains, the gentry of Angus and the Mearns found channels to express both their own faith and their sense of the solidarity of present society with the past. Both Lord Gray and Guthrie of that ilk founded colleges of priests based on their parish churches of Fowlis and Guthrie around 1450 and 1475 respectively. These were furnished not only with a chapter of canons but also with lavish extra aisles and decorated wall-paintings and rood-screens.[11] Though no such colleges existed in the Mearns, Sir Robert Arbuthnott of that ilk had the Arbuthnott aisle added to his parish church in 1505. David Lindsay of Edzell, ninth earl of Crawford, had added an aisle to Edzell parish church: he left instructions in his will that he was to be buried therein, alongside his first wife Janet Gray.[12] Such aisles and their chaplains, dedicated to the saying of votive masses for the founder and his kin, adorned with the patron's coat of arms, were a powerful expression of faith in traditional catholic teaching.

The support given to the extra-parochial friaries and chaplaincies by lairds such as Patrick Paniter, Maule of Panmure and Lindsay of Edzell is indicative of their wish to find ways of realising their Christian faith and their desire to find salvation. It is significant that they often chose to do so by means of their own private institutions, where their sense of the solidarity of kin found religious expression in the requiem mass. Not only the non-residence of the parish clergy formed a barrier to a laird finding similar fulfilment in his parish church. Supervision of most of the parishes in Angus and the Mearns was in the hands of men from outside the shires. The bishop of Brechin was a Hepburn; David Beaton of St Andrews and Arbroath was from Fife. Even when a laird had retained patronage of his local church, his rights could be overcome by litigation at Rome. When Arthur Boece, treasurer of Brechin, and Charles Fotheringham, parson of Edzell, used the device of resignation-in-favour in order to exchange benefices, their successful supplications at Rome overrode the rights of the patron of Edzell, the earl of Crawford.[13] When Mr John Hay, provost of Guthrie, died in 1530, John Garden supplicated for provision at Rome, claiming that the patronage fell to the Pope under the Lateran statutes. The nominee of Guthrie of that ilk, whose family had founded the collegiate church and endowed it, had to face litigation at Rome to secure his title. It is questionable whether Mr James Strachan, who held Guthrie from 1536 to 1577, obtained the provostry by his undoubted skills as a procurator at Rome or by nomination by Guthrie as a local candidate.[14] A devout laird could be forgiven for concluding that the system of providing priests to benefices worked mainly in favour of the skilled Scots lawyers at Rome, to whom local interests were of little account. Many must have felt a deep grievance that they were obliged to pay teinds to support an unresponsive official hierarchy — while at the same time requiring to support a 'private sector' of their own choice with further resources. The church's institutional structure had become counter-productive.

The case of David Straiton in Woodstone, burnt for heresy in 1534, is instructive. John Knox reported that Straiton's offence sprang from 'haterent against the pride and avariciousness of the priests'. Instead of paying teinds on fish caught in his boats, he was said to have caused his servants to cast the tenth fish back into the sea for the prior of St Andrews to collect at his leisure. Following excommunication for non-payment, he was accused of heresy. This led him to inquire further into his beliefs by discussion with other local lairds — John Erskine of Dun and his own nephew George Straiton apparent of Lauriston — and by hearing portions of the Scriptures read. As a result, he refused to recant at his trial and was hanged and burnt in August 1534.[15] Straiton's 'heresy' was in fact simple anti-clericalism: a refusal to submit to the financial and legal disciplines of the church. He was sustained in his opposition by an acute sense of the inappropriateness of the hierarchy to the cause from which it claimed authority, by the fellowship of like-minded equals, and by a growing personal knowledge of Scripture. There was nothing distinctively 'Lutheran' or especially doctrinal in his individual revolt, which had its origins in his experience of the abuses of the official church.

Straiton's anticlericalism was widely held. The mood sprang from a mixture of reactions: from lay resentment of the privileges of the 'first estate', from the exactions of teinds and minor dues to which the clergy were entitled, from a growing conviction that neither privilege nor stipends could be justified by any compensating value to the community. During the 1530s, it was a mood encouraged by James V, who sought to exploit it for his own purposes. The connection between James's sponsorship of Sir David Lindsay's satirical attack on the clergy and the crown's endemic poverty was made by M. Mahoney, who concluded:[16] 'By his (James V's) support of anti-clericalism, he attempted to force the clergy into meeting his demands for taxation'. The particular mechanism by which the King sought to raise funds from the clergy was the creation of a College of Justice, for which James claimed £72,000 over four years — although little enough of these funds reached the newly-created senators of the College. Some credit for the creation of the College has been given to Pavia-trained Sir Thomas Erskine of Brechin: it is tempting to speculate that Sir Thomas may also have been associated with the anticlerical aspects of his master's policies.[17]

Heresy, like beauty, is very much in the eye of the beholder. Though David Straiton was convicted, friar William Arth's Dundee sermon against abuse of the process of excommunication was found orthodox by Mr John

Major — whose opinion the friar had sought when accused of heresy by John Hepburn, bishop of Brechin.[18] Personal status and political power had a great deal to do with the classification of opinions. Though Sir David Lindsay of the Mount's criticisms of the clergy were severe, they won royal approval; on the other hand, Richard Carmichael, a young chorister, was compelled to burn his bill for words said in his sleep.[19] Dr Sanderson notes that most of those known to have been convicted of heresy were of 'humble social standing', Mr Patrick Hamilton — and David Straiton — hence being exceptional.[20] Because the evidence for heresy is thus conditioned both by whom it was practicable to accuse and by the scanty nature of surviving documents, it is difficult to assess the extent to which distinctively protestant opinions had taken root in Angus and the Mearns before the mid-century English wars further complicated the picture.

Criticism of the clergy might count as the faithful — though hurtful — words of a friend like friar Arth, who in England refused to renounce the authority of the Pope. Study of the Scriptures — the reading of the New Testament — had been popularised throughout the learned world of Europe by Erasmus, who remained within the Roman church to his death. Although a volume of modern research has been devoted to tracing the influence of Luther and other European theologians in pre-Reformation religious dissent in Scotland, much remains speculative.[21] Opinions, unlike diseases, are not necessarily transmitted by contact. Students — especially students of theology — are not necessarily clones of their professors. While it is possible to deduce that literature and opinions stemming from the Lutheran continent were infiltrating east-coast Scotland during the 1530s,[22] attribution of fully-fledged 'Lutheranism' to particular individuals is well-nigh impossible. The modern desire to describe John Erskine of Dun as 'Lutheran' from as early as the 1530s must therefore be questioned.

Possibly educated at Aberdeen,[23] the laird of Dun has been noted as one of those who, around 1534, studied the New Testament with Straiton in Woodstone. Also in 1534, Erskine gave surety for the release of four laymen including Fullerton of Morphie-Fraser, imprisoned for their part in releasing sir George Gilbert from the bishop of Brechin's prison. Gilbert was held on a charge of heresy in that, while in Germany, he had married.[24] In 1535, Dun's nearest burgh, Montrose, was listed as one of the east-coast ports through which heretical books were imported; in 1538, George Wishart fled from Montrose after being accused of heresy by John Hepburn, bishop of Brechin, for teaching the New Testament in Greek.[25] There is little here to demonstrate that the laird of Dun was a convinced 'Lutheran' in any sense beyond that of the hostile invective of sixteenth-century polemic. What can be said is that John Erskine's circle, aided both by protestant literature and humanist learning, were progressing along the route Luther himself had followed — from loyal opposition to the flawed institutions of the Roman church towards a new, more internal spirituality, based on personal study of the Scriptures and girded by a reformation of doctrine.[26]

In assessing the weight of this evidence for a centre of Lutheran heresy based at Dun in the 1530s, it is important to remember that the laird of Dun was in political terms junior to his uncle, Sir Thomas Erskine of Brechin, secretary to King James V: a man described by Buchanan as 'papisticae factioni deditissimus'.[27] If supportive of anticlericalism, Sir Thomas took care, like his master, to be so from the stance of a 'faithful friend' of Rome. While the secretary's influence was undoubtedly sufficient to guard his nephew against any active hostility from either the bishop of Brechin or archbishop James Beaton of St Andrews, it should also be assumed that John Erskine lacked the independent standing needed to support novel theological views. The evidence should be pressed no further than to conclude that he was devout, inquiring, and personally acquainted with the Scriptures and with the oppressive aspects of the official church of his day. It is wholly improper to deduce, as Hewison did, that the accident of his killing a priest in the bell-tower of Montrose had any necessary connection with his later career as a leading reformer.[28] The laird of Dun no doubt continued to attend Mass; he was to marry his French second wife according to catholic rites accompanied by court festivities at Linlithgow in January of 1538/9.[29]

What applies to the laird of Dun also applies to the group of lairds from north Angus and the Mearns that formed part of the circle of Sir Thomas Erskine of Brechin — the lairds of Kinnaber, Craigo, Morphie, Mathers, Benholm, Haulkerton, Pittarrow, Thornton, Arbuthnott, Auchinleck, Edzell, Kinnaird and others.[30] While these lairds (who had all secured royal protection on 13 March 1533/4 on the secretary's departure abroad as ambassador) looked to Sir Thomas as their patron, it could not be in their interests to foster religious dissent of a character directly opposing the policies of the king he served. It may be significant that Andrew Straiton of Lauriston, brother of David in Woodstone, was not on the list of lairds associated with the lord of Brechin only months before David Straiton's trial for heresy. If so, the burning of David Straiton — who unavailingly appeared to expect mercy from King James — may have served not only as a warning to the young laird of Dun but also to bring Straiton of Lauriston under the umbrella of the king's secretary. By 1541, Andrew Straiton was to marry Isobel, daughter of one of the key friends of the house of Dun, Lindsay of Edzell: his claim to the disputed lordship of Gray seems to have been handled by Sir Thomas to their mutual advantage.[31] Lacking a lead from the lairds of the area, the dammed-up waters of frustrated faith were held back from flooding into the newly-dug protestant channels of the 1530s. Only in the burgh of Dundee, where individualism had greater scope, was a growing stream of heresy apparent.[32]

This picture was to change rapidly with the death of James V, on 13 December 1542, after which 'the hearts of men began to be disclosed'.[33] On the national scene, the earl of Arran became governor and found his own protestant-inclined beliefs convenient in attempting to strike an alliance with Henry VIII's England. During the few months of Arran's competition with David Beaton for control of the government of Scotland, a window of opportunity was opened for proto- and crypto-protestantism to try its wings as a political grouping. This was the period of which Knox wrote, when:[34]

> Then might have seen the Bible lying almost upon every gentleman's table. The New Testament was borne about in many men's hands.

Thus men whose own religious opinions alone would never have served to bring them into open conflict with the church were brought to do so by a turn of the political wheel. Whether protestantism was taken up for spiritual or cynical motives hardly matters. Under the severe rule of James V, supported by a conservative episcopate, protestantism as a political option remained embryonic. Once born, however, the movement could not be returned to the womb. Further, under Arran's sponsorship, criticism of the church moved into new ground. Whereas David Straiton's criticism of the lives of the clergy and the oppressive legalism of the church was, if heresy at all, an attack on the margins of catholic belief, Arran deliberately raised a question at the heart of the protestant revolt from Rome — the doctrine of purgatory. Sadler, the English ambassador to Scotland, reported on the first of April that the governor had talked 'all dinner-while' on the need to reform the church. On the ninth, he reported that Arran believed:[35]

> that houses of religion were first founded to pray for souls in purgatory and if there were no purgatory (as was his opinion) their foundations were vain . . .

Though a considerable simplification of traditional catholic practice, Arran's views summarises conventional Scots lay piety of his period. As has been noted, the requiem mass was the most frequent of church services, and the bulk of lairdly and burgh charity, legacies and endowments was directed at sponsoring such prayers. If, however, the prayers of the living — whether of laymen, priests, monks or friars, could not avail to shorten the time spent in purgatory by their deceased kin, not only the existence of the houses of religion targeted by Arran for expropriation was put in jeopardy; the host of private altars and chaplaincies were threatened with a loss of purpose and meaning. The basic 'unspoken assumption' of current catholic practice was under attack:[36]

> that the more the clergy were multiplied and the more masses were said, the healthier society would become.

Within Angus and the Mearns, the death of James V meant the loss of power of Sir Thomas Erskine of Brechin, ousted by Arran from the post of secretary. A period of confusion followed, during which the lairds of the two shires sought security in new groupings under new patrons. Sir Thomas, who despite his loyalty to King James's pro-French alliance had maintained personal links to both the English government and the exiled Douglases,[37] now attempted to recover power by joining the onslaught on his former ally Beaton.[38] March of 1542/3 proved somewhat late to change sides. The English were unconvinced of Erskine's sincerity and Arran refused to reinstate him. Further, backed by an interdict imposed on the diocese of St Andrews and the proximity of Easter, Beaton was allowed to enter into ward in his own castle of St Andrews by the end of the month: Erskine's threats to expose the cardinal must have earned Beaton's enmity at just the time when the latter's star was again ascending. Out of favour with both of the contending parties of the state, Sir Thomas proved unable to withhold the obligations undertaken by David Lindsay of Edzell in August of 1543: October saw the raid on Finavon Castle, undertaken by Cardinal Beaton's clients in Angus with the tacit consent of the governor.[39]

The total lack of support gained by Lindsay of Edzell from his friends shows the completeness of the collapse of the party of the former secretary. New dispositions of alliance were made. In the Mearns, the majority appear to have cultivated the protection of the earl Marischal: and in doing so, allied themselves for the moment with the English, protestant faction in Scotland. Among those reportedly enthusiastic clients of Henry VIII in December of 1543 were both the earl Marischal and the master of Marischal, with the 'northland men'.[40] The strength of this faction can be estimated from the remission they obtained as a body in June 1544 for crimes which included breaking the acts restraining the disputing of the Scriptures and reading prohibited books.[41] Among those with the Keiths in 1543-44 from the former Erskine party were Robert Arbuthnott of that ilk, David Barclay of Mathers (deputy-sheriff of Kincardineshire), Alexander Strachan of Thornton and John Wishart of Pittarrow. John Erskine of Dun's friend George Straiton apparent of Lauriston was named. Archibald Douglas of Glenbervie was listed — a valued and close kinsman of the Douglas earls. So too were several of the lesser Mearns lairds: Wood of

Balbegno, Ramsay of Balmain, Melville of Harvieston and Falconer of Ballandro. Together, these lairds represented the most powerful section of the shire.

How far was this union of Mearns lairds a protestant alliance? Certain consistencies can be found. John Wishart of Pittarrow's house in the Mearns had wall-paintings satirically attacking the craft and ambition of the Papal Curia.[42] Pittarrow himself was to be a staunch supporter of the reformed kirk after 1560, though disliked as collector of the thirds. Similarly, Arbuthnott of that ilk and Douglas of Glenbervie were present at the Reformation parliament of 1560: the latter was an elder of the kirk. George Straiton of Lauriston also attended the Reformation parliament: he retained close links with John Erskine of Dun through his life.[43] The leader of these lairds, William earl Marischal, though later a supporter of the government of Mary of Guise — being reported at Mass with her in 1552 — at this time was one of those who attended George Wishart's preaching at Dundee. Indeed, he is said to have offered Wishart a northern base for ministry.[44] The link between the Mearns lairds and the Keiths seems somewhat temporary, however: the creation of the particular events of 1543. The close ties between the lesser tenants-in-chief of the Mearns have been noted before: after Arran's brief flirtation with political protestantism their links seem to have included a predilection towards heresy.

In Angus, there was less unanimity. To the basic conflict between Arran and Cardinal Beaton, two further factors had been added. Henry VIII had released from England both the exiled earl of Angus, lord of the regality of Kirriemuir, and various of the Scots lords taken prisoner at the Solway, including Patrick Lord Gray, sheriff of Forfar. Angus and Gray were intended by King Henry to be, and were to prove to be, his agents in securing support for Henry's 'British', pro-protestant policies. Also returned to Scotland to protect his family's reversionary interest on the crown was the earl of Lennox — whose dynastic rivalry with Arran and the Hamiltons brought him into alliance with Angus at much the same time as Beaton re-established his hold over Arran, in the late autumn and winter of 1543.

Together with the earls of Marischal, Lennox, Cassillis, Glencairn and Rothes, English reports listed lords Gray, Glamis and Ogilvy as Angus' chief kinsmen and friends during August, September and October of 1543.[45] The latter three apparently refused to come to the infant Mary's coronation unless the treaties with England were enforced. Ogilvy's position, however, seems in hindsight rather more obscure. Lord Gray was actually his son-in-law: and the name of Angus counted for much in the shire of which Gray was sheriff. On the other hand, Ogilvy was hereditary bailie of Beaton's abbey of Arbroath and stood first in the list of the cardinal's supporters in Forfarshire. In consequence, two contradictory reports have come down to us regarding Lord Ogilvy's actions in September. Sadler reported on 5 September 1543 that he had heard that Lords Gray and Ogilvy had sacked the abbey of Arbroath. He added, significantly, that he could not tell whether this was true. On the other hand, Ogilvy was also credited with preventing damage to the fabric of the abbey by the author of the *Diurnal of Occurrents*.[46]

This 'sacking' of Arbroath abbey, though exaggerated in repute by sources based in Edinburgh to the south, formed part of the final struggles by Arran against the resurgent Beaton. Linked in the *Diurnal's* account with the assault on Arbroath was the 'great heresie' in Dundee. The 'heresie' took place on 31 August, shortly after the official signing of the English treaties which provoked a riot in Edinburgh against the governor. Arran was later to confess to having inspired the attack on the two friaries at Dundee.[47] Indeed, the 'riot' had all the signs of planning. A leader could be identified, Mr Henry Durham, undoubtedly related to doctor Michael Durham, the late King James V's physician, one of those who had influenced Arran towards protestantism.[48] The objectives of the 'heresie' were also clear. No altars or churches belonging to the burgh were touched: instead, the mob invaded the friaries, one of which — the Franciscan — was outside the burgh's walls. Iconoclasm was the order of the day: the ornaments, images, vestments and candlesticks were destroyed. The mob also carried away the clothing, cowls and food supplies of the houses in an effort to prevent further habitation.[49] Lord Gray's attack on Arbroath was reported in Edinburgh on the fifth of September, ironically while the Governor was meeting the cardinal in secret at Callander. It too shared the limited objectives of the Dundee 'heresie', being restricted (by Lord Ogilvie?) strictly to the parish churches of Arbroath — to St Vigeans, the abbey's own parish church, and to the Lady Chapel, which functioned as the parish church of the burgh.[50]

Though permitted and inspired by political considerations, perhaps as a counter-balance to Edinburgh's opposition to Arran, these events in Dundee and Arbroath were of considerable religious significance. Iconoclasm cannot be equated with twentieth-century vandalism: rather, it expressed converts' radical opposition to the symbols they had previously venerated. The symbol retained its power to evoke sentiment; only now the sentiment was negative: hatred instead of worship. As reports of reformation spread from city to city, iconoclasm developed its own cultic traditions equipped with the Old Testament terminology of 'casting down' idols.[51] It marked a rejection of the doctrine of the Mass as a sacrifice, a rejection of the real presence of Christ in the sacrament by transubstantiation of the elements, a rejection of the veneration of images and of the doctrine of purgatory. The Dundee iconoclasm marked the introduction to burgh protestantism (previously characterised by satirical anticlericalism or else by private piety) of an activism previously associated with the reformation in the Swiss cities and with Zwingli, and probably imported by George Wishart.[52]

The alignment of political forces during James V's reign had not been conducive to religiously-based political groupings. Events between 1543 and 1550 were to prove the exact opposite. The various campaigns by Scottish and English armies during the 'Wars of Rough Wooing' have been thoroughly discussed elsewhere and need not be repeated here. In general, English objectives remained stable throughout the period: to punish the Scots for reneging on the treaties of Greenwich, to advocate the marriage of Mary, queen of Scots, to Edward, prince of Wales, and hence the ultimate object of a united, protestant, realm — a 'Great Britain'.[53] Any ally of the English was expected to support this complex of objectives and hence was brought within the scope of a protestant alliance. As the major Scots opposition factions — those of Angus and Lennox — followed Arran's earlier example in availing themselves of English support, all active clients of these earls were at least exposed to the option of protestantism. Further, the military and diplomatic activities of the English occupation force at Broughty Castle confronted several Angus lairds with an English offer of alliance that they could hardly refuse. In consequence, the number of lairds and others from Angus directly or indirectly associated with heresy in this period is considerable.

The sanctuary given by Dundee to friar Alexander Dick has already been mentioned. Leading those who shielded him against the secular and ecclesiastical authorities in 1532 was James Scrymgeour of Dudhope, constable of Dundee c.1504-1546 and additionally provost on occasion in the 1520s.[54] Through his mother, Scrymgeour was kin to Patrick Lord Gray, and the two neighbouring lairds were close associates. Scrymgeour stood surety for Gray in 1536, and was joint surety with him in the books of council for the sum of 10,000 merks payable for his infeftment in the lordship.[55] Taken prisoner at the Solway, Scrymgeour was privately ransomed and had licence to travel through England to France for the benefit of his health in April of 1543. One of those who were given royal protection in connection with the constable's expected absence from Scotland was Mr Henry Durham — the leader of the attack on the Dundee friaries. Apart from his heir, John Scrymgeour of Glaister, and other Scrymgeours, Dudhope also listed among his friends and kinsmen

Alexander Durham of Grange, James Durham in Ardestie, Patrick Gardyne
of that ilk, John Ramsay of Laws, John Baldovie of that ilk, Thomas
Fotheringham of Powrie, Andrew Oliver of Gagie and a number of
burgesses of Dundee.[56] These lairds were from estates in the hinterland of
Monifieth, in south Angus. Durham of Grange's first wife had been an
Erskine: during the 1530s he had been a client of Sir Thomas of Brechin.
His heir William was to be one of Angus' leading protestants. Gardyne of
that ilk was a further refugee from the party of James V's secretary.[57] With
their patron supportive of the anticlerical element in Dundee from the
1520s and a close ally of Patrick Lord Gray, Scrymgeour's party was
undoubtedly implicated in the Dundee 'heresie' even if the now-aged
constable was himself abroad.

Patrick, fourth Lord Gray, was himself one of the most inveterate of the
Scots allies of the English, supporting their cause from 1543 to 1548, with
occasional interruptions.[58] As his following was considerable, he was much
sought after by the various English and Scottish factions, one correspondent
going so far as to assert:[59] 'Gif ye haif the lord Graye ye haif fra Taye north'.
More than three hundred men (according to John Knox) had attempted to
defend him from Cardinal Beaton and governor Arran in November 1543.
Gray had with him then George, earl of Rothes and Mr Henry Balnaves.[60]
Prominent among their supporters was Robert Carnegy of Kinnaird, with
his sons. Other Angus lairds included Lyall of Balmedy, Mortimer of
Flemington and Gilbert Reid in Colliston.[61] Further friends of Gray were
listed in the joint remission they had with him for remaining from hosts
called for September and November of 1545. As well as Whitelaw of
Newgrange and Gray of Dunninald were named Wenton of Strathmartin,
Fotheringham of Powrie and Charteris of Kinfauns. On 19 March 1546/7,
Charteris and Powrie, Strathmartin, Maule of Panmure and Scrymgeour of
Dudhope were chosen by Gray to act for him in his dispute against Lord
Ruthven concerning the provostry of Perth. Eight days earlier, at the castle
of St Andrews (at the time occupied by those who had slain Cardinal
Beaton), Gray had, together with Norman Leslie the master of Rothes,
James Kirkcaldy of Grange, Mr Henry Balnaves and Alexander Whitelaw
of Newgrange, obliged himself to hand Broughty Castle to the English and
to attempt to recover Perth to hold it on behalf of Edward VI.[62] Gray's
connections — whether based on kin, shared political or shared religious
interests — were broad indeed, and included many of the most powerful
lairds of southern Angus.

Among these supporters a number of lairds are known to have been
associated with Gray in 'assuring' to the English. Said to have 'enticed and
seduced' him 'to the faith and opinion of England' was Alexander ('Sandy')

Whitelaw of Newgrange. By 3 March 1548/9, Whitelaw had been escheated for assisting the English take possession of Broughty Castle, and then for assisting their burning of Dundee and Forfar; for acting as a messenger to and from the English and disponing subsidies on their behalf; and for going into unlicensed exile in England. Whitelaw was married to Egidia Gray, (sister of Gray of Buttergask); in his absence, she was to be prosecuted for assisting the enemy, as was Janet Hume, wife of Andrew Gray of Dunninald after the latter's decease. Six further Grays and other servants of Lord Gray had remissions in 1549 for their part in withholding Broughty Castle.[63] In 1548, after English policy had turned towards repression, Gray complained to Luttrell that his associates were being harassed by both sides and requested that Thomas Strachan of Carmyllie should not be attacked from Broughty:[64] 'consyderand that he is my frende and is assurit'.

John Scrymgeour of Glaister and Dudhope, constable of Dundee, has been mentioned as having suceeded his predecessor James as an ally of Lord Gray. As provost of Dundee, he had signed the articles of 27 October 1547 by which the burgesses bound themselves to be 'faithful setters forth of God's Word' and also true and faithful to the English king. Earlier that year, he had refused to obey orders of the Scottish council to arrest John Scott and seize his press, then operating in Dundee. When Lord Gray, during one of his pro-Scottish phases, was entrusted by Arran with the defence of Dundee, John Scrymgeour was one of those jointly named with Gray in the licence. Nevertheless, Arran had the constable's lands of Dudhope sequestered in 1552 in order to extort composition for a remission for treasonable support for the English: Scrymgeour was forced to sell some lands in consequence.[65]

A second group of 'assured' lairds in Angus were those whose lands lay around Broughty, and hence were in direct danger of burning unless they made their peace with Sir Andrew Dudley, the English garrison's commander. Into this category come William Durham of Grange, Thomas Maule apparent of Panmure, Henry Lovell of Ballumbie and David his brother, James Anderson in the (North) Ferry, Mr Alexander Auchinleck in Murroes, and David Ramsay at the Bridge of Monifieth.[66] The relations between these lairds and the English were by no means identical, however. Robert Maule of Panmure and his heir Thomas were seized from their own house of Panmure and taken prisoner to Broughty by 'Inglismen' and 'certain Scotishmen then favourers of Ingland'. The laird was shot in the leg during the episode and sent as prisoner to the Tower of London, Lord Gray obtaining the release of Thomas Maule.[67] Lovell of Ballumbie appears to have been a more willing ally of the English. Sir Andrew Dudley reported on 20 December 1547 that he had been well received in Dundee by Gray,

Durham of Grange and Lovell of Ballumbie. Lovell was one of the 'gentlemen of Angus' who were instrumental in bringing the earl of Argyll to negotiate with Dudley, so that Argyll (on receiving 1000 crowns) promised support for the king's 'godly purpose' instead of besieging Broughty further. Later in 1548, Lovell was prepared to give a note of surety to the Broughty garrison for the re-entry into ward if required of a prisoner they had released.[68]

Other magnates linked with Angus and the Mearns apart from Gray had dealings with the English during this period. On 24 May 1544, Lennox and his Scots allies sallied from Glasgow to test their strength against Arran: Lennox was defeated, and fled to England leaving the earl of Glencairn as his deputy in the west. With Lennox at Glasgow Moor were the earls Marischal and Crawford, as well as George earl of Errol. Marischal's links with protestant Mearns lairds, his hearing of George Wishart at Dundee and his support of Lord Gray have already been noted. Arran had given David Lindsay of Edzell, ninth earl of Crawford, few reasons for supporting him. Crawford was known in England as one bound to the earl of Angus.[69] In 1548, Crawford, Marischal, Rothes and Errol were among those reported by Patrick Lord Gray to favour the English 'godly purpose, thai beande honestly entyrtaynit'.[70]. Another who later obtained a remission for his support of Lennox in 1544 was Robert Graham of Morphie, who had Erskine of Dun as his curator in his youth: he had been one of those protected during Sir Thomas Erskine of Brechin's absence. Later, he was to attend the Reformation parliament and become an elder of the reformed kirk.[71] James Wood of Bonnyton also had a remission for his part at Glasgow Moor, as did Robert Carnegy of Kinnaird who thus continued his opposition to Arran. Carnegy's remission also covered the offences of absence in England without licence and intercommunication with the English in order to subvert royal authority. Among the eighteen others for whom Carnegy secured pardon for these offences were Reid of Colliston, Mortimer of Flemington, the vicar of Strathmartin (a Mortimer) and Mr Alexander Forrest, parson of Logie Montrose.[72]

In addition to these, John, earl of Buchan, whose chief house was at Auchterhouse, had a remission for assuring. John, Lord Innermeath, whose lands in Angus included Redcastle, assisted the English at Broughty and was accused of spoiling the lieges and fire-raising. Lord Glamis, one of Lord Gray's earlier accomplices, was fined for refusing to be part of the assize to try Innermeath — who had the earl of Crawford as his surety.[73] Glamis was presumably cognisant and approving of friar John Roger's preaching in the parish church at Glamis in 1543-44, before the latter's arrest and subsequent death at St Andrews castle.[74] Fraser of Durris, Wood of

Balbegno, Wishart of Logie Wishart and Strachan of Thornton required remissions for remaining from the various hosts levied during the wars. Agnes Ogilvy, daughter of James Lord Ogilvy, widow of Sir Thomas Erskine of Brechin's son Thomas and wife of Keith of Canterland, had a remission for resetting Norman, master of Rothes, after the murder of Cardinal Beaton.[75]

English reports from Broughty often indicated frustration that this volume of potential support never seemed to fulfil its early promise. In his report of 22 March 1547/8, Sir John Luttrell had optimistic plans for winning the entire war by a campaign in Angus. If only 300 light horse might be provided, Patrick Lord Gray could bring in the entire shire — for 'they might be daily burned'. With such support, Perth could be taken; and then Fife, surrounded by 'frontier wars' in Lothian and Angus. 'And if Argyle be entertained, how could the Governor abide?'[76] Although the garrison at Broughty was from the first in touch with many of the gentlemen of Angus 'who favour the word of God', most appeared to be waiting 'to see how the world go'. Others of these gentlemen only feigned protestantism to save their crops from burning. It was one thing to ask for a supply of English Bibles and testaments, and 'other English books of Tyndale and Frithe's translation', but quite another to render oneself open to a charge of treason.[77] Wyndham, the English naval commander, put it bluntly to Somerset: the men of Angus would speak fair words but would perform nothing unless compelled by fire and sword.[78]

There were those in Angus who cannot be linked with the occupying force at Broughty. The lairds of the central parishes, Guthrie of that ilk and Gardyne of that ilk with their respective kins, do not appear after Gardyne's protection as one of Scrymgeour's friends in April 1543. Cardinal Beaton's kin by marriage, the Grahams of Fintry and of Claverhouse, and his tenants Ogilvy of Balfour and Garden of Leys do not appear to have assured, though Fintry's castle of Mains was left unburnt when the Broughty garrison destroyed neighbouring Powrie.[79] Although the former leader of Beaton's friends in Angus, Lord James Ogilvy of Airlie, had been close to Lord Gray and involved in the iconoclasm of 1543, his name soon disappeared from the lists of clients in English reports: he, together with Lord Glamis and the earl Marischal joined Argyll's forces besieging Broughty in November 1547, shortly before his death.[80] The master of Ogilvy had earlier been killed at the battle of Pinkie, fighting with a contingent from Angus under the earl of Angus. Also slain at Pinkie were John Allardice of that ilk, Alexander Fullerton of Kinnaber, Richard Melville of Baldovie, William Ramsay of Balmain — all lairds from the Angus/Mearns border — as was Thomas Fotheringham of Powrie and

Andrew Haliburton of Pitcur.[81] Knox suggested that many of those who were 'professors of the evangel' fought under Angus at Pinkie: Melville and Ramsay may well have been among those he had in mind.[82] After his participation in the battle of Glasgow Moor, Robert Carnegy of Kinnaird seems to have made his peace with Arran, being nominated by the governor to be a Lord of Session in 1547, and acting as intermediary between Huntly and the governor in 1548. Also reported on 17 March 1547/8 as one who knew the mind of Mary of Guise, Carnegy was successfully to make his own way as a legally-trained government servant: he was involved in no more defeats after that of 1544.[83]

John Erskine of Dun, though certainly a protestant by the middle 1540s, did not seek to ally himself with the English. In April and May of 1542[84] the laird of Dun had licences with his cousin Thomas (eldest son of Sir Thomas of Brechin), his own son John, his kinsman Mr William Erskine and John Lamby of Dunkenny to travel abroad.[85] From the diary of James Melville, it is learned that with John apparent of Dun went Richard Melville younger of Baldovie, and that it was to study first under Maccabeus and then Melanchthon that they travelled.[86] From this tour stems John Erskine of Dun's reputation as a 'Lutheran': though conventionally and conveniently assumed, it is actually unclear whether the laird of Dun accompanied the two younger men to the schools. The fact that Thomas Erskine disappeared while abroad, being taken prisoner in unknown circumstances, suggests that the party met not only with learning but with mixed fortunes — which may explain why John Erskine of Dun returned to Scotland via England after only a year's absence, a licence being requested for him of the English government on 19 April 1543. This seeming link between one of Scotland's leaders of the reformed kirk and continental scholars is tantalising: perhaps the most that can be deduced from the known facts is that Dun's spiritual travels were now taking him in a specifically protestant direction, and that he brought back with him a Frenchman, Pierre de Marsilier, to teach Greek at Montrose grammar school.[87]

Much more certain are John Erskine's links with George Wishart, the former Montrose burgh schoolmaster. Having returned to Scotland in the summer of 1543 with the Greenwich treaty commissioners, Wishart rented a house at Montrose 'next unto the church except one' and began a preaching ministry, undoubtedly under the protection of Erskine of Dun, who had been infeft by his uncle as hereditary constable of the burgh on 9 February 1541/2.[88] Dun's growing prominence as a focus for protestant dissent, together with his uncle's continued hostility to Beaton and Arran, led to John Erskine being imprisoned in Blackness at the same time as the cardinal and the governor burned many 'lymmeris' at Dundee in January

1543/4.[89] The English invasion presumably having led to his release, the burgh of Montrose petitioned that the laird of Dun, together with Leighton of Usan and David Wood of Craig, be commanded to enter the burgh with 'their armed folks' to defend it against the English fleet.[90] By 25 October, 1544, he was in sufficient favour with David Beaton to merit an invitation to ride with the cardinal to parliament. That other prisoner of 1543, Patrick Lord Gray, had also around this time accepted an 'invitation' to form part of the cardinal's household.[91] Yet in 1545, Erskine was once again associated with George Wishart when the preacher retired northwards for recuperation after his ministry to plague-stricken Dundee: it was against Dun's advice that he left the security of Montrose for the journey to the south that led to his arrest and eventual execution.[92] Perhaps something of Wishart's own fearlessness had communicated itself to John Erskine.[93] At any rate, the laird of Dun's first steps as a national leader of the nascent Scottish protestant movement were taken in association with this apostle of the Swiss evangel. In later years, John Erskine's theology was to show little difference from the first Helvetic Confession of 1536, translated into Scots by Wishart.[94]

Though the laird of Dun had undoubtedly reached a protestant theology by 1545, he was to take a leading part in defending Angus against the English. He had been expected to support the invading protestants: they considered him one of the 'most faithful, godlie and wise men' north of Dundee.[95] The French, too, heard a rumour that Dun was to join Cassillis and Marischal in assuring.[96] In fact, he lent the burgh of Dundee three cannons in order to resist an attack by the English fleet in December 1547, and (in exchange for a feu of lands in Logie Montrose) gave funds for the rebuilding of St Andrews castle after it had fallen to the French.[97] In June of 1548, the burgesses of Dundee were again ordered to serve under Dun's command in order to resist the invaders.[98] After the arrival of the French troops in Scotland, John Erskine (who had married a French wife) acted as a liaison officer during the campaigns at Musselburgh, Haddington and Roxburgh. Having been wounded, he retired to Montrose in time to take personal command of local forces that repelled a landing by eight hundred Englishmen from admiral Clinton's fleet.[99] John Erskine's father and grandfather had been killed at Flodden; several of his friends and neighbours from north Angus were killed at Pinkie: patriotic defence of his country was the tradition of his house. Mr William Lamb, parson of Conveth and personally known to Dun, was to produce an argued defence of Scotland's traditions and independence.[100] Only when Mary of Guise attempted to garrison with French troops the fort Dun had constructed near Montrose did Erskine object — his rights as constable seemed threatened. This variance had been smoothed over when he gave the Queen Mother a bond of manrent on 30 September 1549.[101]

It has been said that 'As a distinctively popular movement, protestantism had no deep roots in Scotland'.[102] It is, however, questionable how far one ought to look for 'popular movements' in sixteenth-century Scotland. Modern research confirms the view that violence and direct action — though prevalent — were restricted both by tradition and law, and often unleashed to further deliberate ends.[103] Society comprised groups of lairds bound together under the general leadership of magnates: groups which were often, but not exclusively, based on kin. In assessing the strength of religious dissent in Angus and the Mearns before 1550, it is important to recognise that the scattered and apparently isolated incidents of a preaching here, a Bible-reading there, had greater significance than may at first sight appear. As Dr Sanderson has suggested, [104] '. . . the kind of activites of which people were accused were not the sort of thing one did on one's own'. The iconoclasm at Dundee, the preaching at Glamis, Wishart's tours, were important both religiously and politically: their motivation was similarly dual. Between the years 1543 to 1550, all the magnates of Angus and the Mearns — the earls of Crawford and Marischal, the lords Gray, Glamis and Ogilvy — were at some time directly linked with protestant dissent. The constables of both Dundee and Montrose supported known heretics. Rather than the movement traditionally recognised under the single leadership of John Erskine of Dun,[105] a more fractured, more political protestantism can be traced which spasmodically coalesced around the earl Marischal, the Gray-Scrymgeour axis, the burgh of Dundee and the laird of Dun. Under the stimulus of persecution from Cardinal Beaton and bishop John Hepburn, and under the pressure of choice compelled by the English wars, the movement developed from the anticlericalism of the 1530s towards a full-blooded protestantism in touch with Lutheran Germany, the Swiss and the English.

Before 1550, the movement was held in check by the arrival of powerful forces of conservatism from outside the region — Beaton and Arran in person in 1543/4; the armies of Arran and Argyll during the period of the occupation of Broughty. Argyll had assistance from his uncle, Donald Campbell, abbot of Coupar, who on occasion provided troops to counter raids from Broughty and lent his house at the abbey for negotiations.[106] The traditional patriotic resistance to an invader displayed by Erskine of Dun helped to keep the movement divided. So too did the atmosphere of suspicion that surrounded assuring to the English. Lord Methven's analysis of the 'assured Scots' for the benefit of Mary of Guise can certainly be sustained from study of the English clients in Angus. Methven reported that some of the assured had new options of the Scriptures, others acted out of fear to obtain safety; still others sought to make personal gain out of the national danger.[107] M.H. Merriman agrees with another sixteenth-century assessment, that of John Lockhart, that the 'godlie' who supported the English were a small minority.[108]

Once again, however, it must be stressed that Arran's 'godly fit' and the English occupation provided the essential opportunity for protestantism to become a viable political option. After 1542, both leaders and followers began to use religious attitudes to identify friends and opponents. This was an essential stage if a reformation of the church was ever to be accomplished. Growing lairdly impatience with the existing institutions of the church began to be organised and channelled along the protestant path, using English resources, conventicles and field-preaching. A bypass to the route of 'reform-from-within' was opened once Wishart had testified with his life to the possibility of radical change. It is impressive simply how many lairds in Angus and the Mearns took part in political groupings associated with religious dissent: a clear majority in the Mearns, probably around half in the shires together. This was a 'protestantism' that took its structure not primarily from shared doctrines or religious practice — these were to come later — but from collective political opposition to forces that defined themselves as religiously orthodox. Lairds, already asked questions regarding their own identities, loyalties and security by the political and economic pressures of their period, were now in addition asked questions regarding their salvation. Already experienced in providing for their own practice of religion, used to choosing their own religious 'experts', they began to find answers to their own and the nation's crisis from the new preachers — who happened to be protestant. The addition of a political dimension to the prevalent anticlericalism was in any case a powerful mixture. By 1550, protestantism — still somewhat inchoate, fragmented and latent — had achieved a wide base in these two east-coast shires, and was fast consolidating itself. The growing movement had new aspirations of its own and was on the verge of developing new institutions for itself, outside the structure of the existing church.

NOTES

1. I.B. Cowan, 'Some aspects of the appropriation of parish churches in medieval Scotland', *RSCHS*, xiii (1959), pp.203-222.

2. I.B. Cowan, 'Some aspects', pp.215-333 especially.

3. I.B. Cowan, 'Patronage, Provision and Reservation', in *The Renaissance and Reformation in Scotland*, ed. Cowan/Shaw (Edinburgh 1983), p.75f.

4. I.B. Cowan, *The Scottish Reformation* (London 1982), pp.72-88; especially his discussion of the opinions of Sir David Lindsay of the Mount.

5. See F.D. Bardgett, 'Faith, families and factions' (Edinburgh PhD 1987), Ch. 2 for further discussion of this point.

6. F.D. Bardgett, 'Faith, families and factions', ii, appendix A.a. no. 176 for a biography of Bishop Hepburn in note form.

7. Sir George Gilbert was rescued from the bishop's prison in 1534; *ADCP*, pp.426-8.

8. F.D. Bardgett, 'Faith, families and factions', ii, appendix A.a. no. 175 and A.c. no. 107 for Mr John Hepburn's career as treasurer and minister of Brechin.

9. John Durkan discusses further the role of chaplains in his 'Chaplains in Late Medieval Scotland', *RSCHS*, xx (1980), p.91f.

10. F.D. Bardgett 'Faith, families and factions', ii, appendix A.1 lists local altars identified at Brechin, Dundee and elsewhere.

11. M.R. Apted and W. Norman Robertson, 'Late Fifteenth Century Church Paintings from Guthrie and Fowlis Easter', *Proceedings of the Society of Antiquaries of Scotland* xcv (1961-2), p.262f. Also, I.B. Cowan, *Reformation*, p.61.

12. Mrs P.S.-M. Arbuthnott, *Memories of the Arbuthnots of Kincardineshire and Aberdeenshire* (London 1920), p.28; also, WRH, Inventory of writings belonging to the Right Hon. John, Viscount of Arbuthnott, Lord Inverbervie, NRA(S) 5, nos. 258, 260, 369. J.G. Low, *Edzell Castle, past and present* (Montrose 1900), p.41; JRL, The Craw.mss., 1.1.14: 2.1.1.

13. F.D. Bardgett, 'Faith, families and factions', ii, appendix A.a. nos. 034, 122.

14. F.D. Bardgett, 'Faith, families and factions', ii, appendix A.a. nos. 139, 337.

15. *Knox's History*, i, pp.24-25; J.M. Scott, *Martyrs of Angus and Mearns* (Arbroath 1885), pp.78-98.

16. M. Mahoney, 'The Scottish hierarchy 1513-1565', *IR*, x (1959), pp.49-52.

17. W.S. Reid, 'Clerical Taxation: the Scottish alternative to the dissolution of the monasteries', *Catholic Historical Review*, xxxv (1948), p.140. £1,400 per year was also granted.

18. *Knox's History*, i, pp.15-17.

19. *Knox's History*, i, p.19.

20. M. Sanderson, *Cardinal*, p.78. Dr Sanderson incorrectly modernises Straiton's name as 'Strachan': p.80.

21. J.K. Cameron, 'An early example of Scots Lutheran piety', in D. Baker (ed.), *Studies in Church History* (Oxford 1979), p. 133f; G.W. Locher, 'Zwingli's influence in England and Scotland' in *Zwingli's Thought: New Perspectives* (Brill, 1981) p.214f: J.K. Cameron, 'Aspects of the Lutheran Contribution to the Scottish Reformation', *RSCHS*, xxii pt.i (1984), p.1f; G. Wiedermann, 'Martin Luther versus John Fisher: the debate on Lutheran Theology at St Andrews', *RSCHS*, xxii pt.i (1984), p.13f; G. Muller, 'Protestant theology in Scotland and Germany in the early days of the Reformation', *RSCHS*, xxii pt.ii (1985), p.103f; D. Shaw, 'Zwinglian Influences on the Scottish Reformation', *RSCHS*, xxii pt.ii (1985), p.103f; G. Wiedermann, 'Alexander Alesius' Lectures on the Psalms at Cambridge, 1536', *JEH*, xxxvii no.1 (1986), p.15f.

22. M. Sanderson, *Cardinal*, p.84; *James V Letters*, p.327: 'From Germany is the shortest passage by sea to Scotland, and there are wide firths penetrating to the heart of the country by way of which the foul teaching is imported with the merchandise' (James V to Paul III, 5 Jan. 1536/7.)

23. T. Crockett, 'The Life of John Erskine of Dun' (Edin. D. Litt. 1924), pp.8-9. Aberdeen, possibly as a result of its new commitment to renaissance scholarship, seems to have been a centre for unorthodox thought in the early sixteenth century: A.A.M. Duncan, 'Hector Boece and the Medieval Tradition', in *Scots Antiquaries and Historians* (Abertay Historical Society, Dundee 1972), p.6; I.B. Cowan, *Reformation*, p.93.

24. ADCP, pp.426-8. Gilbert is omitted from M. Sanderson's *Cardinal* app.3. A sir John

Gilbert, possibly his brother, was vicar of Montrose hospital and closely associated with the laird of Dun, provost and constable of the burgh. See F.D. Bardgett, 'Faith, families and factions', appendix A.a., nos. 143, 144, 145, 146.

25. Crockett, 'Life of John Erskine of Dun', pp.21-27, 34.

26. Sanderson, *Cardinal*, pp.72-93 discusses the difficulty of quantifying the extent and doctrinal depth of early Scots 'Lutheranism'. R. Gill, *Theology and Social Structure* (Oxford 1977), pp.68-9 distinguishes four levels of theology and its effects, arguing that non-professional strata are less accessible to study.

27. *Spald.Misc.,* ii lxxxiv.

28. A. Hewison, *The Covenanters* (Glasgow 1908), i. p.14, suggested that Dun 'at home had done effective work' (for the reforming movement) 'by dispatching a priest'. Erskine's instrument of assythment for killing sir William Foster, see: *Spald. Misc.,* iv, p.27f.

29. Crockett, 'Life of John Erskine of Dun', p.37.

30. *ADCP,* p.420: see Ch. 1, n.56.

31. 'Mearns Genealogie', *Third Spald. Misc.,* ii 213; *RMS,* iii, 2407; F.D. Bardgett, 'Faith, families and factions', i, pp.35-6.

32. I.E. Flett assessed the strength of protestant thought in Dundee in his 'The conflict of the reformation and democracy in the Geneva of Scotland' (St Andrews M.Phil. 1981), Ch. 1. Fifteen Dundee merchants were convicted of heresy in 1538/9, at which time James Rollok, John, James and Gilbert Wedderburn fled from the burgh to safety abroad: ibid., pp.18-9. It had been to Dundee that friar Alexander Dick had fled and found protection in 1533; Flett demonstrates, however, that traditional civic catholicism continued without interruption: ibid., pp.10-11.

33. *Knox's History,* i, p.40.

34. *Knox's History,* i, p.45.

35. *L&P Henry VIII,* xviii (1), nos. 348, 391.

36. J. Durkan, 'Chaplains in Late Medieval Scotland', *RSCHS,* xx (1980), p.91.

37. *Spald.Misc.,* ii, 193: undated letter of James to Erskine: '. . . weit ye that it is murmuryt hyr that ye sould a spolkyn with Gorge and Archebald Dougles in Ingland ( ) quhylk wase again my command . . . And mayre atouyer the cuntre sayes that ye weyll tayk sylver to put by my matrys . . .' Sir Thomas received plate worth £109 10s 11d as a gift from Henry VIII during the embassy of 1535: *L&P Henry VIII,* ix, 45, 48, 53, 73.

38. *L&P Henry VIII,* xviii, pt. i, nos. 152, 154.

39. M. Sanderson, *Cardinal*, pp. 160-176 discusses in detail the national politics of 1543.

40. *The Hamilton Papers,* ii, 234.

41. *RSS,* iii, 820.

42. *The Hamilton Papers,* ii, 406; C. Rogers, *Life of George Wishart* (Grampian Club, London 1876), p. 20.

43. Attendance at the 1560 parliament: *APS,* ii, 525/6.

44. *The Hamilton Papers,* ii, 406; C. Rogers, *Life of George Wishart* (Grampian Club, London 1876), p.22.

45. *The Hamilton Papers,* ii, no. 55: *L&P Henry VIII,* xviii, pt. 2, no. 174.

46. M. Sanderson, *Cardinal*, p.175; *L&P Henry VIII,* xviii, pt. 2, no. 133; *Diurnal,* p. 29: 'they . . . wald haue destroyit Abirbrothok kirk, war not the lord Ogilbie.'

47. I.E. Flett, 'The Geneva of Scotland', p.25; *Hamilton Papers,* ii, 38.

48. Ms. Dundee town charter chest, cited in I.E. Flett, 'The Geneva of Scotland', pp.37-8; *Knox's History,* i, 48.

49. Ms. Dundee town charter chest, cited in I.E. Flett, 'The Geneva of Scotland', pp.37-8.

50. *RSS,* ii, 636: gift of escheat of John Ouchterlony, 17 Feb. 1543/4.

51. T.F. O'Dea, *The Sociology of Religion* (2nd ed. N.J. 1983), pp.41-43; D. McRoberts, 'Material destruction caused by the Scottish Reformation', *Innes Review,* x (1959), p.131; D. Shaw, 'Zwinglian Influences', *RSCHS,* xxii, pt.2 (1985), p.123.

52. D. Shaw, 'Zwinglian Influences', *RSCHS,* xxii, pt.2 (1985), p.123; contrast J.K. Cameron, 'Scots Lutheran Piety', *Studies in Church History* (1979), p.147.

53. M.H. Merriman, 'The assured Scots: Scottish collaborators with England during the rough wooing', *SHR*, xlvii (1978), pp.10-34; also, 'The struggle for the marriage of Mary, queen of Scots' (London Ph.D., 1975). M.L. Bush, 'The rise to power of Edward Seymour, Protector Somerset' (Cambridge Ph.D. 1964) with *The government policy of Protector Somerset* (London 1975); also, M. Sanderson, *Cardinal*, pp.160-230. For the literature/propaganda associated with the campaigns, R.J. Lyall (ed.), *Ane Resonying* by William Lamb (Aberdeen 1985).

54. *ADCP*, p.372; *RMS*, iii, 435, 996. I. E. Flett, 'The Geneva of Scotland', p.21 suggests that Scrymgeour also sheltered Alexander Alane in his escape from Scotland via Dundee in 1528.

55. *RMS*, iii, 1423; Pitcairn, *Trials* i/i 177★; *ADCP*, pp.516, 531.

56. *Hamilton Papers*, i, 252; *ibid.*, i, 523; *RSS*, iii, 194. For the protections, issued 2 April 1543; SRO, Dalhousie mss, GD 45.15.1.

57. *RMS*, iii, 304; *ADCP*, p.420.

58. Sir Francis Mudie gives a detailed narrative of Gray's involvement during these years in 'The Rough Wooing', *Broughty Castle* (Abertay Historical Society no. 15, 1970).

59. *Scottish Correspondence of Mary of Lorraine*, ed. A.I. Cameron (SHS no. 27), p.113.

60. *Knox's History*, i, pp.53-55.

61. *RSS*, iv, 2234.

62. *RSS*, iii, 1541; *RPC*, i, 64; *CSP(S)*, i, 4.

63. *RSS*, iv, 138; SRO, Justiciary Courts, JC 1.6 f.8r-v, JC 1.6 f.10v; and Pitcairn, *Trials*, i/ii 344★. Examples of Whitelaw's correspondence on behalf of 'his master' Lord Gray are *CSP(S)*, i, nos. 60, 110, 111, 119, 202, 208. *RSS*, iv, 416 for the remissions to the Grays etc.

64. *Scottish Correspondence*, p.279.

65. *CSP(S)*, i, 71; *RPC*, i, 69; *CSP(S)*, i, 322; *RSS*, iv, 1797; *RMS*, iv, 431, 1616, 1729.

66. *RSS*, iv, nos. 87, 93, 112, 2132, 688, 58.

67. SRO, Dalhousie mss, GD 45.26.53 f63v.

68. *CSP(S)*, i, 107, 148; *Scottish Correspondence*, p.273.

69. *Diurnal*, p.32; *RSS*, iv, 7, 2372, 2504; *Hamilton Papers*, ii, 251. The ninth earl had also refused to attend the host raised to recapture the castle of St Andrews: WRH, The Haigh Inventory, ii, p.53.

70. *CSP(S)*, i, 323.

71. *RSS*, iv, 2452; SRO, Scott of Brotherton mss, GD 70.351; *ADCP*, p.420; *APS*, ii, 525/6; JRL, The Craw. mss. box P bund.vi, no. 16.

72. *RSS*, iv, 2608; *RSS*, iv, 2339.

73. *RSS*, iv, 2110; *RSS*, iv, 536, Pitcairn, *Trials*, i/ii, 344★.

74. M. Sanderson, *Cardinal*, p.280.

75. *RSS*, iii, 3047; iv, 188, 2738, 2544; iv, 1281.

76. *CSP(S)*, i, 203.

77. *CSP(S)*, i, 56, 73, 74.

78. *CSP(S)*, i, 185.

79. Sir F. Mudie/D.M. Walker, *Mains Castle & the Grahams of Fintry* (Abertay Historical Society no. 9, 1964), p.6. Fintry, with Maxwell of Tealing and Baldovie of that ilk, was associated with Lord Gray and Scrymgeour of Dudhope in a commission to defend Dundee against attack, 27 August 1548: *CSP(S)*, i, p.163.

80. *CSP(S)*, i, 94.

81. *Scots Peerage*, i, 18; SRO, Barclay-Allardice mss., GD 49.47; *RSS*, iv 150 and *ibid.*, 1420; T. McCrie, *The Life of Andrew Melville* (Edinburgh 1824), i, p.10.

82. *Knox's History*, i, 99; Melville's son Richard had been sent to the continent with John apparent of Dun to study under Melanchthon; Ramsay had been with those Mearns lairds who discussed the Scriptures: Melville, *Diary*, p.12; *RSS*, iii, 820.

83. *ADCP*, p.567; *CSP(S)*, i, 212; *Scottish Correspondence*, p.223; Fraser, *Southesk*, i, p.26.

84. Crockett, 'Life of John Erskine of Dun', p.43 agrees with *HMC, fifth report*, p.639,

no.58 in rejecting the date of 1537 attributed by the editor of *Spad.Misc.*, iv, 30 to this journey abroad.

85. *Spald.Misc.*, iv, 30, 43.

86. *The Autobiography and Diary of Mr James Melville*, ed. R. Pitcairn (Wodrow Society 1842), p.12.

87. Crockett, 'Life of John Erskine of Dun', p.44; *Spald. Misc.*, ii, 205; *Hamilton Papers*, i, 359.

88. Rogers, *'Life of George Wishart*, p.19; SRO, Erskine of Dun mss., GD 123.59.

89. *Diurnal*, p.31; this event is omitted by M. Sanderson in *Cardinal*.

90. NLS, ms.5407, f.2.

91. *Spald. Misc.*, iv, p.45; Crockett, 'Life of John Erskine of Dun', p.49; M. Sanderson, *Cardinal*, p.187.

92. *Knox's History*, i, 64.

93. Crockett describes Dun thus: 'John Erskine's vacillations command our interest, if they fail to secure our respect, and one pictures him as a man of somewhat easygoing nature, not ungenerous, readily receptive to new impressions, genuinely pious, but intellectually disposed to discipleship rather than leadership'. 'Life of John Erskine', p.51.

94. Roger, *Life of George Wishart* reprints Wishart's version of the Confession.

95. I.E. Flett, 'The Geneva of Scotland', p.41.

96. *Scottish Correspondence*, p.184. *CSP(S)*, i, 176 suggests that 'D(un)' assured with Gray around 27 Feb. 1547/8. In fact inspection of the original of this document — PRO, SP 50.3 — suggests that 'Dun' is too short a word to fit the hole in the manuscript after the initial 'D' which is all that remains of the name of Gray's supporter. 'Dudhope' would fit the space and known allegiances at the time.

97. *CSP(S)*, i, 107; NLS (Chartulary of the priory of St Andrews) ms. 17.1.3b; my thanks are due to Dr John Durkan for this reference.

98. *RPC*, xiv, 5.

99. Crockett, 'Life of John Erskine of Dun' gives a detailed account of this period of Erskine's life, based on the contemporary narratives of Buchanan and Jean de la Beaugue.

100. *Ane Resonyng*, ed. R.J. Lyall (Aberdeen 1985), pp.x-xiv.

101. PRO, State Papers, SP 13.68.

102. I.B. Cowan, *Reformation*, p.89.

103. J.M. Brown, 'Bonds of Manrent in Scotland before 1603' (Glasgow Ph.D., 1977), pp.3-4; J.M. Brown, 'Introduction', in *Scottish Society in the fifteenth century* (London 1977), pp.1-5; K.M. Brown, 'The nobility of Jacobean Scotland', *History Today* (December 1984), p.15.

104. M. Sanderson, *Cardinal*, p.79. By contrast, Professor Cowan concentrates only on the known heretics and not on those who sponsored, facilitated and protected them: *Reformation*, Ch. 5.

105. There seems to be no reason to assign Alexander Strachan of Brigton (of Kinnettles) to any group led by Erskine of Dun: Brigton, however, is three and a half miles from Glamis Castle. I.B. Cowan, *Reformation*, p.102.

106. *CSP(S)*, i, 176, 192. The abbot of Coupar had subscribed Beaton's 'secret bond' and joined the Privy Council on Arran's reconciliation with the cardinal: *Hamilton Papers*, i, 632; ii, 33.

107. *Scottish Correspondence*, pp.240-241.

108. M.H. Merriman, 'The assured Scots', *SHR*, xlvii (1968), p.34.

CHAPTER 3

'The Nycht Is Neir Gone': the 1550s

With the ending of the English wars and the succession of Mary Tudor in place of Edward VI, a period of uneasy calm descended on Scotland. Between 1547 and 1554, the earl of Arran gradually surrendered the government to Mary of Guise. Archibald, earl of Angus, died in 1557; the earl of Lennox remained in exile in England. A new generation of political leaders was being born: Lord James Stewart, in particular, Mary queen of Scots' half-brother, was beginning to find a following. In Angus, too, a turn of the kaleidoscope produced a new political pattern. Pinkie had removed many lairds: the deaths of Cardinal Beaton and James Lord Ogilvy beheaded one of the Angus factions soon after the dissolution of that of Sir Thomas Erskine. The national kin-groupings of the Campbells and the Hamiltons explored possibilities in the shire. Meanwhile, the ending of the wars had united protestantism with traditional Angus patriotism and, for a time tolerated by the government, heresy gathered strength — especially among the Mearns lairds linked to John Erskine of Dun.

One expression of patriotism in this period was to call for reform of the church. The same love of Scotland that motivated John Erskine of Dun to fight against the English invaders was behind Mr Robert Wedderburn's appeal to the 'first estate' to reform itself:[1]

> Quhar for (o my sone speritualite) i exort the that thou cause al thy membris concur to gyddir to mak reformatione of the sklanderous abusione that ringis amang them ande ther eftir, thou sal treit vnite and concord be/tuix the uniuersal legis of scotland . . . to that effect that ze my three sonnis noblis clergie & Lauberaris may pas in ane faythful accord to resist the cruel inuasions of zour dissaitful and incredule ald enemeis.

Wedderburn's *The Complaynt of Scotland,* written in the context of the English invasions, viewed the 'thre plagis' that had almost brought the country to 'extreme ruyne' — 'fra veyr fra pest and fra hungir' — as God's judgment upon the sinfulness of all the three estates of the commonwealth.[2] Through the literary medium of 'Dame Scotia' he appealed in turn to the 'Dame's' 'eldest three sons' to reform those evils that deformed each estate.[3] The vicar of Dundee's main criticism of his own estate of the realm was that the lives of the clergy did not match their teaching. God had given them authority and pre-eminence in order that they might instruct the ignorance of the rest of the commonwealth: failure in this regard was therefore worthy of double punishment. Though 'Dame Scotia' had little specifically wherewith to reproach the clergy, they were blamed for the vices — sensual appetite, avarice and arrogance — of the commons and nobility. The pupils followed the example of their teachers and ignored the teaching. The spread of heresy was the result:[4]

> . . . doubtless thy abusione and the sinister ministratione of thy office is the special cause of the scisma and of diuers sectis that trublis al cristianite, & quhou beit that the rute of thir scismes and sectis be/in germane denmark and ingland zit nochtheles the branchis of them are spred athort al cristin realmis in sic ane sort that tha hef maye fauoraris nor aduersaris for diuers men desiris ane part of the temporal patrimonye of the kyrk be caus of the abusione and euyl exempil of the kyrk men . . .

Wedderburn viewed the life of Scotland as one entity: to him the political, economic and religious lives of the nation were simply aspects of a single commonwealth. Malfunction in one area brought consequences throughout the system, for God's just and providential rule underpinned the whole. Reform of the church to him was not simply a technical or ecclesiastical concern: it was at the root of the evil days currently experienced. Viewing heresy as a result of current abuses, *The Complaynt* logically opposed the policy of burning heretics as treating the symptoms and not the cause of the disease:[5]

> And this plag and scisma sal neuyr be reformit for na statuis, lauis, punitions, bannessing, byrnyng, hayrschip nor torment that can be deuisit quhil on to the tyme that the speritualite reforme ther auen abusion.

The argument of *The Complaynt* provided a coherent scheme of cause and effect based on presuppositions of the nature of society (a commonwealth) and the sovereignty of God.[6] Conservative and backward-looking in his vision of an ideal nation, Wedderburn cited extensively from the Greek and Roman classics, from French, Italian and Scottish literature and legend. His major source was the Bible, which was cited throughout the work and viewed as authoritative.[7] His was a learned version of the mentality which, in the less educated, attached great weight to portents and other supernatural phenomena that could indicate the judgments of God as surely as the course of history.[8]

It is likely that Mr Robert Wedderburn's tract originated in opposition to memories of Mr George Wishart's preaching in Dundee. Wishart had earlier viewed plague as the hand of God, revealed in judgment. He, however, had interpreted the plague to strike Dundee in 1545 as the divine punishment that he had predicted when he was forced to abandon preaching in the burgh. Though Wishart had linked plague with rejection of God's Word,[9] others of the protestants with English links had seen a wider pattern in events. John Elder in a private letter concluded that the pest, hunger, fire and sword of 1545 were God's punishment of those who had gone back on their sworn word and cast aside the solemn treaties of Greenwich.[10] Wishart, Elder and Wedderburn shared the same view of causation: that God's judgments were active in the world. Their description of current events was the same. Wedderburn, however, sought to consider the protestant heresy as one of the plagues of judgment; Wishart viewed his preaching as part of the cure sent by God to remedy the nation's evils. *The Complaynt* was published in France in 1550 and dedicated to Mary of Guise.[11] It sought to use a shared Christian world-view and authorities revered by all shades of learned opinion in order to support a policy that linked reform of the church with patriotic revival of the nation and with opposition to England.

In the struggle between Mary of Guise and the earl of Arran for political supremacy, both sides looked for allies. At various points between 1548 and 1558 both sides followed a policy of religious toleration and of reform of the church from within. Wedderburn's *The Complaynt* fits a context when the abuses of the first estate were generally recognised: when the debate had moved to the character of the coming reform, rather than whether reform was necessary at all. The defeat at Pinkie threw Scotland into dependence on France: Arran, discredited, obtained the French duchy of Châtelherault and began to surrender power to Mary of Guise. Yet even in eclipse, the duke's political authority was not wholly removed. He secured the archbishopric of St Andrews for his half-brother John and the abbey of Arbroath for his son, Lord John Hamilton. Archbishop John Hamilton as *legatus a latere* was responsible for a series of reforming councils of the Scottish church — councils which seem to have owed little if anything to Rome, had connections with projected Catholic/Lutheran reforms in the diocese of Cologne, and might — had circumstances been favourable — have led to a Henrican-style reformation in Scotland.[12] Meanwhile, Mary of Guise deployed French gold and influence to conciliate and win over nobles who had previously favoured the protestant cause, including the earl Marischal and John Erskine of Dun.[13] After the murder of Cardinal Beaton and the ending of the English wars, events conspired to put church reform on the political agenda, and to give certain reformers limited political credit.

It may be that Mr Robert Wedderburn was one of those reformers who had attracted the notice and patronage of Mary of Guise. Earlier, he had been associated with the burning of an effigy of Cardinal Beaton, had been suspected of assisting the castilians at St Andrews, and was presumably acquainted with his brother John's production of the *Gude and Godlie Ballatis*.[14] The vicar of Dundee's positive approach to reform suited the mood of the burgh in the early 1550s. I.E. Flett's study of the burgh found examples of traditional piety — a concern for the upkeep of altars, for observance of the feast days. On the other hand, Flett also discovered that funds that previously would have been devoted to wax candles for the altars were increasingly channelled to the poor in the 1550s. The iconoclasm of 1543 had not been without some lasting effect. Burghal piety was beginning to discover new, more cost-effective means of expressing itself as belief in the sacrifice of the Mass and the treasury of the saints waned. Further, the magistrates defended their own schoolmaster Thomas Macgibbon when the abbot of Lindores, attempting to assert his own rights in the school, objected that Macgibbon's teaching was unorthodox.[15]

Although the date of the various songs and pieces now collected as *The Gude and Godlie Ballatis* is uncertain, several must have been current in this period and sung in Dundee — expressive of a continuing anticlericalism. The strongly polemical songs 'Hay now the day dallis' (with its refrain, 'The nycht is neir gone'), 'Preistis, Christ beleue', 'Remember man, remember man' and 'The Paip, that Pagane full of pryde' seem to date from this period.[16] Dundee's role as a centre for the import of European reformed works was probably increased by the return from exile of James Rollock, conservator of Scots trade at Campvere.[17] In Dundee the years from 1550 to 1558 seem to have seen an entrenchment of protestant sentiment in the burgh, which was beginning to affect the conduct of affairs. As these years were ones in which it was not the policy of church or state to persecute religious dissent, actual trials for heresy did not occur. A lack of criminal convictions does not imply a waning of the reform movement. It is difficult to believe that the impact of reformed doctrine was not behind the new oath laid down for the Dundee baxter craft on 23 November 1554, notable for its emphasis on preaching and omission of traditional Marian devotion.[18] Yet whether the doctrines so expressed were protestant, or reformed catholic in the style of archbishop John Hamilton, remains unclear. The climate of affairs was in favour of ecclesiastical reform: protestantism itself was gaining ground in the popular mind, but Dundee's protestants still lacked the essential political strength to surface as an openly-organised congregation.

The development of religious dissent in Dundee was not without significance for the rest of Angus. The relationship between the landward lairds and the burgh merchants was symbiotic. If the Dundee merchants made their best profits by exporting wool-fells, it was from the estates of the Braes of Angus that they first purchased these. David Lindsay, ninth earl of

Crawford, charged that 1,100 sheep had been rieved from his lands during the spulzie of Finavon.[19] His successor, David Lindsay of Edzell, owned 1000 sheep jointly with his wife Dame Helen Lindsay on her death in 1579.[20] Of necessity, the Lindsays of Edzell — as with the earls of Crawford, the Ogilvies of Airlie and the other large landowners — required regular dealings with trusted burgesses of Dundee. The Crawford muniments reveal that Dame Katherine Campbell, countess of Crawford, had wider connections. She left to her son Lindsay of Edzell the silver cup she had instructed Robert Clark, burgess of Montrose, to purchase for her in Paris while she attended the court of the queen-regent. She acknowledged debts owed by her to James Robertson, merchant-burgess of Edinburgh, for delivering certain merchandise she had ordered: other sums were owed to an Edinburgh 'ipothecar'.[21] Clark was to become one of the regular bailies of Montrose, a close associate of provost John Erskine of Dun and probably related to him by marriage.[22] Robertson may have been one of Edinburgh's protestants associated with the earl of Morton in the 1570s.[23] Although the religious opinions of these particular burgesses cannot be discovered before 1560, it would have been along similar routes and by similar relationships that dissenting literature and opinions were imported by Dundee and Montrose merchants[24] and disseminated to the lairds of Angus and Mearns from these 'power-stations' or 'stations of high tension'.[25] It is notable that the lairds most obviously associated with religious dissent in Angus and the Mearns during the 1540s were grouped in clusters around these east-coast burghs.[26] Mr Robert Wedderburn testified to the popularity of heresy in his experience when he wrote that, around 1550, the new sects 'hef maye fauoraris nor aduersaris'.[27]

Among Mary of Guise's gestures of conciliation were the moves taken in 1550 to release the various Scots held captive in the French galleys following the fall of St Andrews castle. John Knox had been freed somewhat earlier, in 1547.[28] His preaching tour of 1555 and 1556 had a significant impact on the direction to be taken by church reform in Scotland. The main thrust of Knox's teaching, according to his own account, was the idolatory of the Mass, and hence the necessity for those 'who had a zeal to godliness' not to compromise their faith by occasional conformity. Knox tells us that it was John Erskine of Dun who called a gathering over supper in his lodging at Edinburgh to debate this question: that those that were present were convinced by Knox's reasonings, and that John Erskine followed up the initiative by hosting the preacher for a month at Dun, 'whereunto resorted the principal men of that country'. The close connection evident between John Knox and John Erskine of Dun during Knox's 1555-6 tour was to remain a feature of their careers. It seems likely that Knox was responsible at this time for Erskine's final break from the Roman church — and that the laird of Dun brought several of his neighbours out of the old church with him. Knox paid two visits to Dun in these years: of the second, he reports:[29]

> From thence he departed the second time to the Laird of Dun; and teaching them in greater liberty, the gentlemen required that he should minister likewise unto them the Table of the Lord Jesus, whereof were partakers the most part of the gentlemen of the Mearns; who, God be praised, to this day constantly do remain in the same doctrine which they then professed, to wit, that they refused all society with idolatry, and bound themselves, to the uttermost of their powers, to maintain the true preaching of the Evangel of Jesus Christ, as God should offer unto them preachers and opportunity.

Knox's success in winning these 'gentlemen' to his radical viewpoint has added significance in view of the growing likelihood of reform sponsored from within the church: conversion of Erskine of Dun and other protestant leaders to an understanding of the Mass as idolatry pre-empted any possibility that they would be prepared to settle for compromise reforms on the lines of Cologne.[30]

That the Mass was idolatry was no new opinion of John Knox's. While serving as a minister in Edward VI's England in 1550, he had defended his preaching against the Mass before the Council of the North, convened at Newcastle upon Tyne. He developed his thesis by way of contrasting the Lord's Supper with the Mass. Whereas the former was in token of remembrance for the death of Christ, the single sacrifice for sin, the Mass was held to be itself a sacrifice that could persuade the Almighty to remit sin. According to Knox, the Lord's Supper was a gift from God to man — whereas the Mass was a sacrifice offered by man to God. In the Supper, the participants acknowledged themselves redeemed from sin and death: through the Mass, the worshippers sought forgiveness. For the Supper, all (including the president) sat, dressed alike, and ate and drank together; in the Mass, the priest was distinguished by his position at the altar and by his vestments — he alone participated in the elements. Knox concluded that the Mass was idolatry — being an invention of man, set up to worship God — and also an abomination, in that it falsely claimed to remit sins.[31]

Knox's view of the Mass was one with his views of the Roman church — that it was the church of the antichrist. This was the view he had argued in his first public sermon, given while serving as chaplain to the castilians at St Andrews castle. In it he defined views he was to hold life-long, that there could be no compromise between the 'immaculate spouse of Jesus' and the 'synagogue of Satan' led by the Pope, 'the man of sin'. Arguing that the Roman church was that empire, predicted in the book of Daniel, that was to devour the saints, Knox passed on to condemn as unscriptural such practices as celebration of holy days, fasting and vows of celibacy. In 1555, he concentrated on establishing the polarity of the Lord's Supper from the Mass: yet this polarity took its force from the basic identification of the existing religion as an anti-church.[32] At a deeper level yet, the argument against both church and Mass took force from its conceptual framework: the antichrist was a creature of the Last Days, his rule the final challenge to the saints before Christ's victorious return. Living as they were in a world where the traditions of centuries were facing challenge, people of the sixteenth century were prone to understand their times in terms of this final crisis. The works of both Mr Robert Wedderburn and Sir David Lindsay of the Mount contain this eschatological perspective.[33] Though Knox did not lay emphasis on eschatology apart from its use in lending weight to his appeals for patient endurance,[34] it formed a most satisfactory basis for his analysis of the current state of Scotland and its church — and for proposed radical remedies.[35]

It was to this view of the world and the Roman church that Knox persuaded the laird of Dun and the gentlemen of the Mearns in 1555 or 1556. Its implications were clear: they could no longer participate in the ceremonies of the unreformed church, and were bound instead both to create their own parallel institutions and to seek to destroy those of the antichrist — they were committed to participation in the cosmic struggle against 'principalities and powers'. In consequence, they commissioned Knox to celebrate the Lord's Supper for them as a token of their new-found unity and commitment, and he, recognising them as a congregation of believers, agreed.[36] Before 1555-56, the protestant movement in Angus and the Mearns had been a diverse mixture of popular anti-clericalism linked with lairdly political factions; a mixture of simple Biblically-based piety and occasional discussion-groups over supper. Knox provided both the conceptual cement to link these together and the prophetic, charismatic authority to spur on his hearers to commit themselves to positive action.[37]

Who, then, were these 'gentlemen' — 'the most part of the gentlemen of the Mearns' — who had thus become foundation-members of the 'congregation of Angus and the Mearns'? As Knox fails to give their names, only speculation is possible. He does, however, add the information that at the time he wrote part one of his History (1566) the same men were still constant in their faith.[38] Certainly, the Mearns lairds of this period present the appearance of a close-knit group. After the earl Marischal, Archibald Douglas of Glenbervie (inherited 1513, died 1570) was probably the most influential in the shire. In 1544, he had a remission for breach of the acts forbidding disputing about the Scriptures and for reading certain imported books. In 1563, he was to attend the General Assembly as commissioner for the Mearns; and earlier that year, had committed himself to consult John Erskine of Dun as superintendent on the stipends to be paid to the minister and readers out of the teinds of Glenbervie owed to Mr Robert Erskine, the parson. Glenbervie's ties to the Erskines were not just neighbourly: his daughter Margaret married John of Balhaggartie, heir of Sir Thomas Erskine of Brechin, in 1550. When on 28 February 1557/8 Archibald Douglas infeft his heir William as fiar of Glenbervie, John Erskine of Balhaggartie was a leading witness to the charter, which was drawn up by John Erskine of Dun's own notary Mr Andrew Elder and attested by the sheriff-clerk for Kincardine, Robert Milne — both of whom were to serve in the reformed church. Archibald Douglas of Glenbervie supported the Reformation in parliament in 1560: he seems a suitable candidate for consideration as one of Knox's auditors in 1555-6. [39]

Closely associated with Douglas of Glenbervie was Alexander Falconer of Haulkerton (fiar 1544, inherited 1557) who had married Douglas's daughter Elizabeth around 1544. Both Glenbervie and Alexander's father, David Falconer of Haulkerton, had had protections as friends of Sir Thomas Erskine of Brechin in 1533-4: John Erskine of Dun had chosen David Falconer to represent him at an arbitration in 1546. Alexander Falconer was first witness at his brother-in-law William Douglas's infeftment as fiar, and was appointed overman, together with James earl of Morton, to Archibald Douglas's executors in the latter's will of September 1570. Although no direct evidence of either Haulkertons' association with the reformed kirk exists, their links of choice and of kin with Douglas of Glenbervie and Erskine of Dun make both David and Alexander Falconer candidates for having partaken of the Lord's Supper at Dun in 1555-6. [40]

George Straiton of that ilk and of Lauriston (inherited c.1546, dead by 1575) has already been mentioned as one of those who read the Scriptures with Erskine of Dun and David Straiton before the latter's execution. He too had had a remission in 1544 for offences associated with heresy and was to participate in the parliament of 1560. In 1568, he was to support the strongly protestant regency of Moray against those who preferred the claims of Mary queen of Scots. [41] On 27 February 1560/61, George Straiton of that ilk, John Erskine of Dun and Alexander Falconer of Haulkerton were chosen by John Wishart of Pittarrow as judge-arbiters nominated by him to settle a boundary dispute. [42] Such judges were chosen both for their local knowledge and as trusted friends of the parties — of both parties, where possible. Clearly a respected member of this tight fellowship of Mearns lairds, Straiton seems to have joined Erskine of Dun in making the transition from the time of questioning they shared in the 1530s to an explicit protestant commitment in the 1550s.

About the allegiance of John Wishart of Pittarrow (inherited 1525, died 1585) there is little room for doubt. Wishart was another of Sir Thomas of Brechin's party who had been remitted for opinions tending to heresy in 1544; he was one of the few northern lairds who supported Lennox and Angus at Leith in 1543/4. Frequently invited to witness charters issued by such as Douglas of Glenbervie and Erskine of Dun, Wishart was prominent among the Lords of the Congregation in 1559-60, associated with Lord James Stewart, prior of St Andrews, and in favour with the ultra-protestant English ambassador Randolph — being described by the latter as 'a man mervileus wyse, discryte and godly, with owte spotte or wryncle'.[43] In that Sir John's career had involved a more active opposition to Cardinal Beaton and governor Arran, his protestant credentials might be said to be more consistent even than Erskine of Dun's. Whereas the latter was to find his vocation in the reformed church, Wishart as Comptroller and Collector-General of the Thirds was to follow his father as a servant of the crown, under the patronage of the Lord James.[44]

Other lairds can still be added to this list of possible communicants in 1555/6. Alexander Ogston of Fettercairn was to be a commissioner to the Assembly in 1563 and a king's man in 1568; he married Margaret Strachan, relict of the William Ramsay of Balmain who had been involved with heresy before 1544.[45] Robert Graham of Morphie (infeft as a minor, 1511; died 1593) was under the tutorship of John Erskine of Dun as a young man and one of Sir Thomas's friends in 1533/4; he fought for Lennox at Glasgow Moor in 1544. Archibald Douglas of Glenbervie agreed to be a surety for him in 1556; he signed the Band of the Scottish Nobility 'to set forward the Reformation of Religion' in April 1560 and became an elder of the new kirk.[46] John Strachan, eleventh laird of Thornton, had been part of Sir Thomas Erskine's following, had absented himself from the host at Pinkie but attended the 1560 parliament, having had a feu-charter to lands in the parish of Conveth from Lord James Stewart as prior of St Andrews. He consistently supported the protestant regents during the civil wars.[47] John Allardice of that ilk (inherited as a minor 1547) might have been brought to Dun by his curator, John Wishart of Pittarrow: he was to marry Beatrix Keith, daughter of the earl Marischal in 1558.[48] The deputy-sheriff of the Mearns, David Barclay of Mathers, had close ties with the Erskines, being married to a Jean Erskine and acting as bailie for Sir Thomas of Brechin in 1550. He had been associated with heresy before 1544 and with Douglas of Glenbervie as a surety for the laird of Morphie in 1556. As he had been succeeded by his son George in 1563, however, it cannot be said that he exactly fulfils the criteria given by Knox for those at Dun in 1555/6.[49] Other likely candidates are Henry Fullerton, portioner of Craigo, and William

Fullerton of Ardoch — both close neighbours of Dun, the latter John Erskine's chief factor and to be associated with him in the administration of the church in Angus and the Mearns as a collector of the thirds there.[50]

Few of the lairds of the Mearns remain to be considered. William Ramsay of Balmain's heir David, though a king's man in 1568, was still a minor in 1555.[51] William Lundie of Benholm had been linked to the Erskines, but the estates during the 1550s had been inherited by an heiress and a minor, Elizabeth Lady Benholm.[52] Little is known of Walter Wood of Balbegno and William Rait of Hallgreen, but both may have retained conservative sympathies: perhaps because they seem not to have found a place among the kin and friends of the lairds so far discussed. Wood of Balbegno, of course, was kin to David Wood of Craig who himself held lands in the Mearns in addition to his own property south of Montrose, having the feu of lands in the barony of Newlands from the abbey of Arbroath in the time of cardinal David Beaton. Craig, the former comptroller, was commissioned in 1552 to raise troops in Angus to serve in France; he was to support Mary queen of Scots until his death in 1566.[53]

The position of Robert Arbuthnott of that ilk seems to have remained conservative rather longer than many of his neighbours. In the Arbuthnott aisle and its associated chaplaincy, his house had a substantial and recent investment in orthodoxy. The history of the Arbuthnotts written by their distinguished protestant member, Mr Alexander Arbuthnott, principal of King's College, Aberdeen, makes this clear. Robert's father, David of that ilk, was described by Mr Alexander in the following terms:[54]

> yis was ane single mane and of gryt estima[t]ion in ye Mernis, quho be his wysdome, magnificence, liberalitie, godliness, honor[able] houshalding, nomber off dependeris, and be mony notable deidis he nowreit and advancit ye hous . . .

The building of the aisle was the chief claim advanced by principal Arbuthnott for his forefather's godliness: '. . . quhow zelus he wes in decorning and biging of halie bigingis' was shown by the edifice itself (which can still be admired as part of the modern parish church of Arbuthnott) and by the fact that the funds for the construction were found by the laird himself, without call upon his tenants. Further, he mortified a yearly rent of £10 Scots to the chaplain,[55]

> leist so gorgus ane building suld haif apperit to haif bein buildit in vaine or be ye negligence of ye keiparis mycht haif decayd . . .

As well as the example of his father's piety, Robert Arbuthnott also had a kinsman who had become a Dominican friar following the defeat at Flodden 'for devotionis caus to leif ye warld'.[56] A commitment to the Reformation could seem to Arbuthnott to involve an unfilial attitude at odds with traditional veneration of kin.

The career of the laird of Arbuthnott in the 1530s and early 1540s in fact conformed to that of his neighbours: he was of the party of Sir Thomas Erskine of Brechin, and he had a remission for illegal discussion of the Scriptures in 1544. His connection with the Keiths, however, seems to have been through his marriage to Christine Keith c.1536, rather than from any religious convictions. On 10 February 1544/5, he had a charter to the kirklands of Arbuthnott from Cardinal Beaton 'for defence of the church against Lutherans and others'. Christine Keith's will when she died in 1553 left £6 to the priests on the day of her funeral and an additional 40s for processions and masses: the lady of Arbuthnott died, in fact, in the traditional faith. It was probably not until 1560 or soon after that Robert Arbuthnott of that ilk joined the congregation of the Mearns.[57]

Finally, the position of the Keiths remains to be discussed. William, earl Marischal, had been one of the focal points of the protestant movements at the time of George Wishart. He had been one of the Scottish lords of whom, with Patrick Lord Gray, the English expected most in 1547-8.[58] Nevertheless the earl was reported at Mass with the queen-regent in 1552.[59] Probably personally favourable to at least some aspects of protestantism, the earl had estates widely spread throughout Scotland that could be endangered by unwise actions. Besides, his second son, Mr Robert Keith, had been granted the abbey of Deer in 1544 and appears to have remained catholic by conviction during his life. The earl's eldest son and heir, however, William master of Marischal, was a close associate of James Stewart, prior of St Andrews. The master was part of the inner circle of the Lords of the Congregation.[60] Had either the earl or the master of Marischal been present at Dun in 1555/6, Knox would certainly have recalled it: in fact, he recounted that the earl was 'allured' to hear him preach in Edinburgh, and was so 'contented' that the earl asked him to write a tract for transmission to Mary of Guise. This was the 'pasquil' she later handed on to archbishop James Beaton of Glasgow. It was Alexander earl of Glencairn, however, not the earl Marischal, who was bold enough to hand Knox's message to Mary.[61] In 1555 and 1556, the lairds of the Mearns were prepared to entertain Knox and his message in the safety of their own shire: it was another thing again to venture open support for such a hothead as Knox at court, even though the regent was wooing the support of the reforming lords.

When Knox returned to Geneva, he left behind within the Scottish movement for the religious reform a small number of influential men who were committed protestants. He had celebrated the Lord's Supper not only at Dun, but for the earl of Glencairn in the west and at Calder House in Lothian. He had had contact not only with Glencairn and Marischal, but with Argyll and his heir, Lord Lorne; with Lord Erskine, with Lord James Stewart, half brother to Mary queen of Scots. These men were among the most powerful in the kingdom. Already linked to each other by ties of marriage,[62] after 1555 they became a political faction whose programme included a reform of the church on protestant lines. Leadership was in the hands of the younger men — Lord James, Glencairn, Lord Lorne. Those protestants most deeply committed in the 1540s — Marischal and Gray — were reluctant again to be drawn into conflict. John Erskine of Dun and Mearns lairds like Wishart of Pittarrow therefore represented valuable continuity.

As the Lords of the Congregation — as they were to become known — developed from an association of like-minded men, becoming first a faction and then a military force, they developed further links with each other. John Erskine of Dun seems to have been a guiding figure among the small group of families that formed the privy kirk of Edinburgh: he was also to be found dining at St Andrews with the sub-prior there, John Winram.[63] Growing ties between the prior, Lord James Stewart, and Wishart of Pittarrow have been mentioned. Ecclesgreig and Fordoun parishes had their parsonages appropriated to the priory: these were the parish churches for the lairds of Mathers, Lauriston and Pittarrow. After the Reformation, they were to be served by canons of the priory.[64]

Overshadowing the growing influence of Lord James Stewart in the Mearns was that of the Campbells of Argyll in Angus. This was associated with two people: abbot Donald Campbell of Coupar and Dame Katherine Campbell, countess of Crawford. The link between these two Campbells was long-standing. In 1539 Dame Katherine Campbell's first husband, the master of Ogilvy, together with his father, had given his bond to serve and defend the abbot and convent of Coupar in exchange for a grant of the bailiery of Coupar to the house of Airlie and the lands of Clintlaw and Auchindorie to the master and his new wife.[65] The couple had a further lease to Meikle Forter in 1540.[66] When both James Lord Ogilvy of Airlie and his son died in 1547, Dame Katherine became both tutrix to the heir and executrix of the estate. Acting with her as curators were Thomas Ogilvy of Wester Craigs, abbot Donald Campbell of Coupar and John Lord Erskine.[67] From 1547 to 1563, James fifth Lord Ogilvy was to remain a minor, subject (though to a decreasing extent) to the guidance — both economic and political — of his mother, the abbot, and his uncle Thomas of Wester Craigs.

Of these two Campbells, abbot Donald had the closer ties with the earl of Argyll — being in fact brother to Colin, third earl, and hence uncle to Archibald the fourth earl.[68] It was in the company of Argyll that Donald Campbell had signed Cardinal Beaton's Linlithgow Bond: the abbot had been associated with Argyll's attempts to besiege the fort of Broughty, on one occasion inspiring a raid of 150 horse and foot raised by himself.[69] Between 1549 and 1554, Châtelherault attempted without success to obtain papal provision of the abbot of Coupar to the bishopric of Dunkeld, from which see the earl of Argyll held Castle Campbell in Dollar Glen.[70] In 1554, however, abbot Donald became Keeper of the Privy Seal — a post he held until 1562.[71] Archibald, earl of Argyll, appears to have steered a middle course between, first, Cardinal Beaton and governor Arran, and then between Mary of Guise and Châtelherault, whose sister he had married. In consequence his uncle, having been brought into the ranks of the officers of state under Arran, retained the Seal under the queen-dowager.[72]

Dame Katherine was the daughter of Finlay Campbell of Corswell and sister to John Campbell of Cawdor, in Nairn. As her sister married Alexander Lord Fraser of Lovat and her brother was commendator of Ardchattan, in Argyll, she retained widespread connections with the Campbell interests even after her remarriage (1550) to David Lindsay of Edzell, ninth earl of Crawford.[73] During the 1550s her husband was a 'lame-duck' earl, at odds with the master of Crawford, his adopted son, and technically holding only a liferent of the earldom.[74] While the earl had the liferent, however, David Lindsay master of Crawford was starved of funds — he claimed to have 'nocht ane merkis land be yeir of ye haill erldome' to call his own.[75]

The conflict between the ninth and tenth earls of Crawford can be traced in the Crawford muniments. The master having come of age in 1551, he sought to reduce his prior settlements with the earl as over-burdensome, especially the donation to the house of Edzell of the superiority of the baronies of Fern, Edzell and Newdosk and the lordship of Glenesk. A contract was agreed whereby the master would cease these actions for reduction provided the earl would redeem wadset lands to the sum of 2,700 merks. This agreement of 14 April 1551, however, specified that the earlier contracts of 10 April 1546 (the master's marriage to Cardinal Beaton's daughter), 15 April and 9 August 1546 (bonds of service by the master to the earl) would be ratified. These included a warranty by the earl to infeft the master in the whole earldom — he therefore neglected to register the 1551 agreement with the books of the Lords of Council. The master thereupon sued the earl for breach of contract and had a cursing pronounced against him for breach of oath. In return, the earl claimed that the master had broken the terms of his bonds of 1546 not to alienate property without consent and not to pursue the earl at law: by 1556, both parties had the other excommunicated. By 27 March 1557, the master had secured orders from the lords warding the earl in Dumbarton Castle for failure to fulfil the registration promised in 1551: Mary of Guise transported the warding to Edinburgh Castle, as Dumbarton was 'a cald, ruinous place'. The contract was finally registered on 16 March 1557/8; but the earl was to die that year, leaving Dame Katherine as tutrix to their sons, including David Lindsay of Glenesk, heir of Edzell.[76] During the years 1558-1560, Dame Katherine therefore held in her hands the affairs of the house of Edzell as well as retaining influence over the house of Airlie through her son the Lord James and his most active curator, abbot Donald of Coupar.

It is tempting to describe the shire of Angus during the 1550s as suffering a temporary power-vacuum: Airlie and Glamis were held by minors, as was the earldom of Angus itself by 1557. Crawford and the Lindsays were locked in legal warfare. Patrick, Lord Gray, whose death for treason had been sought by the French towards the end of the wars of 'The Rough Wooing', was only released from ward in 1554 by Mary of Guise, and faced a variety of lawsuits brought by burgesses of Dundee who sought at his hands reparations for damage by the English. In 1557 while with the army on the English border, he was again taken prisoner and hence he was in effect absent from the shire for most of the 1550s.[77] John Scrymgeour, constable of Dundee, having had his estate of Dudhope sequestered, appears to have retired to his own lands of Glaister, in Argyll; John Scrymgeour, younger, became constable.[78] It was the provost, however, James Haliburton, tutor of Pitcur, who increasingly exercised control over the burgh. For politics, like nature, abhors a vacuum. The temporary eclipse of the natural leaders of Angus society simply gave an opportunity for others to take their place. Abbot Donald Campbell and Dame Katherine Campbell, with their links to Archibald earl of Argyll, were offered an opportunity for increasing Campbell power in Angus in the years 1557-1560.

Bishop John Hepburn of Brechin died in the spring of 1557,[79] thus providing Donald Campbell with his third opportunity to add a bishopric to his abbacy. Duly nominated for the vacant see by Mary of Guise, he made arrangements for the necessary finance to 'expedite' bulls from Rome conferring papal authority. The sources of these funds are of interest. Undoubtedly the abbot's sudden need for cash was behind the precipitate feuing of the estates of Coupar noted by Dr Sanderson, though the process may have been overtaken — perhaps perverted from feuing to occupiers to feuing to the abbot's kin — by the onset of the Reformation.[80] While negotiations were proceeding with prospective feuars, however, the abbot borrowed 500 merks from his kinswoman Dame Katherine, and her husband the ninth earl of Crawford.[81] By 11 February 1557/8, he was able to provide half of the twelve hundred crowns he had contracted with Timothy Cagnoli, Edinburgh's resident Italian banker, to make available in Rome to Mr James Thornton, Campbell's agent there. The remaining £858 Scots the abbot obliged himself to pay, and named as his sureties John, Lord Erskine, and Robert Carnegy of Kinnaird.[82] On 23 July 1558, Cagnoli issued a discharge for the balance of these funds.[83]

It would appear, however, that an element of the funding for the bulls was earmarked for disbursement only when and if the Pope should agree to provide Donald Campbell to Brechin. Once the abbot had provided the full amount required, Cagnoli, acting under contract, placed an amount equal to the contingency fund in the hands of a third party — James Baron, burgess of Edinburgh. Baron was authorised to pay out these resources to the abbot in the event of Mr James Thornton notifying him that they were not required. Baron[84] discharged Cagnoli for this reserve on 16 March 1558/9 to a total of £1,327 13s 4d Scots. In May of 1559, Campbell's junior agent at Rome, John Row, wrote that the Pope, though increasingly difficult to interview, was not disposed to grant the bishopric while Campbell retained his abbacy, and was displeased by the abbot's recent adoption of secular clothing.[85] By July of 1559, Thornton had authorised repayment of the funds: presumably the Pope had finally rejected the nomination of Donald Campbell.[86] Some monies were repaid direct to the original subscribers, the earl of Argyll and Dame Katherine Campbell.[87] Thwarted at Rome, the abbot of Coupar was to continue his quest for the bishopric of Brechin through protestant channels.

Since 1540, considerable changes had taken place in the chapter of Brechin. Mr James Hamilton, a natural brother of the duke of Châtelherault, had obtained the deanery in 1545. His ambitions do not seem to have lain in Angus, however: having been an unsuccessful candidate for the archbishopric of Glasgow in 1547, he obtained the parsonage of Cadder — the subdean of Glasgow's prebend — in 1550. In 1553, Mr James was provided to the bishopric of Argyll, retaining the parsonage of Cadder, in exchange for the deanery of Brechin. The other party to this benefice exchange was the bishop-nominate of Argyll, Mr William Cunningham, brother of Alexander earl of Glencairn. Hamilton thus gained the political tool of a bishopric — even if an inconsiderable one.[88] Cunningham gained control, under the old bishop, of the chapter of Brechin — and was vicar-general of the diocese after Hepburn's death.[89] By the summer of 1557, therefore, the temporalities of Brechin were in the hands of John Erskine of Dun as the bailie to the earl of Argyll, while spiritual control was in those of a brother of the earl of Glencairn, of all the protestant earls the most loyal to the cause.[90]

Several links can be established between dean William Cunningham and Dame Katherine Campbell, châtelaine of Edzell. When David Lindsay, ninth earl of Crawford, appointed Dame Katherine as his executrix the notarial instrument was witnessed by both abbot Donald Campbell and the dean of Brechin.[91] Dean Cunningham issued an instrument releasing Dame Katherine from excommunication on 10 October 1559; unfortunately the document relates only that the penalty had been imposed for 'certain ecclesiastical offences', so the historian's curiosity is thwarted.[92] It is unlikely that the dean could have been ignorant of a feu-charter agreed by the chapter on 20 November 1557 that granted various lands to Dame Katherine and her husband.[93] Other members of the chapter related to the house of Edzell and its long-standing friends, the Erskines of Dun. The parson of Finavon, Mr David Lindsay, had had his rival's claims bought out by the ninth earl of Crawford. Mr David had been one of those who witnessed the precept whereby Sir Thomas Erskine of Brechin infeft John Lord Erskine in his feu of the lordship of Brechin in exchange for the barony of Balhaggartie in Mar.[94] James Pitcairn was to set his archdeanery in tack to Arthur Erskine, Lord Erskine's brother, and had previously witnessed charters drawn up for John Erskine of Dun.[95]

The appointment of Mr William Cunningham, therefore, strengthened existing ties between the chapter of Brechin and the houses of Edzell and Dun. Certainly the most important of these was Mr Robert Erskine's tenure of the prebend of Glenbervie. Mr Robert was a brother of Erskine of Brechin: uncle of John of Dun. He had obtained Glenbervie by 1526, and his considerable career had included the provostry of Trinity College, Edinburgh, and the deanery of Aberdeen. In 1552, he added the parsonage of Arbuthnott to his collection of benefices, retaining the deanery and Glenbervie. Mr Robert was no stranger to Edzell: he had witnessed the bond of the master of Crawford to the ninth earl in 1546; his subscription occurs in 1549 and 1554 on tacks of teinds to the earl and Dame Katherine by David Lindsay, parson of Finavon. He was one of the chapter who had agreed the tack of lands to the earl and his wife in 1557. Mr Robert's participation in the affairs of the chapter of Brechin seems to have increased in the 1550s, and on occasion he was appointed to act for John Hamilton, archbishop of St Andrews, in granting legatine confirmation of feu-charters associated with the diocese.[96]

Apart from the arrival of dean Cunningham, the most significant newcomer on the chapter of Brechin was John Hepburn, natural son of bishop John Hepburn. Born around 1530, he was described at Rome as a scholar, of Brechin diocese, in 1541: and as under the age of eighteen years when his agents supplicated for his provision to the perpetual vicarage of Montrose in 1543. By 1549, he was subscribing with the chapter as treasurer of Brechin, and in 1556 the young man matriculated at St Salvator's College at St Andrews. Mr John Hepburn was obviously a significant presence at Brechin: he — despite his youth and junior prebend — presided over the chapter in the absence of dean Cunningham when the feu was granted to David Lindsay, ninth earl of Crawford. At the Reformation, he was accepted as the first minister of Brechin by the assembly of December 1560; by 1563, he was to be one of the first commissioners of the Assembly, with authority to plant kirks in Moray and the north.[97] By 1558, under the leadership of dean Cunningham and Mr John Hepburn, the chapter of Brechin was no longer the conservative — even reactionary — body it had been under the old bishop.

Whereas Campbell and Erskine influence had increased on the chapter of Brechin, a Hamilton had gained the abbey of Arbroath. Lord John Hamilton, Châtelherault's second son, had had bulls providing him to the abbey issued in Rome in 1551. Nevertheless, their service was delayed until 1553, so that they reached Scotland in January of 1553/4. R.K. Hannay speculates that Mary of Guise sought to prevent John Hamilton obtaining the abbey until his father had finally stepped down as governor of Scotland in her favour.[98] The arrival of a Hamilton in place of James Beaton at Arbroath signalled changes in the use of the patronage of the abbey. Whereas Ogilvy of Balfour had been graniter, now this post was granted to John Carnegy, natural son of Robert Carnegy of Kinnaird, and gifted administrator. John Carnegy had a grant in 1554 of the barony of Ethie, previously feued by the abbey to his father. During the 1550s, he also added to his lands held from the abbey the baronies of Seaton and Dunnichen.[99]

These gains by John Carnegy were only part of a wider association by his father, Sir Robert, with the Hamilton interest. Since his opposition to the governor at Glasgow Moor in 1544, Robert Carnegy had had a successful and profitable career as a lawyer and diplomat in government service. Created a Lord of Session on 4 July 1547, he had been Justice-Depute for the trial of the earl of Rothes for the murder of Cardinal Beaton — at which an assize acquitted the earl. In 1548, Carnegy shuttled between Scotland and England, negotiating between Huntly and Arran, and arranging the release by the French of various of the St Andrews castilians. Having facilitated Huntly's escape from England, he became keeper of the Great Seal and had the profits of the Seal while Huntly, the chancellor, was abroad. In 1551, as treasurer-clerk, Carnegy was in charge of the Scottish deputation to finalise the peace-treaties. In 1553 and 1554, he was a Scottish commissioner named to treat with English counterparts for pacification of the borders. His diplomatic skills were most tested, however, when he became an intermediary between Arran and France in the negotiations whereby Arran was granted the dukedom of Châtelherault in exchange for resigning as governor. For a time Arran's agent in France for the duchy, Carnegy appears to have retained the confidence of both Mary of Guise and the Hamiltons. In 1557, he was appointed ambassador to England by the queen-dowager, while remaining treasurer-clerk.[100]

On this latter occasion, Sir Robert made his will before leaving Scotland: a document, dated 1 April 1557, that is of considerable interest.[101] Unusual in being written by a layman in person, the will began abruptly with the briefest of clauses bequeathing the soul to God. Traditional wills included phrases praying for the intercession of the Virgin and the saints — as late as 1570, the earl of Montrose's last will would be so worded.[102] No pious legacies to priests and clerics at the time of the funeral were mentioned by Sir Robert — as they had been by Christine Keith, Lady Arbuthnott, in 1553.[103] Committed protestants, however, tended to include references to their trust in Christ for salvation, and made legacies to the poor.[104] The laird of Kinnaird's will suggests that he was a practical man, not committed to catholic orthodoxy, but with a conventional faith in God as judge and ultimate disposer of the affairs of men. Sir Robert Carnegy left as overmen to his executors John Hamilton, archbishop of St Andrews, and bishop Robert Reid of Orkney, both men supportive of catholic reform in the 1550s.

Besides his connection with the Hamiltons and his service of the government of Mary of Guise, Sir Robert also had links with John, Lord Erskine — one of those who had heard John Knox in 1555-56. In 1550, Lord Erskine had increased his presence in Angus by acquiring the feu of the lordship of Brechin and Navar — part of the royal estates — from Sir Thomas Erskine. Although the lordship was extensively sub-infeudated, it conferred actual possession of the castle of Brechin, the offices of chamberlain and bailie of the lands for the crown, and patronage of the Maisondieu of Brechin.[105] Sir Thomas had already accepted William Carnegy as preceptor of the Maisondieu and approved feucharters of the lands of the hospice to Sir Robert; Lord Erskine was to accept both Mr David and Mr Robert Carnegy as preceptors during the 1550s. The latter was in addition subdean of Brechin, occurring from 1556.[106] Both Lord Erskine and Sir Robert were involved in 1558 with the financial measures taken in the attempt to secure the bishopric of Brechin for abbot Donald Campbell.[107]

One further document related to Sir Robert Carnegy of Kinnaird merits discussion. In a dispute in 1555 against David, master of Crawford, Sir Robert chose as his arbiters John Wishart of Pittarrow, John Erskine of Dun, James Wood of Bonnyton and Alexander Livingston of Dunipace.[108] Apart from his protestant neighbours, the laird of Kinnaird chose another of the queen-dowager's minor government servants — Livingston of Dunipace, a lord of the College of Justice, keeper of the Great Seal and director of chancellery.[109] More conservative in religion than his co-arbiters, Dunipace had granted lands and an annual rent to the friars of St Andrews in 1552.[110] Livingston's interests in Angus and the Mearns were in fact quite extensive. He had been involved in settling the uproar caused when John Leighton of Usan had murdered his mother (Helen Stirling) and her serving girl: Leighton of Usan was married to Janet Livingston.[111] Further, the eleventh laird of Thornton, John Strachan, was married to Livingston's daughter Margaret; and Livingston obtained lands in the Mearns from Thornton's neighbour, Straiton of that ilk, during the 1550s. The laird of Dunipace also had links with the Erskines — when Sir Thomas of Brechin and Lord Erskine had signed their charters of excambion at St Andrews, Dunipace was one of the witnesses, together with Barclay of Mathers, the bishop of Orkney and Lord James Stewart, the prior of St Andrews.[112]

Between the deaths of Adam Wallace (1550) and Walter Milne (1558), no-one in Scotland was executed for heresy. Professor Donaldson suggests that toleration was 'congenial enough to Mary of Guise, who was probably by inclination neither a zealot nor a persecutor'.[113] In any case, it was in the queen-regent's interests to conciliate as many sections of Scottish society as possible in order to win approval for the marriage of her daughter Queen Mary to the dauphin of France. The death of Edward VI and the subsequent reign of the catholic Mary Tudor in England had removed the opportunity for an English alliance and spared Scots protestants the necessity of choosing between their faith and their nation. Mary of Guise's need to win over national support for her assumption of the regency also dictated a gentle approach to lairdly consciences — Châtelherault had played the protestant card before, and could conceivably do so again. The years from 1550 to 1554, and from 1554 to 1558, were therefore years marked by a kind of political consensus in Scotland.

Mary was able to call upon the traditional willingness of lairds from Angus and the Mearns to serve the crown. John Erskine of Dun was employed on the commission for Queen Mary's marriage, just as his uncle had earlier assisted the negotiations before James V's weddings. Sir Robert Carnegy of Kinnaird served as treasurer-clerk and ambassador; abbot Donald Campbell of Coupar was keeper of the Privy Seal, Alexander

Livingston of Dunipace was director of chancellery. The service offered by these lairds was, however, service to the crown — and not necessarily to Mary of Guise herself. Donald Campbell remained essentially a Campbell and closely followed the policies of the earl of Argyll. The abbot also had links with the Hamiltons, under whom he had originally received office — as did Robert Carnegy. Châtelherault may have surrendered the government: but he remained first person of the realm, and retained substantial influence throughout Scotland, including Angus. Nor had he finally given up the struggle against Mary of Guise — though from 1554 he was hampered by the need to preserve his funds from France and by his son the earl of Arran's presence in France, where his protestantism had incurred official displeasure by 1557. When Mary of Guise looked for her own party in Scotland, she looked to her French advisers, officials, diplomats and troops.[114]

In the meantime, under archbishop Hamilton's leadership, moves were made to attempt a reform of the church. Viewed by the lights of such as Mr Robert Wedderburn, this could fit the generally patriotic consensus tone of these years: reform was admittedly overdue, and in any case suited the politics of both the Hamiltons and Mary of Guise. The undesired consequence, however, was to give the explicitly protestant reformers something of a free hand. John Knox was able to complete a programme of preaching even more extensive and theologically radical than Wishart's — and leave Scotland a free man. After 1556, the country was not to be free from unauthorised protestant preaching: both Angus and the Mearns had what passed for regular ministries. In any case, it must be remembered that the situation before 1555 had greatly changed since the 1540s. Knox had intended a mere fleeting visit before taking up his call to the congregation at Geneva — he had found himself, almost accidentally, the focus of national interest.[115] 'Privy kirks' — illegal protestant congregations — probably existed in Dundee, the Mearns and Edinburgh continuously after his tour. James V had tolerated — even sponsored — anticlericalism to suit his purposes. His widow now tolerated the more dangerous phenomenon of protestantism: it served to pressurise the hierarchy to commit themselves to reform, and it retained valuable friends for her. Nevertheless, protestant expectations were running high. Until 1558, patriotism, protestantism and policy developed side by side in uneasy harmony. After 1558, Mary of Guise was to provoke a union against her of patriots, protestants and her political opponents, the Hamiltons: she was left with very few active supporters indeed.

NOTES

1. *The Complaynt of Scotland, by Mr Robert Wedderburn*, ed. A.W. Stewart (STS 1979), p.127. Stewart's view on the authorship is adopted.

2. *Complaynt*, p.136.

3. *Complaynt*, p.135.

4. *Complaynt*, p.126.

5. *Complaynt*, p.126.

6. R. Mason, 'Covenant and Commonweal', *Church, Politics and Society*, ed. N. Macdougall (Edinburgh 1983), pp.108-112.

7. A.W. Stewart's introduction to *The Complaynt*, pp.xxi, xxvii.

8. See *Diurnal*, p.321; *Knox's History*, i, p.124.

9. *Knox's History*, i, pp.60-63.

10. *L&P Henry VIII*, xx (2), no.573.

11. A.W. Stewart's introduction to *The Complaynt*, p.x.

12. G. Donaldson, *James V to James VII*, pp.78-84; J.H. Burns, 'The Political Background', *IR*, x, pp.210-215; J.K. Cameron, 'Catholic Reform', in *RSCHS*, xx (1979), 111-115; T. Winning, 'Church Councils in sixteenth-century in Scotland', *IR*, x, pp.311-337.

13. Marischal was part of the queen-mother's entourage for her visit to France in 1550 and received financial support from her: NLS, Balcarres papers 29.2.5 f.142. Erskine was one of the commissioners sent to France in 1557 to negotiate the marriage of Mary queen of Scots, and had signed a bond of manrent with the queen-dowager in 1549: G. Donaldson, *James V to James VII*, pp.80, 89.

14. I.E. Flett, 'The Geneva of Scotland', p.52. A.F. Mitchell argues that *The Complaynt* shows evidence of knowledge of some of the songs: *The Gude and Godlie Ballatis*, ed. A.F. Mitchell (STS 1897), p.xxxix.

15. I.E. Flett, 'The Geneva of Scotland', pp.50-56.

16. *The Guide and Godlie Ballatis*, ed. A.F. Mitchell, pp.192-207. In 1552 parliament passed an act against the singing of 'ballattis, sangis, blasphematious rymes': *APS*, ii, 438f.

17. I.E. Flett, 'The Geneva of Scotland', p.53.

18. A. Maxwell, *Burgh Laws*, p.322 cited Flett, *op.cit.*, p.65.

19. WRH, The Haigh Inventory, i, p.71-2.

20. JRL, The Craw. mss., 5.1.4.

21. JRL, The Craw. mss., 3.1.16. Herbert Gledstanes, a frequent notary for Edzell charters, is among those listed by Sir Francis Mudie as part of the 'Protestant pro-English party' of Dundee in the 1540s. JRL, The Crawford mss., 1.1.14: *Broughty Castle* (AHS 1970), p.17.

22. SRO, Burgh records, B.51.1.1 (protocol books Richard and James Guthrie), fs.2r,4r (John Erskine of Dun acknowledging a debt to William Erskine and his wife Isobel Clark); also fs.41v,62v.

23. M. Lynch, *Edinburgh and the Reformation* (Edinburgh 1981), p.155.

24. *Knox's History*, i, p.25: 'the knowledge of God did wonderously increase . . . chiefly by merchants and mariners, who, frequenting other countries, heard the true doctrine affirmed . . . Amongst whom were Dundee and Leith'. Knox referred to the late 1530s and 1540s.

25. In France, 'the towns were power-stations of the Reformation', being heirs of the lines of communication developed over the years between the different regions: M. Prestwich, 'Calvinism in France, 1555-1629', in *International Calvinism* (Oxford 1985), p.81; which also cites C.H. Haskins's metaphor taken from the transmission of electricity, p.77. Dr M. Lynch argues that the development of the reformed religion within Scottish burghs could be a 'stop-go' process, subject to delay and compromise. Nevertheless, burgh caution in altering the traditional cult did not necessarily compromise the role of burgh merchants as purveyors of ideas and literature: M. Lynch, 'From privy kirk to burgh church; an alternative view of the

process of protestantism', in *Church, politics and society,* ed. N. Macdougall (Edinburgh 1983), pp.93-94.

26. Around Dundee: Lord Gray, Scrymgeour of Dudhope and Dundee, constable of Dundee, Lord Glamis, Strachan of Carmyllie, Durham of Grange, Lovell of Ballumbie. Around Montrose: Erskine of Dun, Melville of Baldovie, Straiton of Lauriston.

27. *Complaynt,* p.126.

28. W. Stanford Reid, *Trumpeter of God* (Michigan 1974), p.68.

29. *Knox's History,* i, pp.120-122.

30. Dr M. Lynch suggests that in general in the 1550s, 'the initiative had passed . . . to a Catholic reform movement': *International Calvinism,* p.226. He somewhat discounts this success of Knox's.

31. Knox, *Works,* iii, pp.64-75: 'A vindication of the doctrine that the Mass is idolatry'.

32. K. Firth, *The Apocalyptic Tradition in Reformation Britain* (Oxford 1979), pp.114-118 discusses the basic text in *Knox's History,* i, p.186f.

33. Firth, *Apocalyptic Tradition,* pp.111-113 discusses *The Complaynt* by Wedderburn and Lindsay's *Monarche.* Further evidence of interest in eschatology in Angus comes from an entry dated 1561 in the protocol style book of sir Alexander Ramsay (1530-1563). SRO, Banff Charters, GD 83.1092, pp.23-25.

34. Bardgett, 'Faith, families and factions', i, addenda to Ch. 7 for a detailed comparison of the use made by John Erskine and John Knox of eschatological thought.

35. Knox shared his identification of the Pope with the antichrist with those English protestants for whom this equation 'provided the central organising principle for a whole view of the world'. P. Lake, 'The Significance of the Elizabethan Identification of the Pope as Antichrist', *JEH,* xxxi (1980), p.161.

36. R.L. Greaves, *Theology and Revolution in the Scottish Reformation* (Michigan 1980), pp.104-5.

37. J. Ridley, *John Knox* (OUP 1968), p.231.

38. W. Croft Dickinson, *Knox's History,* i, xci.

39. Bardgett, 'Faith, families and factions', ii, appendix B, no. 043; *RSS,* iii, 820; SRO: CC 1.1a; RD 1.6 f.106r; *Prot.Book Cristison* nos.449, 441; *RMS,* iii, 1254 and Bardgett, 'Faith, families and factions', ii, appendix A.a no. 097 and A.c nos. 049, 155; *APS,* ii, 525/6.

40. Bardgett, 'Faith, families and factions', ii, appendix B, nos. 056, 057; *RSS,* iii, 820; SRO, Erskine of Dun mss, GD 123.1; *RMS,* iii, 1254; SRO, Edin.tests. CC 8.8.12 f.34v.

41. See Ch. 2, ns. 15-18, *RSS,* iii 820; Bardgett, 'Faith, families and factions', ii, appendix B no. 269; *APS,* ii, 525/6; Fraser, *Douglas Book,* iii, p.212.

42. WRH, The Arbuthnott Inventory NRA(S) 5 no. 378.

43. Bardgett, 'Faith, families and factions', ii, appendix B, nos. 288, 289; *ADCP,* p.420; *RSS,* iii, 820, 857, 948; *RMS,* iv, 908; Kinnaird, Southesk Charters box no. 4 bund no. 2; *CSP(S),* i, nos. 480, 550, 959.

44. Mr James Wishart of Pittarrow was Justice-Clerk and Advocate, 1513 x 1524: *ADCP,* pp.4, 211. Sir John was a Lord of the Articles and a member of the Council by the summer of 1560: *CSP(S),* i, 879; *RPC,* xiv, 300.

45. Bardgett, 'Faith, families and factions', ii, appendix B no. 223; SRO, CC 1.1a; Fraser, *Douglas Book,* iii, 212; and see Ch. 2 n.82.

46. Bardgett, 'Faith, families and factions', ii, appendix B no. 092; SRO, Scott of Brotherton mss GD 70.351; *ADCP,* p.420; *RSS,* iv, 2452; SRO, Reg.Deeds RD 1.1 f.262v; *CSP(S);* i, 751; JRL, The Craw. mss. box P bund. vi no. 16.

47. Bardgett, 'Faith, families and factions', ii, appendix B no. 266; *ADCP,* p.420; *RSS,* iii, 2938, iv, 2544; *RMS,* iv, 1941; *APS,* ii, 525/6; Fraser, *Douglas Book,* iii, 212.

48. Bardgett, 'Faith, families and factions', ii, appendix B no. 003; *RMS,* iv, 1337.

49. Bardgett, 'Faith, families and factions', ii, appendix B no. 016; *ADCP*, p.420; *RSS*, iii, 820; SRO, Dalhousie mss GD 45.16.960; SRO, Reg.Deeds RD 1.1 f.262v.

50. Bardgett, 'Faith, families and factions', ii, appendix B nos. 072, 069, DAC prot.bk. no. 7 (Alexander Wedderburn) f.18v; SRO, Reg.Deeds RD 1.9 f.226r.

51. Bardgett, 'Faith, families and factions', ii, appendix B no.233.

52. Bardgett, 'Faith, families and factions', ii, appendix B nos. 163, 164.

53. Bardgett, 'Faith, families and factions',ii, appendix B nos. 293, 230, 297; AUL, Arbuthnott writs ms. 2764 bund.v: no. 286; *RMS*, iii, 2741 for five feus of kirklands; *RPC*, i, 132; *RPC*, i, 380-1; SRO, Edin. tests. CC 8.8.11 f. 158r.

54. AUL, ms. 2764: 'Originis et incrementi Arbuthnoticae familiae descriptio historicae' (trans. Mr William Morrison), fs.78-9.

55. AUL, ms. 2764 'Arbuthnoticae familiae', fs.80-82.

56. AUL, ms. 2764 'Arbuthnoticae familiae', f.77.

57. *ADCP*, p. 420; *RSS*,iii, 820; *RMS*, iii, 1545, 3065; AUL ms. 2764 bund. vi no. 351; and see Bardgett, 'Faith, families and factions', ii, appendix B no. 005.

58. See Ch. 2, n. 45.

59. *Hamilton Papers*, ii, 406.

60. *RSS*, iii, 830; *CSP(S)*, iii, 221; *CSP(S)*, i, 1057.

61. *Knox's History*, i, 122-3.

62. Lord E. Percy, *John Knox* (London 1937), pp. 230-231.

63. *Knox's History*, i, 119, 120; *Copiale Prioratus Sanctiandree*, ed. J. H. Baxter (Oxford 1930), pp. xxvii.

64. Bardgett, 'Faith, families and factions', ii, appendix A.c. nos. 082, 019.

65. SRO, Airlie mss., GD 16.7.1; WRH, The Haigh Inventory, ii, 74; RFVA, ASPA vol. 105, May 1540.

66. WRH, The Haigh Inventory, ii, 74.

67. SRO, Airlie mss, GD 16.24.178.

68. *C.A. Chrs.*, ii, 276.

69. M. Sanderson, *Cardinal*, p. 167; *CSP(S)*, i, 176.

70. *RSS*, iv, 310; *ADCP*, pp. 595, 600, 623-5; *RPC*, i, 86f; *RSS*, iv, 1679, 2142. During this period, Donald Campbell had also been in consideration for the archbishopric of Glasgow: R.K. Hannay, 'Some Papal Bulls among the Hamilton Papers', *SHR*, xxii (1925), p.34.

71. *RMS*, iv, 941, 1436.

72. M. Sanderson, *Cardinal*, p. 187, 190; G. Donaldson, *All the Queen's Men* (London 1983), p.40.

73. WRH, fo. The Haigh Inventory, ii, 74, 75, 86; *RMS*, iv, 987, 539.

74. See Ch. 1, no.42-53.

75. WRH, The Haigh Inventory, i, 100.

76. WRH, The Haigh Inventory, i, 100; ii, 65; i, 95; ii, 68-9 and 65; also, JRL, The Craw. mss 1.1.13.

77. He had been sent into ward in 1550 when Mary of Guise paid a visit to France — *Scottish Correspondence*, p.341; Ogilvy of Inchmartine, Monorgund of that ilk and Maule of Panmure were released by Mary in 1554 from their obligation that he would not escape. BL, Egerton ms 1819, f.10; *ADCP*, p. 628; *RMS*, iv, 384, 407, 1020; see also; *Broughty Castle*, Sir Francis Mudie and others (Abertay Historical Society pub. no. 15, 1970), p.32.

78. *Broughty Castle*, Sir Francis Mudie and others, p.32.

79. Bardgett, 'Faith, families and factions', ii, appendix A.a. no. 176.

80. M.H.B. Sanderson, *Scottish Rural Society in the 16th Century* (Edinburgh 1982), pp.90-93.

81. SRO, Reg.Deeds RD 1.2 f.359r.

82. SRO, Reg.Deeds RD 1.2 f.380v. For Cagnoli, CA Chrs. ii, 204.

83. SRO, Reg.Deeds RD 1.3 f.57r.

84. SRO, Reg.Deeds RD 1.3 f.228r.

85. *C.A. Rent.,* i, 108-9 prints the letter.

86. SRO, Reg.Deeds RD 1.3 f.472r.

87. SRO, Reg.Deeds RD 1.3. f. 343r.

88. Hannay, 'Some Papal Bulls' *SHR,* xxii, p.37

89. Bardgett, 'Faith, families and factions', ii, appendix A.a nos. 164, 079.

90. Mahoney, 'The Scottish Hierarchy', *IR,* x (1), p.41 comments of this conjunction: 'In December of the same year, Glencairn, Erskine and Argyll signed the 'Godlie Band'. There is thus the suspicion that Cunningham was closely associated with the leading reformers'.

91. JRL, The Craw. mss., box E ii; WRH, The Haigh Inventory, ii, p. 76.

92. JRL, The Craw. mss., 3.1.6.

93. *RMS,* v, 884.

94. SRO, Dalhousie mss., GD 45.16.960.

95. Bardgett, 'Faith, families and factions', ii, appendix A.a. no. 273.

96. Bardgett, 'Faith, families and factions', ii, appendix A.a. no. 104. Mr. Robert Erskine's attitude towards church reform is questionable. As dean of Aberdeen, he subscribed the chapter's petition to the bishop in 1559 that sought to implement reforms agreed at provincial councils. It is difficult, however, to see how Mr Robert could have been serious in signing a document that called for clerics to be resident in their parishes, to preach, and to avoid the company of suspected heretics: *Spald.Misc.,* iv, p.57. A copy of the dean and chapter's counsel was retained in the Dun Papers.

97. Bardgett, 'Faith, families and factions', ii, appendix A.a no. 175 and A.c. no. 107.

98. Hannay, 'Some Papal Bulls', *SHR,* xxii, p.41.

99. SRO, RH 4.96 (prot.bk.Pettilock), ff. 19v, 89r; SRO, Northesk mss, GD 130 box 1 bund. 3, bx 2 bund. 4; *RMS,* v, 197.

100. *ADCP,* p. 567; C. Rogers, *Memorials of the Strachans* (Grampian Club no. 27, 1877), pp. 27-9; *CSP(S),* i, 212; Franser, *Southesk,* i, 26-7 and 28-9; *ADCP,* p. 609: *CSP(S)* i, 376, 379; *RPC,* i, 150; Kinnaird, Southesk Charters box no. 6 bund. no. 1.

101. Kinnaird, Southesk Misc. box 3, bund. no. 32; Fraser, *Southesk,* i, p. 50.

102. SRO, Edin. tests. CC 8.8.4 f.178r.

103. See above, n.57.

104. SRO, Edin.Tests.CC 8.8.3 f. 172v-175r: testament of William Durham of Grange. See also Ch. 7 for a general discussion of the value of testamentary evidence.

105. *RMS,* iv, 434, 440; SRO, Dalhousie mss.,GD 45.16.960; Strathmore writs (NRAS 885), box 197.5. The Strathmore writs were made available by consent of Strathmore Estates.

106. Bardgett, 'Faith, families and factions', ii, appendix A.a. nos. 058, 054, 055, 057.

107. See above, n. 82.

108. SRO, Reg.Deeds RD 1.1 f.175r: 20 July, 1555. The master chose Douglas of Kilspindie, Ogilvy of Wester Craigs and Crichton of Ruthven.

109. *RSS,* iv, 65, 554. Livingston was a regular witness to royal charters until August 1560: *RMS,*iv, 1388.

110. *RSS,* iv, 693, 1620.

111. *RSS,* iv, 263, 272, 607, 787; *RMS,* iv, 570.

112. *RMS,* iii, 2893; iv, 814, 815, 816; and see note 105 above.

113. G. Donaldson, *James V to James VII,* p. 86.

114. Donaldson, *James V to James VII,* p. 86. J. Durkan, 'James, Third Earl of Arran: The Hidden Years', *SHR,* lxv (1986), p. 161f.

115. Lord E. Percy, *John Knox,* pp.228-9.

CHAPTER 4

The Reformation Crisis

The Scottish Reformation, when it came in 1559-1560, came in the shape of a political crisis: of a *coup* — even a counter-coup — by the Lords of the Congregation against the French queen-regent, Mary of Guise. In triggering this coup, the lairds of Angus and the Mearns were to play a leading role. The situation had certain paradoxes. Angus and the Mearns were by no means socially radical shires, yet they supported a religiously radical cause. Despite the ambiguities and shifting alliances of the wars of 'The Rough Wooing', these lairds had a tradition of loyalty and service to the Scottish crown: yet in 1559, they took a lead in instigating armed opposition to the regent. These oddities were in fact more apparent than real. Whereas during the wars against England patriotism had been in conflict with protestantism, in the late 1550s both came together as an example of the phenomenon (not unknown in late twentieth-century British politics) of radical-conservatism and as opposition to the pro-French policies of the queen-mother.

In John Knox's retrospective narrative of the events of 1557-1558, the seemingly close relationship between the leading protestants and Mary of Guise is striking. A perceptible coolness dividing the friars from the queen-regent was mentioned by those lords who wrote in Knox in March 1556/7, summoning him to return to Scotland.[1] Summons against the protestant preachers were discharged: little was done to punish the tumult on St Giles' day in Edinburgh.[2] According to Knox, Lord James Stewart, the prior of St Andrews, negotiated on behalf of the regent with the earl of Argyll, promising in her name a thoroughgoing reform of the church and 'more other promises than we list to rehearse' in exchange for parliament's assent to an act conferring the crown of Scotland jointly on Mary queen of Scots and her husband, Francis, the dauphin of France.[3]

The climax of this cooperation between the protestant faction and Queen Mary of Guise came at the time of the 1558 parliament called to confer the crown matrimonial on Francis. In advance of this, the regent made it known that she would tolerate continued unauthorised preaching at public protestant assemblies — except in Edinburgh and Leith. During the parliament, proposals for reform were not brought forward at her request. Finally, in letters to Calvin, 'we did praise and commend her for excellent knowledge of God's word and goodwill towards the advancement of his glory . . .'[4] At the same time, 'both by word and writing' those who suspected the regent's sincerity were sharply criticised. It seems likely that Knox himself, still at Dieppe, was one of those so rebuked. His narrative, in the interests of emphasising Mary's hypocrisy, may well have also over-emphasised the naivety of the 'simple and pure of heart' who thus trusted her.[5] After allowing for his anger, passion and occasional chronological errors, the picture that remains is that of the regent successfully winning support for the French marriage and the coronation of Francis by a policy of divide and rule: by making promises to both the clergy and the protestants, by playing off the interests of the duke against those of Lord James Stewart.

The policy being followed by the Congregation was a bold one — nothing less than a reformation of the church in Scotland with or without the consent of the regent. Since 1557, the protestant leaders had consulted together and acted in concert.[6] Their policy had two sides to it: on the one hand, they continued to seek reform at the hands of the queen-regent; on the other, they sought to extend the areas open to protestant preaching by direct action. Several of the petitions of this period emphasise that their preferred course would be a reform sponsored by the government. The 'First Oration' prefaced its specific petitions thus:[7]

> . . . we, knowing no other placed in this realm, but your Grace, in your grave Council, set to amend, as well the disorder ecclesiastical, as the defaults in the temporal regiment, . . .

When in December of 1558 archbishop John Hamilton summoned the protestant preachers to face the church courts at St Andrews, the Congregation appealed for a hearing before the regent:[8]

> Beseeching your Grace as you ought of duty, and as you are placed of God above his people, take our cause, or rather the cause of God, to be tryed most justly according to the holy Scriptures, before yourself; and put inhibition to the said Bishop to proceed further until tryall be taken, as said is.

On that occasion, trust in the regent was not entirely misplaced: at her request, the case was continued and not for the time pursued when the summons expired in February 1558/9.[9]

Benefiting from the period of toleration, the momentum of the protestant movement gathered pace in Angus. Although Knox's preaching tour of 1555/6 had concluded with his return to Geneva, other preachers continued the work. Knox's History mentions Paul Methven at Dundee, and 'divers others in Angus and the Mearns'.[10] One of these others was John Brabner, who by October 1560 was to receive a suit of black clothes as a gift from the council of Aberdeen,[11]

> for his labours, cuir and diligence in time bygane in preching, teching and administratioun of the sacraments without any recompension.

That Brabner was not elected minister at Aberdeen may be explained by the fact that he seems, even by the standards of his day, to have been an extremist, 'ane vehement man for inculcating the Law and pain thereof . . .'[12] Methven, however, who at this time was preaching in Fife and Angus as well as Montrose and Dundee itself, 'was ane more myld man, preaching the Evangel of grace and remission of sins in the blood of Christ . . .'[13] Methven and Brabner were held to be the 'chiefest ministers in the country'; among those who heard their preaching was the old laird of Panmure, Robert Maule. Indeed, his kinsman and biographer, commissary Maule, narrates that the laird had them in his company and that at this time, shortly before his death, he embraced the reformed religion. Also credited with the laird's conversion was his youngest son Robert, 'ane godly person' who 'did mightily walk beside his Father, instructing him in the chief points of Religion' and reading the Scriptures to him, the laird being himself illiterate.[14] Presumably Robert Maule of Panmure was one of those who, according to Knox, 'began openly to abrenounce their old idolatry and to submit themselves to Christ Jesus, and unto his blessed ordinances'.[15] The laird's conversion did not, however, prevent him from being buried (1560) in the choir of the kirk of Panbride, 'before the High Altar at the North Wall'.[16] The new religion could bring comfort and assurance of salvation to the penitent: in this simple form, it could also co-exist with the respect for rank and veneration of kin that marked the relationship between the Angus lairds and their parish churches.

There were other illegal preachers in Angus and the Mearns besides Paul Methven and John Brabner. When finally the preachers were accused before the courts, John Erskine of Dun became cautioner for the appearance of friar John Christison to underly the law for offences connected with heresy allegedly committed at Perth.[17] Christison had been a grey friar in the Montrose house: by April 1560, he was to subscribe documents as the minister of Glenbervie and was to serve the church there for twenty years.[18] The friar may well have been a regular preacher in the Mearns, and introduced to Perth in order to assist the capture of the burgh for the reformed cause. While any of the comparatively large number of ministers in Angus and the Mearns may have begun their preaching careers before

1560, no further names from this period can be known for certain — beyond that of John Erskine of Dun himself, one of the earliest of those who 'exhorted their brethren'.[19] A few of his close associates may be picked out as possible candidates: Mr Thomas Anderson, 'a man of mean gifts bot of singular guid lyff' was schoolmaster at Montrose and its minister by 1563. Mr William Gray was similarly schoolmaster at Logie Montrose and minister at Dun itself. Both Richard Melville, laird of Baldovie, and his brother Mr James were approved as ministers and preachers by the assembly of December 1560, and may well have exercised ministry before that date.[20]

Dundee continued to be the power-house of protestantism in south Angus. Methven had been regularly preaching since July 1558;[21] in January of 1558/9, the burgh council issued edicts which, if they did not formally 'establish' the new kirk, served to underpin it by the creation of a proper moral climate.[22] As for the physical environment, the sacking of Dundee by the English had done much to remove the traditional symbols of the catholic faith — the various altars and chapels of the burgh. The chapel of the Virgin in the Wellgate, for example, was described as waste when feued in 1563; in 1550, its patron the constable had presented as chaplain Mr George Scott, vicar of Glassery and Longforgan, former writer of accounts to James V. Patrick Lyon, burgess of Dundee and brother of Lyon of Haltoun of Eassie, was presented in April 1559 to the chaplaincy of St Adwall, Virgin and Martyr, within the parish kirk of Dundee. He later could prove his possession of the chapel only by evidence of his having lifted and disponed its annual rents. Chaplain of St James the Apostle was Mr Thomas Scrymgeour, chanter of Brechin — a kinsman of the chapel's patron. In general, presentations to chaplaincies in Dundee during the 1550s seem to mark a new stage in the secularisation of the church's assets while the chapels themselves were abandoned.[23] Active opposition to those who may have sought to maintain the old faith within the burgh may be indicated by the failure to pay dues to Mr John Hamilton, vicar of Dundee from 1558. In January 1560/61, he claimed that he had had from his benefice 'not one penny yir thrie zeiris bypast'.[24]

The period from January to March 1558/9 saw an increase in tension between those advocating catholic and those for protestant reform, the regent now coming openly on to the catholic side. Perhaps as a response to archbishop Hamilton's summons against the preachers, the 'Beggars' Summons' was issued, dated from first January 1558/9. This propaganda tract, based upon a prior English model, purported to be a claim by the 'blynd, cruked, beddrelles, wedowls, orphelingis and all uther pure . . .' of Scotland against the friars. In pseudo-legal language, it gave warning to the friars to remove from the hospitals they occupied, which, it was claimed, belonged of right to the poor.[25] The source of the 'Summons' is unknown. The organisation of duplication and distribution of this tract, however, resembles the later circulation by the protestants to all the French military commanders. John Erskine of Dun had first-hand knowledge of a hospital which had been annexed to a friary — Mr Patrick Paniter had reclaimed lands feued to Dun in order to re-endow the Montrose Hospital as a friary. After the Reformation, John Erskine obtained possession of the building as a poor-house.[26]

Although similar warnings to the friars had been published before, the significance of that known as the 'Beggars' Summons' was that it set a time-limit. By law, superiors wishing to rid themselves of tenants had to give forty days' notice before the term-day of Whitsun. May 14, 1559, was therefore the day by which the friars had been warned 'to flit and quit'.[27] With the long-drawn-out negotiations regarding the French marriage and the matrimonial crown concluded, all sides sought a solution to the growing religious crisis. Archbishop Hamilton summoned a further Provincial Council of the Church, which met in March. Easter fell on 26 March, and provided the first major test of the new determination of both the protestants and the regent to decide the course of church reformation.

During Lent, royal proclamations were read at selected burghs, including Dundee and Montrose, threatening death to any who did injury or violence to priests, attempted to disturb the traditional services, or ate flesh during the period of fast.[28] When Easter itself came, the regent and her household flamboyantly and unitedly celebrated in traditional manner. Paul Methven equally publicly preached at a communion-season at Dundee, administering[29] 'the sacrament of the Altar in a manner far different from the divine and laudable use of the faithful Catholic Church'. The subsequent criminal charges brought against Methven specified that he had served a congregation that included burgesses from both Montrose and Dundee; which fact, together with the arrival of friar Christison from Montrose at Perth, suggests that the protestant leadership of Angus and the Mearns were staging a planned counter-offensive against the regent's new role as a defender of the faith. If so, they were successful: Perth's burgh authorities continued to tolerate protestant preaching despite the regent's commands. Perth had been viewed by Scots and English as one of the key strategic towns of Scotland during the late 1540s. A challenge to the regent's authority had been given. Her response was to summon the preachers to underlay the law at Stirling on May 10 — just before Whitsunday — accusing them of violating the lenten proclamations. To support their clients,[30] the town of Dundee, the gentlemen of Angus and Mearns, passed forward with their preachers to Saint Johnston (Perth), without armour, as peaceable men, minding only to give confession with their preachers.

In the past, such conflicts had been resolved amicably. In the new climate of resolve of spring 1559, this conflict became critical.

Who were these 'gentlemen of Angus and Mearns' who thus provoked the train of events that led to the Scottish Reformation? 'The faithful of Dundee', it was reported, 'exceeded all the rest in zeal and holiness, preferring the true religion to all things temporal'.[31] The anonymous chronicler named Dundee as the chief area in Scotland where open protestant services took place following the summer of 1558. Leading his list of the other areas of 'greatest fervency' were the Mearns and Angus — in that order. The unity of the lairds of the Mearns has already been commented upon. Following Knox's tour of 1555/6, he had maintained a private correspondence with John Wishart of Pittarrow.[32] Pittarrow was a leader among those who, in May of 1559, garrisoned Perth in order to defend their Easter preachers.[33] He was to be continuously with the forces of the Congregation until their victory in the spring of 1560.[34] With Pittarrow and Dun himself, Knox's narrative shows that John Ogilvy of Inverquharity was among the Congregation at Perth, on one occasion accompanying John Erskine of Dun to negotiate with the regent.[35] Inverquharity was bailie of the regality of Kirriemuir, and hence owed allegiance to the earl of Morton, tutor to the young earl of Angus. Morton, though he had signed the 'First Band' in 1557, required the regent's continued support in order to defeat the claims of the countess of Lennox to the earldom of Angus and hence failed to accompany the Congregation in the field. His bailie, however, was present.[36] Mr James Haliburton, provost of Dundee, with William Lord Ruthven, provost of Perth, completes the role of those from Angus leading the congregation in May 1559.[37]

How far were the motives of these early protestant leaders religious and how far political? The relationship between these areas of life and thought in Angus and the Mearns differed little from that in the rest of sixteenth-century Europe. The whole of life was imbued with religion: Mary of Guise's Easter sacrament was equally a political and a religious symbol.[38] If politics is about competition for the exercise of power to determine issues, then the 'politics of principalities and powers' may be as well religious as secular, depending on the motives of the groups concerned — and, indeed, was frequently both at once.[39] The question, therefore, should be re-phrased: how far did men take part in the political activity of the Reformation from religious motives, and how far from secular ones? How far did they allow their faith to override their more temporal concerns — or vice versa? John Erskine of Dun seems a clear example of one whose protestant faith was the mainspring of his activities in this period. Associated closely with the French army during the English wars, he had given Mary of Guise his bond of manrent in 1549; Knox described him as 'most addicted to please her in all things not repugnant to God.'[40] Dun's ties with Mary of Guise must have made him an enthusiastic listener to the regent's promises of reform once the French marriage was negotiated: together with Lord James Stewart — also associated by Knox with this policy — he had been a commissioner to France in 1557. Dun had a gift from the regent of £500 from the treasury's 'readiest fruits', possibly to assist with his incurred expenses.[41] Dun's political influence — such as it was — came from his receipt of patronage from the regent. Lord Erskine, his chief, constable of the castle of Edinburgh, maintained a deliberately low profile as a loyal servant of the crown, beyond faction — he sought thereby to regain the earldom of Mar, to which he had a hereditary claim.[42] John Erskine of Dun had much at stake when, for the sake of his religion, he determined to continue his support for the preachers he had maintained, despite their horning and the royal letters 'inhibiting all men under pain of rebellion to . . . support them.'[43]

Like the laird of Dun, James Haliburton, provost of Dundee, had taken a lead in the defence of Angus from the English at Broughty. As a reward for his services, he had been granted an annual pension of £500 a year by Mary of Guise.[44] He, too, stood to lose much from his refusal to arrest or hinder Paul Methven. Indeed, taking their careers as a whole, Mr James Haliburton and the lairds of Dun, Pittarrow and Inverquharity do seem to have allowed their faith to dictate their political attitudes in the late 1550s. Having increasingly enjoyed a limited freedom of conscience and religious practice under Mary of Guise's policy of toleration, they sought both to defend this freedom and to extend it to others. It must be remarked that these lairds — presumably with their closest friends and converts like Maule of Panmure — still formed a minority of the politically powerful houses of Angus, if not of the Mearns. The tenth earl of Crawford took a conservative religious stance all his life; by May of 1558, both the duke of Châtelherault and the earl of Argyll were still apparently staunch supporters of the regent — the Campbell and the Hamilton interests in Angus were therefore not yet by the side of the congregations of the Mearns, of Montrose and of Dundee.[45] In consequence, it was 'but a very few and mean number of gentlemen' who renewed the occupation of Perth on May 22 in the face of the advancing army of the French and of nobles loyal to Mary of Guise.[46]

The Word could not after all do it alone; policy and power determined where it should get a hearing.

Professor G.R. Elton's dictum[47] is well exemplified by the course of the Scottish Reformation. Those who first rallied in the name of God to defend 'his ministers' could not have resisted the Regent, her French troops and Scots lords beneath the walls of Perth in 1559 if aid not had been forthcoming to them from those less committed to the protestant cause. Saved on May 29 by the arrival of the earl of Glencairn with substantial forces from the west, the Congregation also won over to their side the earl of Argyll and Lord James Stewart, prior of St Andrews. It was at the invitation of the latter that the lairds of Dun and Pittarrow, and Mr James Haliburton, were invited to attend at St Andrews 'for reformation to be made there'.[48] Subsequent events — the recapture of Perth, the taking and loss of Edinburgh, negotiations with the English; the eventual victory of the Congregation with the aid of an English fleet and army, and the opportune death of Mary of Guise — belong rather to the history of Scotland than of Angus and the Mearns.

Nevertheless, the ill-assorted coalition that had victory in Scotland in the summer of 1560 was reflected in the smaller mirror of Angus. The decision by the young Archibald, earl of Argyll, to join with the Congregation brought other Campbells to the cause.[49] In Angus, abbot Donald Campbell of Coupar and his ward, James Lord Ogilvy of Airlie, adhered to the Congregation. On May 19, the abbot of Coupar was reported to have 'put on secular weed'.[50] The abbey itself must have been in danger of the same treatment that was meted out to Scone. An element of bargaining probably took place as the abbot agreed to the Lords' conditions for taking Coupar under their protection:[51]

> Imprimis that he incontinent reforme his place of Cowper Putting down and birnyng oppinlie all Idolis and Imagis and tubernacuilis tharin destroying and putting away all altaris. And that na mess be thair done heiraftir nowthir privillie nor opinly. And that the superstitiouse habit of his monkis with their ordour ceremoneis and service as you call it be removit. And that na prayaris be usit in the kirk but in the Inglishe toung. And thai according to the scriptouris of God.

Donald Campbell was also required to support the Congregation in all future conventions and parliaments, and at that time to pass forward with his men 'to the forthsetting of the glorie of God'.

The adherence of abbot Donald Campbell to the Congregation undoubtedly brought his kinswoman Dame Katherine Campbell and her eldest son, James Lord Ogilvy, into the reformed camp. By June 1559,

Ogilvy was reported amongst the army raised to retake Perth after St Andrews had been reformed.[52] By July, his name was listed with the victors at Perth.[53] In April of 1560, the English ambassador at Edinburgh reported:[54]

> Friends daily increase: the last is Lord Ogilvy, a well disposed young gentleman, — who came well attended, and will not diminish one of his number until he see the end of the matter.

The fifth Lord Ogilvy's support for the Reformation was uncharacteristic of his later life — a supporter of Mary queen of Scots, he was to become one of the catholic lords who troubled her son's reign.[55]

By September 1559, John Knox was able to report that Brechin was among those burghs where a protestant ministry was established.[56] This, too, was a consequence of Donald Campbell joining the congregation. The abbot had been seeking the bishopric of Brechin for some years — by midsummer of the year 1559 he had been rejected by the Pope. Nevertheless, bishops-nominate were not without rights in their diocese. Although Donald Campbell's tenure of the see is not generally recognised in works of reference — or even in the present plaque of record within his cathedral — it seems that he did exercise some jurisdiction over the city and chapter. An extract from the court book of Brechin survives in the Airlie muniments, testifying that on 9 January 1559/60, James Lord Ogilvy of Airlie was elected a freeman of the burgh and chosen as provost under the abbot of Coupar, the postulant bishop of Brechin.[57] Although accorded the trading privileges of a royal burgh, and a member of the Convention of Royal Burghs since 1555, Brechin was in fact a burgh of barony whose superior was the bishop.[58] Equipped with bailies and a common council, the citizens managed their own affairs. As superior, the bishop had the right to preside over the council and annually to appoint one of the bailies. Apart from the bishop, no separate provost had existed before James Lord Ogilvy was so 'chosen'. Although most other details of the reformation of Brechin in the autumn of 1559 remain obscure, the combined influence of the abbot of Coupar and James Lord Ogilvy seems to have been that which persuaded the council to conform.

Some have suggested that the chapter of Brechin cathedral may have provided a focus of resistance to the Reformation.[59] There is in fact only evidence that two of the chapter opposed the Reformation. Indeed, given the conforming leadership of the bishop-postulate and the dean, it would be surprising if more had gone against the tide of affairs.[60] Although only Mr John Hepburn (treasurer and son of the late bishop Hepburn) served in the new church, the dean, archdean, chanter, canon-vicar and the prebendary of Glenbervie can all be associated with lairds and kin who accepted the Reform.[61] Of the remainder, Mr David Lindsay, prebendary of Finavon, appears to have died c.1560; Mr George Hepburn, the chancellor, seems to have been largely non-resident — by 1580, he was to feu not the chancellor's manse, but the waste land where it was once situated. The burgh's former schoolmaster, the canon-pensioner and vicar of Panbride, sir William Laing, and the subdean Mr Robert Carnegy, were both associated with Sir Robert Carnegy of Kinnaird — a crown servant not especially committed to catholic orthodoxy.[62] It seems most unlikely that any of these men would have provided serious opposition to the Reformation.

Opposition there was in Brechin, however. Once the Lords of the Congregation had purported to depose Mary of Guise from the regency, they began to act in her place — issuing writs under the privy seal in the name of Francis and Mary, king and queen of Scots. Abbot Donald Campbell had been Keeper of the Seal since 1554 and would retain possession of the office until 1562.[63] One such writ was issued on December 14, 1559, specifically discharging the jurisdiction of the Commissary courts of Brechin, the Council being informed that 'certain wicked persons within the City of Brechin, malevolent members of the . . . Antichrist,[64] had disobeyed a previous, general, edict. The identity of the Commissary and Scribe of Brechin thus identified as an early recusant is uncertain. Mr John Cockburn, prebendary of Kilmoir, had been a close associate of bishop John Hepburn since the 1530s and had acted as commissary during the 1550s. As one of the few remaining old guard on the chapter, his continuing to maintain the courts of the church might have been expected. On the other hand, sir James Robertson subscribed as clerk to the chapter in 1553 and was commissary in 1555, and so better fits the definition of the opponent specified in the privy seal writ. Both men were still alive until Robertson's death c.1562. As the writ issued instructions not just to the commissary but to all the tribunal's members, it may not, in fact, be necessary to choose between Cockburn and Robertson — both may have resisted the Reformation in 1559.[65]

One further document evidences opposition on the chapter of Brechin to the Reformation. On 29 November 1559, the Lords issued a further privy seal writ instructing all clerics to compear at St Andrews to profess the new faith, on pain of losing their benefices.[66] This threat resulted in a variety of priests appearing to join the Congregation and confess their faith before the kirk session of St Andrews on 3 February 1559/60.[67] The prebendary of Burghill, however, sir Robert Abercromby, failed to conform. On 12 April 1560, the Lords of the Council purported to deny the fruits of Burghill to

Abercromby and gave authority to James Hepburn, a previous claimant of the benefice, to uplift them in his place.[68] The canon of Burghill may not have conformed at the Reformation — it seems likely, however, that the more pressing reason for the sequestration of his benefice was his dispute with James Hepburn, and hence probably with the new minister, Mr John Hepburn. Abercromby was to retain Burghill to 1587, despite this challenge by James Hepburn and another by John Leslie in 1566. Nevertheless, these two writs of 1559 and 1560 were probably sufficient at the time to secure the accession of the whole chapter of Brechin to the protestant cause.

The decision of abbot Donald Campbell of Coupar to support the Reformation, for all its substantial gains to the Congregation both nationally and in Angus, appears to have been motivated by the threat posed to his abbey and by clan loyalty. Similar political motives persuaded the earl of Morton, from 1557 head of the house of Douglas during the minority of the earl of Angus, not to give the Reformation much active support, despite his personal inclination to protestantism. Because of his youth, the new earl of Angus was unable to take sasine of his lands: during this interim, the crown was therefore entitled to the feudal duty of nonentries. These the regent waived, however, making a gift of them to Morton who in turn subscribed a bond of manrent to her, for himself, his heirs, his kin and his friends.[69]

Rather than levy these feudal casualties from the earldom's tenants to his own gain, Morton preferred to bind his friends closer by in turn waiving the dues in exchange for bonds of manrent to the house of Angus. A series of these are preserved in the National Library of Scotland. The bonds follow a similar pattern, beginning with the acceptance of an obligation to ride on the affairs of 'our sovereign lady' and then to serve the earl of Angus as the subscriber's predecessors had done. As the service was promised explicitly in exchange for the gift of nonentries, so the bonds were limited to continue only until the entry of the heir of the earldom. First to subscribe these standard-form bonds were Thomas Fotheringham of Powrie and David Graham of Fintry, respectively on 9 and 10 December 1557. In February of 1557/8, David Tyrie of Drumkilbo, John Lovell apparent of Ballumbie and James Ochterlony of Kelly subscribed. In April of 1558, John Lyon of Cossins sealed a bond; on 22 July, both James Wood of Bonnyton and John Ogilvy of Inverquharity followed suit. Finally, Thomas Maule apparent of Panmure subscribed on 19 November 1558.[70]

This collection of bonds of manrent gives an interesting insight into the competing claims for loyalty upon Angus lairds immediately preceding the Reformation crisis. Sub-infeudation had spread the tentacles of the Douglas interest widely through the shire: whereas the laird of Drumkilbo owed service as a tenant of the regality of Abernethy, the other lairds were tenants of the scattered lands of the regality of Kirriemuir. Several — Panmure, Ballumbie, Powrie, Fintry — were also tenants-in-chief of the crown in their own right. In the 1540s, the then lairds of Bonnyton, Fintry, Kelly and Panmure had been part of Cardinal Beaton's clientèle.[71] In the early years of the century, Kelly, Powrie and Fintry had been associated with the earls of Crawford. Lyon of Cossins was close kin to the Lords of Glamis: John the eighth lord, however, was a minor. With the earldom of Crawford weakened by the dispute against the house of Edzell, Morton put his service to Mary of Guise to political profit by building friendship with important Angus lairds, who in turn were looking for good lordship.[72]

The consequences for the course of the Reformation of this extension of the Douglas interest in Angus are obscure. John Ogilvy of Inverquharity was not prevented from becoming one of the leading members of the Congregation; nothing is known, however, about the activities of the other Angus tenants in the years 1558-1559. Of Morton himself, a signatory to the 'First Band', Knox wrote: 'who promised to be ours, but did never plainly join'.[73] It seems likely that, given the risks attaching to clear commitment to either side, Morton's clients in Angus would have valued their bonds to the house of Angus as convenient reasons for failure to support any other lord claiming their service. From this inactivity, the tenth earl of Crawford was probably the greatest loser. He was to join with Huntly in inviting Mary queen of Scots to return as a catholic monarch to Aberdeen; yet his course, too, during 1559/60 appears to have been one of inaction.[74]

On 10 September 1559, the young earl of Arran, having newly arrived in Scotland from France,[75] joined the Congregation. By the nineteenth, his father the duke of Châtelherault had also joined. With the Hamilton interest turned against her, the isolation of Mary of Guise from the Scottish political nation was virtually complete. What had begun as defiance of her authority by Dundee, Perth and certain Angus lairds on religious grounds had swelled to become national resistance to French control of Scottish affairs and supposed colonisation of Scottish lands.[76] In a last attempt to retain the duke, she employed Sir Robert Carnegy of Kinnaird as a negotiator between them. Such agents were chosen because of their connections with both sides: it had been Lord James Stewart and the earl of Argyll who had first negotiated on the regent's behalf with John Erskine of Dun outside of Perth. In a public proclamation of her case, she described Carnegy as 'of good credit and reputation'.[77] Although there is no evidence that Carnegy followed the example of the queen-dowager's earlier representatives in deserting her cause, the close links his family was developing with Châtelherault's second son, the abbot of Arbroath, may well have had a higher priority in his mind than his bond of manrent to Mary of Guise — subscribed in the very different circumstances of 1548.[78] Lord John Hamilton, abbot of Arbroath, was one of those who ratified the Contract of Berwick of February 1559/60 and participated in the siege of Leith.[79] The accession of the duke to the Congregation brought the last of the major grouping, with connections in Angus to the cause of Reformation. Arbroath abbey, like Coupar, was spared assault when the men of Angus and the Mearns forcibly reformed Lindores, Scone and the Aberdeen priories in 1559.[80]

It is probable that the majority of the lairds of Angus passively acquiesced in the Reformation rather than fervently supporting it. Many had had previous links with heresy or with English allies; few if any had good reasons for defending the existing church — which all agreed needed reform. The reform of 1560 promised the opportunity for gain for the materially minded, and of spiritual benefits for the religiously inclined. Revolt against Mary of Guise was presented as the 'defence of the realm';[81] men like Mr Robert Wedderburn had equally viewed reformation of the church as a patriotic necessity to avert the wrath of God from the nation. Defence of religious freedom for protestant preaching dovetailed with defence of Scotland from French ambitions: traditionally loyal and patriotic Angus lairds could view the Reformation favourably as according with their former principles. After the initial crisis of May and the fighting around Perth and St Andrews, the part played by men from Angus and the Mearns sharply decreased. In July 1559, they were unable to assist when the Congregation in Edinburgh were threatened by the French;[82] the next occasion when they attended in force was with the Scottish host that met with the English before Leith in April 1560. Knox reported, however, that the 'army was great' for a few days only. The feudal levies and light cavalry provided by northern lairds was little use for a siege of a fortified stronghold. Of the Mearns gentry, only Henry Graham, younger of Morphie, was to sign the Band at Leith, 27 April 1560.[83] The active involvement of Mr James Haliburton with Dundee's armed bands and artillery at Edinburgh and Leith should not conceal the fact that few others from Angus and the Mearns are known to have been associated with the Reformation conflict in the spring of 1560.[84]

Professor Donaldson has described those who supported the Reformation at the parliament of 1560 as 'the party of revolution', characterised by their past Anglophilism, constancy to the reforming cause, and cohesion as a group.[85] Examination of those from Angus and the Mearns at Edinburgh in

August of 1560 reveals not one but several circles of associations. From those who subscribed bonds of manrent to the house of Angus in 1557/8 were the lairds of Powrie, Kelly, Inverquharity and Panmure. All four can be shown to have consistently supported factions associated with a protestant commitment during their careers.[86] The congregation of the Mearns was well represented by seven important lairds: those of Pittarrow, Thornton, Lauriston, Glenbervie, Allardice, Arbuthnott and Morphie. Pittarrow and Lauriston had been linked with John Erskine of Dun as members of the council of the Lords of the Congregation since October 1559.[87] Archibald Douglas of Glenbervie had been described in English reports in 1548 as 'one of the chiefest of that surname, except the earl of Angus'. Associated with heresy in the 1540s, linked by marriage to the house of Dun, Glenbervie was commissioner for the Mearns to the General Assembly of 1563.[88] Robert Graham of Morphie and John Strachan of Thornton had similar consistent records.[89] The name of Robert Arbuthnott of that ilk was new to protestant circles — it has been suggested that his wife's faith remained traditional into the 1550s. His son and heir Andrew, however, was an associate of John Erskine of Dun, lending him £200 in 1555.[90] The commitment of these lairds to the reformed church after 1560 was to remain solid. The triangle of lands whose apex was Dunnottar was a heartland of the protestant faith; yet, even so, the allegiance of northern Mearns, by Deeside, was less secure.

The position of the sole earl of the Mearns, William the earl Marischal, was much less clear-cut than that of the lairds of the shire. His record in the 1540s was as an enthusiastic protestant — and in the 1550s, as a supporter of Mary of Guise.[91] During the crisis of 1559, he appears to have given cautious verbal support to the Congregation — perhaps in order to secure the release of his heir, a captive in England. By the summer of 1560, he could be described as 'neutral' — yet he arrived for the parliament, and was at first welcomed by the English ambassador. By August, it was reported that the Lord James was to be 'earnest' with him to overcome his doubts and delays — finally, he approved the new *Confession of Faith,* but left Edinburgh without accepting the proposed marriage of Arran to Queen Elizabeth — pleading sickness. Though (perhaps) personally a protestant, the earl Marischal had many links to the north of Dunnottar: he held lands from the earl of Huntly, and could be described as one of that earl's friends.[92] Also at the parliament of 1560 was the master of Marischal — a close associate of Moray, and much more in accord with the general sentiment of the Mearns.[93]

All four of the traditional magnates of Angus attended parliament in August 1560. John Lord Glamis and James Lord Ogilvy were, however, still minors.[94] The former was to develop a career as a protestant; the latter as conservative in religion.[95] It seems likely that Lord Ogilvy was present with his curator, the abbot of Coupar, Donald Campbell; and that Ogilvy of Inverquharity appeared with the earl of Morton.[96] Of the other Ogilvies, Patrick of Inchmartine (in Gowrie) was rather closer to Patrick Lord Gray than to Ogilvy of Airlie. Alexander of Clova, though an associate of Lord Ogilvy in the 1570s, was rather more in the company of Inverquharity around 1560. Little is known of David Ogilvy of that ilk — but his heir, Gilbert (succeeded 1560 x 1562), gave Morton a bond of manrent in 1565 and was a king's man in 1568, thus taking opposite sides from the chief of his name.[97] Once again, it must be emphasised that lairds had other loyalties apart from kin: in Angus especially, bonds of choice — of marriage-ties, of personal faith — could cut across the shared surname.

Both David, tenth earl of Crawford, and Patrick Lord Gray took equivocal positions during the summer of 1560. Indeed, they seem to have mutually supported each other in their dealings with the English. On February 10, 1559/60, Randolph reported that the earls Atholl, Errol, Montrose, Marischal and Crawford and lords Gray, Ogilvy, Drummond and Oliphant would do as the earl of Huntly advised them — and that the latter had begun to 'reform religion in his country'. Crawford and Gray came to parliament together with Atholl and Innermeath in July; by August, Randolph was complaining that Atholl and Marischal were making undue delays, that Crawford was finding objections, and that Gray promised support in due course. Atholl, Crawford and Gray were finally reported as agreeing to the proposed marriage between Arran and Queen Elizabeth — but Gray left Edinburgh before expressing this consent in writing.[98] This bloc of northern earls and lords appears to have been suspicious of the Hamilton and Douglas interests that were prominent in 1560 — by working loosely together, they retained a measure of independence.

Lord Gray's bitter experience of the English during the late 1540s may have made him peculiarly sensible of the need to retain links with all parties. His absence in England as a prisoner of the earl of Northumberland from 1557 to December of 1559 meant that he had been removed from Scotland during critical years. The English, indeed, recognised his political worth and deliberately retained both him and the master of Marischal for four extra months: when released, it was on terms — a false step could mean that he was recalled.[99] Gray, therefore, had many reasons for cautious ambiguity in 1560. Letters to him from both Mary of Guise and Mary queen of Scots survive. In the first (11 May 1560) the queen-regent recognised '(that he was) of mynd as yit to preserve in the gude mynd towart zour souerane . . .'[100] She suggested that the actions of the other lords were hardly compatible with due obedience, that they made no headway in the siege of Leith, and concluded by asking whether Gray was prepared to further her cause. By October, Queen Mary was writing to thank Gray for the 'entire affection' he had had to her mother,[101] and to solicit the support of him and his friends in their duty and obedience to herself. Gray, then, despite his protestantism of the 1540s, maintained a friendly and (com)promising correspondence with Mary of Guise and her daughter, at the same time that he was agreeing to the Arran/Elizabeth match — which could have been perceived as a political threat by Mary. The English did in fact recall him to ward: in February 1561/2, the earls of Atholl, Marischal and Mar (James Stewart — later Moray) bound themselves as surety for his not escaping from Northumberland for six months.[102]

Representatives of Angus at the 1560 Reformation parliament were a somewhat ill-assorted group. The magnates attended uneasily — as clients of their sponsors, or as mildly dissenting from the general ethos. There was an Ogilvy group — sheltering under a kinship that concealed different loyalties. There was a group of friends of Morton — a group based on the thinnest of feudal relationships and requiring to be patched together with written pledges. There were commissioners from the key protestant burghs of Dundee and Montrose; and also from Forfar. Compared with the seven lairds from the Mearns, interlocked by marriage, faith and shared political history, this was a disparate set. Where, too, were the other lairds of Angus? Where were Gardyne and Guthrie of that ilk, Ogilvy of Balfour, Graham of Fintry, Wood of Craig or Bonnyton, Carnegy of Kinnaird? John, commendator of Arbroath, and Donald, abbot of Coupar, were in attendance — but they represented factions based outside the shire.

The history of protestantism in Angus had been that of occasional personal piety linked with political factions that had religious colouring. A good many families had had connections with the movement — far more than attended the Reformation parliament and who thus assented to the new *Confession of Faith* and banned the Mass on pain of death. Local catholic leadership was non-existent, or, as bishop John Hepburn had been, discredited both by persecution of heretics and by the growing catholic reform movement. The new faith seems, therefore, to have been accepted in Angus — and welcomed in the Mearns. Though both shires together formed the 'epicentre of the explosion',[103] their reactions can be distinguished. Apart from Erskine of Dun at Montrose and in the Mearns, there was no clear local leadership to unite the Angus lairds. Just as the shire's faction led by Cardinal Beaton had been smaller than that of secretary

Erskine of Brechin, so neither the interests of Campbell nor Hamilton ever achieved more than a marginal hold on Angus loyalties.

The first fifty years of the century had been testing ones for the small independent families of Angus: James V's aggressive forfeitures, the English occupation and crop-burnings, the impact of new standards of living, of new concepts of the world — these made for caution, for solidarity. These lairds would do little to risk their hereditary estates — neither for a conceptual faith, nor for outside interests. Nor would they willingly oppose their neighbours in arms. In such a situation, all the cards were held by those who *were* united: by a covenanting faith, by sharing of the Lord's Supper, by the determination to succeed that follows once the point of possible withdrawal has been left behind. There were those who found that the polarisation explicit in the identification of the Roman church with the antichrist made sense of their experience of current events: of the turmoil of the world, of the abuses of the church, of their own sense of crisis and insecurity. Others found the role offered them as patrons, elders and leaders of the new faith attractive and in continuity with the traditions of their house. Others again saw opportunites to add to their lands. For all these reasons, the Reformation had taken root in Angus and the Mearns.

Yet this religious revolution was based on a firmly conservative mood. At the simplest political level, the duke aimed to reverse Mary of Guise's *coup* in displacing him, the first gentleman of Scotland, from the regency. In a real sense, the political events of 1559/60 were not a revolution but a counter-coup: an attempt to return to 1547, before Pinkie, to remove the French troops, French officers of state and the French regent. The language of the 'revolution' was backward-looking, to the ideal 'commonweal'. Even the eschatology of the period was post-millennial, expecting a decline into actual and spiritual warfare at the end of the age. Knox's aim was to return the church to the golden age of the past purity — that of the 'primitive and apostolic church'.[104] Mary of Guise's own supporters had advocated reform of the church as a patriotic measure. Discontent with the present had led to its rejection in favour of the virtues and ideals and leaders of the past. The parliament of 1560 proceeded to abolish the authority of the Pope in Scotland, forbade priests to say Mass, and accepted the new *Confession of Faith*. This radical-conservative mood, however, was a most insecure basis on which to construct a new 'godly' society. Once positive and practical proposals were brought forward to build a future, the coalition fell apart. General assent was not forthcoming even at the 1560 parliament for the projected marriage between the earl of Arran and Queen Elizabeth of England; nor were the proposals of the Book of Discipline as generally welcomed as the *Confession*. In any case, the return of Queen Mary to Scotland soon produced an entirely new political situation, and one much less favourable to religious radicals.

NOTES

1. *Knox's History*, i, p.132
2. *Knox's History*, i, pp.126-7, 127-9.
3. *Knox's History*, i, p.141.
4. *Knox's History*, i, p.158.
5. *Knox's History*, i, p.141.
6. Their programmes and demands grew bolder as time passed: whereas in 1557, they claimed only vernacular prayers and readings from Scripture in the parish churches, with 'doctrine, preaching and teaching' to be 'used privately, in quiet houses', by 1558 their 'First Oration' sought public preaching with both baptism and the Lord's Supper to be ministered in public in the vernacular. *Knox's History*, i, p.138, 149-152.
7. *Knox's History*, i, p.150.
8. Petrie, *Compendious History*, century xvi, pt. 2, pp.191-192, citing a ms. then in the Dun Papers; see Crockett, 'Life of John Erskine of Dun', p.81.
9. 'Histoire of the Estate of Scotland', *Wodrow Scot. Misc.*, pp.61-2.
10. *Knox's History*, i, p.125.
11. A. White, 'Religion, politics and society in Aberdeen', p.168.
12. Commissary Maule: SRO, Dalhousie mss, GD 45.26.53 f.65.
13. *Knox's History*, i, 148; SRO, Dalhousie mss, GD 45.26.53 f.65; for Methven at Montrose, SRO, Justiciary courts, JC 1.7 f.134r = Pitcairn, *Trials*, i/ii, 406/7*.
14. SRO, Dalhousie mss, GD 45.26.53 f.65. Maule's use of 'country' is, unfortunately, ambiguous. Did he mean Scotland or Angus?
15. *Knox's History*, i, p.148.
16. SRO, Dalhousie mss, GD 45.26.53 f.65.
17. SRO, Justiciary courts, JC 1.7 f.134r = Pitcairn, *Trials*, i/ii, 406/7*.
18. Bardgett, 'Faith, families and factions', ii, appendix A.c. no. 029.
19. *Knox's History*, i, p.148.
20. Bardgett, 'Faith, families and factions', ii, appendix A.c nos. 003, 086, 146, 143.
21. 'Histoire of the Estate of Scotland', *Wodrow Soc. Misc.*, p.67.
22. Excessive drinking was to be punished and brothel keepers banished. Children were prohibited from creating a disturbance in the kirkyard during services and, if under five, were excluded from the church itself. An emphasis on sexual discipline was characteristic of the first protestant council of Edinburgh in 1560. Maxwell, *Old Dundee*, pp.78, 81, 75; M. Lynch, *Edinburgh*, p.91.
23. Bardgett, 'Faith, families and factions', ii, appendix A.a nos. 304, 217, 312; SRO, Scrymgeour-Wedderburn mss., GD 137.3890 and 3891 for Our Lady in Wellgate being waste.
24. SRO, Book of Assumption, E 48.1.1 f.357v and Bardgett, 'Faith, families and factions', ii, appendix A.a no. 165.
25. *Knox's History*, ii, 255; Rev. Brother Kenneth, 'The popular literature of the Scottish Reformation', *IR*, x, p.305.
26. *Knox's History*, i, p.166; see appendix A.a no. 265.
27. *Knox's History*, ii, p.256.
28. *LHT*, x, 416.

29. *Knox's History*, i, pp.158-9; SRO, Justiciary courts, JC 1.7 f.134r.

30. *Knox's History*, i, p.160.

31. 'Histoire of the Estate of Scotland', *Wodrow Soc. Misc.,* p.54.

32. *Knox's History*, i, p.136.

33. *Knox's History*, i, p.173.

34. *Knox's History*, ii, p.497 (index).

35. *Knox's History*, i, p.176.

36. SRO, Ogilvy of Inverquharity mss., GD 205 box 4 bund. 6; NLS, ms.5308 no. 1262; G.R. Hewitt, *Scotland under Morton* (Edinburgh 1982), p.3.

37. Both refused the regent's orders to seize and arrest the protestants preaching in their burghs. Haliburton persuaded Methven to 'avoid the town for a time' — Dundee was frequented by the French troops stationed at Broughty Castle. *Knox's History*, i, p.159; I.E. Flett, 'The Geneva of Scotland', p.48.

38. R. O'Day, *The Debate on the English Reformation* (London 1986), p.133.

39. G.R. Elton's dictum must therefore be misleading: political decisions and actions are inevitable, but it is gratuitous to consider that they are necessarily secular. 'The progress and spread of reformed Churches . . . depended in the last resort on one thing only — the secular politics of principalities and powers.' *Reformation Europe* (London 1963), p.140.

40. SRO, State Papers, SP 13.68; *Knox's History*, i, p.160.

41. Kinnaird, Southesk muniments: ms. in royal letters log-book.

42. *Peerage*, v, 613; G. Donaldson, *Mary Queen of Scots* (London 1974), p.129. Lord Erskine also appears to have retained a catholic faith to at least July 1556, when he (on his succession) surrendered the commend of Dryburgh to marry: SRO, Mar and Kellie mss., GD 124.9.13-21.

43. *Knox's History*, i, p.161.

44. *RPC*, xiv, 9; *RSS*, v, 2897.

45. *Knox's History*, i, pp.164, 173.

46. *Knox's History*, i, p.164.

47. G. Elton, *Reformation Europe*, p.124.

48. *Knox's History*, i, pp.180-1.

49. 'To Saint Johnston, . . . did convene . . . the laird of Glenorchy (Sir Colin Campbell) and drivers others who before had not presented themselves for defence of their brethren.' *Knox's History*, i, p.188.

50. Bardgett, 'Faith, families and factions', ii, appendix A.a no.050.

51. *C.A. Chrs.*, ii, 278 citing 'Two Papers from Argyll Charter Chest', *SHR*, xxi, pp.142-3.

52. *CSP (S)*, i, 474.

53. *CSP (S)*, i, 480.

54. *CSP (S)*, i, 713.

55. G. Donaldson, *All the Queen's Men*, p.191 (index) incorrectly considers the Lord Ogilvy present at the Reformation parliament to have been the fourth lord. See Bardgett, 'Faith, families and factions', ii, appendix B nos. 198-200.

56. Knox, *Works*, vi, p.78; letter to Mrs Anne Locke.

57. SRO, Airlie mss., GD 16.25.49.

58. D.B. Thoms, *The Council of Brechin* (SFBC 1977), pp.20-30; G.S. Pryde, *The Burghs of Scotland* (Oxford 1965), pp.33, 38; cf. Arbroath, p.31.

59. I.B. Cowan, *Reformation*, p.116.

60. G. Donaldson emphasises the importance of leadership: *Scottish Church History*, p.79, discussing rates of conformity in Orkney and Galloway.

61. William Cunningham, Mr James Pitcairn, Mr Thomas Scrymgeour, Mr John Hay, Mr Robert Erskine: Bardgett, 'Faith, families and factions', ii, appendix A.a nos. 079, 273, 312, 169, 104. (Mr John Hay was to be considered 'godly, learned and wise' by ambassador Randolph in 1565: *CSP (S)* ii 192, 196, 198.)

62. Bardgett, 'Faith, families and factions', ii, appendix A.a nos. 206, 173, 191, 057; for Sir Robert of Kinnaird, Ch. 3, nn. 99-112.

63. *C.A. Chrs.*, ii, 278-9.

64. Petrie, *Compendious History*, century xvi, pt. 2, p.215 — citing from the Dun Papers; T. Crockett, 'Life of John Erskine of Dun', p.118.

65. Bardgett, 'Faith, families and factions', ii, appendix A.a nos. 066 and 289. Crockett dated this document to 1560, but the 2nd and 18th year of the reigns of Francis and Mary was 1559, dating inclusively.

66. Petrie, *Compendious History*, century xvi, pt. 2, p.215; cited T. Crockett, 'Life of John Erskine of Dun', p.103. This and the preceding writ also printed in *Keith's History* (Spottiswoode Soc. 1844), pp.246-8. Keith dates both in 1559.

67. *StAKSR*, i, 10-11. In December, Lord James wrote, 'our letters through the country are duly obeyed' and included Angus in the list of sheriffdoms where this was so: *CSP (S)*, i, 597.

68. Bardgett, 'Faith, families and factions', ii, appendix A.a no. 001: this entry includes the full text of the writ.

69. SRO, State Papers, SP 13.78; cited J.M. Brown, 'Bonds of manrent in Scotland before 1603' (Glasgow Ph.D. 1977), no. 522.

70. NLS, ms.25.9.6 nos. 5, 6, 7; 1, 2, 3; 9; 10, 11; 14. Some extant bonds by minor tenants have not been listed; others are damaged. This collection is omitted in the thesis cited in note 69 above.

71. See Ch. 1, note 56.

72. Bardgett, 'Faith, families and factions', ii, appendix B for clarification of the individual lairds mentioned here and throughout.

73. *Knox's History*, i, p.262.

74. *History of the Church of Scotland by Archbishop John Spottiswoode*, ed. M. Russell and M. Napier (Spottiswoode Soc. 1851), i, 328-9.

75. J. Durkan, 'The Hidden Years', *SHR*, lxv (1986), pp.163-4.

76. R. Mason, 'Covenant and Commonweal', in *Church, Politics and Society*, ed. N. Macdougall (Edinburgh 1983), pp.105-112 discusses the switch in the Congregation's appeal from religious to patriotic language.

77. *Knox's History*, i, pp.230, 237.

78. SRO, State Papers, SP 13.59; cited J.M. Brown, 'Bonds of manrent in Scotland before 1603' (Glasgow Ph.D. 1977), no. 521. See Ch. 3, nn. 100-112.

79. *Knox's History*, i, p.308.

80. *Knox's History*, i, pp.188-91 (Scone); *ibid.*, p.186 n.4 (Lindores); W. Moir Bryce, *Scottish Grey Friars*, i, pp.322-4 (Aberdeen). Coupar and Arbroath must have been 'reformed' by their own commendators; no evidence survives to indicate whether they were unroofed at this time or later. D. McRoberts' case is somewhat overstated: 'Material Destruction', *IR*, x, pp.143, 150, 159-160.

81. *Scottish Correspondence*, p.427.

82. *Knox's History*, i, p.200.

83. *Knox's History*, i, pp.312, 316.

84. For the roles of Dundee and its provost, Mr James Haliburton: I.E. Flett, 'The Geneva of Scotland', pp.69-70. T. Crockett 'The Life of John Erskine of Dun', p.111 notes that Erskine appears to have been in Angus during the early months of 1560. He was appointed master of the hospital of Montrose and factor to its fruits 22 Feb. 1559/60; *HMC*, v, p.640 no. 65.

85. G. Donaldson, *All the Queen's Men*, pp. 31-47.

86. Bardgett, 'Faith, families and factions', ii, appendix B gives suggested dates of succession for the following lairds.
Thomas Fotheringham of Powrie (1547-c.1576: see appendix B.063): member of General Assembly 1563; king's man in Angus 1569; his brother a reformed minister; associate of the Lindsays of Edzell. SRO, CC 1.1a (extract Assembly records); Strathmore mss box 235.3; Bardgett, 'Faith, families and factions', ii, appendix A.c no. 065; SRO, Reg.Deeds RD 1.11 353r.

D

James Ochterlony of Kelly (c.1554-c.1557: see appendix B.197): one of the friends of John Lord Glamis chancellor of Scotland; Strathmore mss, box 235 bund. 3 no. 9 (8 Oct. 1577). *Sir John Ogilvy of Inverquharity* (c.1542-1587: appendix B.217): justice-deputy to try witches in Arbroath, 1568; king's man in Angus; supplied troops for the siege at Leith, 1572; a Ruthven raider; SRO, Airlie mss, GD 16.25.4; Strathmore mss box 235.3; NLS, ms. 5308 no. 1259; *RSS*, viii, 1713.

Thomas Maule of Panmure (1560-1600: see appendix B.177): supported the English at Broughty; married his heir to John Erskine of Dun's daughter and two of his daughters to kin of Dun; a king's man and a friend of the Regent Moray and of chancellor Glamis; *RSS*, iv, 93; SRO, Dalhousie mss GD 45.26.53 page 70; Strathmore mss., box 235.3; GD 45.26.53 page 67 and Strathmore mss., box 235 bund.3 no. 9.

87. *CSP(S)*, i, 550.

88. *CSP(S)*, i, 236; *RSS*. iii, 820; Ch. 3, n.46; SRO, CC 1.1a.

89. See Ch. 3, n.47 and for Morphie, above n.87.

90. See Ch. 3, nn. 54-7; SRO, Reg.Deeds RD 1.1. f.148r.

91. See Ch. 3, nn. 58-61.

92. *CSP(S)*, i, 455, 480, 511, 512, 647; *Hamilton Papers*, ii, appendix xxxix; *CSP(S)*, i, 713, 812, 879, 881, 886, 891; *RSS*, vii, 1022.

93. The calendars of state papers include a whole series of personal requests from Lord James Stewart, later earl of Moray, on behalf of the master of Marischal, his brother-in-law, desiring better treatment at the hands of his English captors, who continually demanded that he re-enter captivity and sought a large ransom for his final release. *CSP(S)*, i, 1057, 1134, 1141; *CSP(S)*, ii, 105, 153, 155, 161, 177, 179, 180, 184, 440, 460; dates from 1 Jan. 1561/2 to 5 Jan. 1566/7.

94. The earl of Atholl had the ward of Glamis — but the latter's curators were Morton and Bellenden of Auchnoule: Strathmore mss., NRA(S) 855 box 9.201 and SRO, Reg.Deeds RD 1.5 f.22r. For Lord Ogilvy, see Ch. 3, n.67.

95. Donaldson, *All the Queen's Men*, p.41.

96. Campbell appears as curator to Lord Ogilvy 1558 x 1562: SRO, Airlie mss., GD 16.24.178, GD 16.12.289; besides sponsoring the young man as provost under him of Brechin.

97. *Inchmartine's* son and himself both married daughters of Lords Gray: see appendix B nos. 213, 214. Clova chose Inverquharity to act as arbiter for him in 1561: SRO, RD 1.4 f.166r and had witnessed charters for him in 1556: *RMS* iv 1122, SRO, RD 1.2 f.8r. *Gilbert Ogilvy of that ilk:* SRO, Acts & Decs., CS 7.70 f.23; Strathmore mss., box 235.3 and see appendix B nos. 201, 202.

98. *CSP(S)*, i, 647, 872, 881, 885, 891.

99. *CSP(S)*, i, 519, 591.

100. *CSP(S)*, i, 787; BL, Egerton ms. 1818 ff. 11, 15.

101. *CSP(S)*, i, 912.

102. *CSP(S)*, i, 1075; BL, Egerton ms. 1818 f.17.

103. McRoberts, 'Material Destruction', *IR*, x, p.151.

104. *Knox's History*, ii, p.4.

CHAPTER 5

'The Face of a Public Church Reformed': Parochial Reformation — The First Quarter-Century

'. . . and therefore nothing we desire more earnestly then that Christ Jesus bee universally once preached throughout this Realme, which shall not suddenly be, unlesse that by you, men be appointed, and compelled, faithfully to travell in such Provinces as to them shall be assigned . . .'

The evangelisation of 'all Inhabitants of this Realme' was the prime objective of those who provided spiritual guidance to the Scottish Reformation. In the Book of Discipline, drawn up between May 1560 and January 1560/61, the leaders of the new kirk set forward their plans for the planting and erection of 'Kirkes . . . where none are now'.[1] In undertaking this task, they recognised their obligation to fulfil Christ's great commission — an obligation to which their eschatological perspective added urgency.[2] The means selected to achieve their goal was a new parish ministry of preachers or ministers, exhorters and readers working together with elected elders and deacons, and overseen by ten or so provincial officers of the kirk, called superintendents.[3] Having been accepted as a gifted preacher by the assembly of the kirk in December 1560, John Erskine of Dun was nominated as superintendent of Angus and the Mearns by the Great Council of Lords, and inducted to his province by John Knox in January 1561/2.[4] Though both the size of his province and the nature of his authority were to be modified, John Erskine remained to his death (1589/90) the chief administrator and spiritual leader of the reformed ministry of his two shires. His responsibilities were diverse, including the examination and admission of ministers, consideration of their stipends, provision of their manses and glebes, upkeep of the fabric of churches, liaison with the courts of the church (whether kirk sessions or General Assembly) responsible for punishment of moral transgressions, and maintenance of a personal preaching ministry. Examination of the extent of the reformed kirk's success in achieving a parochial reformation conducive to 'the preaching of Christ Jesus' in Angus and the Mearns from 1560 to 1590 is inseparable from assessment of the career of the laird of Dun.

Assessment of the numerical strength of the new ministry during the 1560s is notoriously difficult,[5] the main difficulty being that no central register specifically designed as a comprehensive list of serving clergy remains from before 1567. Between 1567 and 1568 a Register of Ministers, Exhorters and Readers was compiled and amended on an *ad hoc* basis by deletion and insertion until 1571-2. From 1567 to 1572, lists of ministers and others paid from the thirds of benefices supplement the information of the Register: these accounts of the collectors of thirds are the only general source for the years 1561-1566.[6] Discrepancies between what actually happened in the localities and what was officially known lessen the value of both these records. For example, James Fleming occurs as reader at Ruthven in 1563 according to the thirds and not thereafter in any central source. From a local notary's protocol book, however, it appears that in 1570 as vicar-pensioner and minister he performed a marriage in the parish kirk.[7] Similarly, Mr William Salmond first appears in central records as reader at Dunnottar in 1574, yet in 1569 he was officiating as 'vicar of Clunye Redar and exhortar thair howand pouer for ye ministratioun of ye sacramentis' under authority of a writ from John Erskine of Dun dated 12 October 1569.[8] Conversely, Nicholas Spittal, former provost of Lord Gray's collegiate church of Fowlis and a canon of St Andrews priory, was obviously a minister of some repute by 1566 when he subscribed a letter as one of the 'most qualified' — but as his stipend probably came from Fowlis and the priory, he does not appear in the accounts of the thirds until 1569.[9] Assessing the strength of the new ministry from central sources is unavoidable — yet it must be remembered that these consistently understate the real position.[10]

Angus and the Mearns obviously had in place a good nucleus of a reformed ministry from as early as 1561. Though no central lists of names exist before 1563, the total sums paid as stipends are available for comparison for the three years 1561, 1562 and 1563. By the latter date the superintendent and eighty-two others were receiving cash payments totalling £4082. This was only marginally increased from 1562 — £3,936 6s 8d: and roughly a quarter up on that of 1561 — £3,144 6s 8d.[11] These figures suggest that at least sixty ministers, exhorters and readers were officially recognised by 1561. £3,936 6s 8d was approximately one-fifth of the national payment of stipends in 1562; these sums were the largest payments made to any province in each of the first three years that accounts were kept. Dr Crockett observes that, in 1562, the cash sums expended in Angus and the Mearns were greater than those levied there — while in 1561, income only marginally exceeded expenditure.[12] It may well be that the fact that the Collector-General of Thirds was John Wishart of Pittarrow explains the priority-claim upon his incomes from the thirds enjoyed by the new ministry of his home province. The leading position established by

John Erskine of Dun's province also reflects favourably on the superintendent's diligence in 'planting kirks' and on the welcome given by the lairds of Angus and the Mearns to the reformed church.[13]

By 1563, a minimum of eighty-eight known ministers, exhorters and readers were serving the ninety-one parishes of Angus and the Mearns.[14] These bald figures need analysis, however. Some of the parishes left vacant were small — for example, Ecclesjohn (beside Dun) whose lands were wholly owned by John Erskine of Dun, did have parsonage revenues but it was later to be described as 'of auld ane chapel erectit for pilgrimage'.[15] Other small parishes which were to be deliberately left without the provision of a reader were Ballumbie (beside Monifieth), St Skaa or Dunninald (beside Maryton) and Burghill and Kilmoir (associated with Brechin). Twenty-eight of the reformed ministry of 1563 were actually ministers: six were exhorters, and the rest (fifty-four), readers. In order to provide the preaching ministry considered essential for a reformed kirk, all but a few of the ministers were appointed to more than one parish. Thus the twenty-eight had allocated to them no fewer than fifty-two of the eighty-six significant parishes. This system of linkage was basically geographical, ignoring any previous ecclesiastical allegiances. So Fern and Menmuir from the diocese of Dunkeld were linked with Tannadice, from the Angus deaconry of St Andrews. Mr James Fotheringham was minister of three central Angus parishes: Kinnettles, Meathie and Inverarity; John Christison served the neighbouring Mearns parishes of Fetteresso, Dunnottar and Glenbervie. The untypical appointment of Mr John Hepburn to Brechin and Panbride is probably explained by the pre-Reformation linkage of the revenues of this coastal parish to a canonry of the cathedral.[16] A further twenty parishes were served by their own readers or exhorters, bringing the total of parishes with reformed clergy allocated to them to seventy-two.

Some distinctions in the provision of the new ministry can be made on a geographical basis. By 1563, no minister had been appointed to any of the five Deeside parishes supervised directly by John Erskine of Dun. However, Strachan and Durris did have their own readers; an exhorter served Banchory-Devenick, and Nigg shared a reader with Aberdeen. Alexander Robertson first occurs as reader at Maryculter in 1564: but in 1563, he served at Peterculter and may in fact have covered both parishes from the earlier date.[17] In the Mearns proper, there was virtually total coverage of the fifteen parishes by six ministers and fourteen readers. All but Catterline and Inverbervie had ministers allocated to them: and the latter was served by James Simpson, whose forty-five years of continuous service as a reader in several neighbouring kirks suggests strong local ties.

Table 5.1. Analysis of Ministers, Exhorters and Readers in Angus and the Mearns 1563-90.

	1563	67	69	72	74	76	78	79	80	85	86	88	89	90
ministers	28	35	40	39	32	33	36	36	37	46	43	45	48	59
new this year:		5	5	3	4	2	5	0	3	15	1	6	4	14
exhorters	6	—	—	1	—	—	—	—	—	—	—	—	—	—
new this year:		—	—	1	—	—	—	—	—	—	—	—	—	—
readers	54	50	55	53	74	75	73	72	69	47	41	37	36	31
new this year:		13	5	5	28	10	4	5	3	4	0	0	2	0
graduates	22	20	24	23	22	23	26	28	29	38	35	37	41	50
new this year:		3	4	3	5	4	6	2	3	15	1	5	5	13
beneficed	19	—	—	—	36	37	39	39	44	49	42	46	48	53
TOTAL	88	85	95	93	106	108	109	108	106	93	84	83	84	90
new this year:		18	10	9	32	12	9	5	6	19	1	8	6	14

Service of Pre-Reformation Clergy

	1563	67	69	72	74	76	78	79	80	85	86	88	89	90
beneficed	18	15	16	16	15	13	11	10	10	7	6	7	7	5
friars	2	1	1	1	1	1	1	1	1	—	—	—	—	—
monks/canons	7	8	9	9	7	5	5	4	3	3	3	2	2	3
others	6	3	5	5	5	4	4	4	4	3	2	1	—	—
total	33	27	31	31	28	23	21	19	18	13	11	10	9	8

These figures are derived from source material at the SRO. Their limitations are as follows:
1. They relate to the parishes of Angus and the Mearns surveyed for the purpose of this study — a list which corresponds neither with exact shire boundaries nor sixteenth-century ecclesiastical provinces.
2. They include known clergy and ministers.
3. They are based on central — and hence official — sources.

None of these parishes in the Mearns was left unallocated to some form of reformed ministry — as might be expected from an area that was a stronghold of the new doctrines from well before 1560. Only Newdosk was left without a reader — and that small barony belonged wholly to the neighbouring Lindsays of Edzell, and was probably served from there.[18]

In Angus, the spread of ministers and readers across the shire was virtually complete, though not quite as comprehensive as in the Mearns. Five surprising gaps around Dundee are probably explained by the incomplete nature of the thirds as a source. Nicholas Spittal, one-time provost of Fowlis collegiate church and a canon of St Andrews priory, was minister of Fowlis with Benvie and Longforgan from 1567 to 1574: but, as it has been argued that his service to the reformed church dated from earlier than 1566, he was probably minister of all three parishes by 1563.[19] The small parishes of Liff and Logie-Dundee had had a joint curate with

Invergowrie in 1555/6, and as a trinity were to share a minister from 1576 to 1590: it may be that before 1576 they were also served from Invergowrie.[20] The vacancy at Kirkbuddo is also surprising but probably not significant, as the lands of the parish were held by John Erskine of Dun.[21] More important were the remaining vacancies at Cookston, Farnell and Ethie; Finavon, Airlie with Lintrathen, and Glamis. These gaps are best understood as representing John Erskine of Dun's reluctance to appoint reformed clergy to the home parishes of magnates still cool towards the Reformation. Cookston and Farnell were virtually co-extensive with the lands of Sir Robert Carnegy of Kinnaird — an absentee from those known to have attended the Reformation parliament. Ethie was held by his natural son, Carnegy of that ilk. Finavon and Airlie were of course the seats of the tenth earl of Crawford and James Lord Ogilvy of Airlie, whose careers during the 1560s were to be interlocked as consistent supporters of Mary, queen of Scots. While Lord Glamis did attend the General Assembly of 1563, he had inherited in 1559 as a minor, only purchasing his freedom from the ward of the conservative earl of Atholl in 1561. In 1565, he was to accompany Atholl, Crawford and Ogilvy in the army raised by the queen to counter Moray's rebellion.[22] If these seven significant vacancies are, indeed, adequately explained by the conservative preferences of their heritors (to use this term somewhat anachronistically), then the otherwise general appointment of staff to those Angus parishes retained by the reformers must also reflect a general acceptance of the Reformation by Angus society. Nevertheless, the conservatism of Angus' leading magnates was to pose problems.

Who were these eighty-eight ministers, exhorters and readers? What sort of men served the reformed kirk — and why? These questions are the more interesting because of the complaints raised against John Erskine of Dun in the General Assembly of December 1562.[23]

It was laid to his charge, that there wer manie popishe preistis, unabill and of wicked life, admitted to reading kirkis within his diocie. 2. That some zoung men wer rashlie admitted to the ministrie, and to be exhortaris, without such trial and examinatioun as ar required in the Book of Discipline. 3. That gentilmen of vitious lives wer chosen to be elderis in divers kirkis. 4. That sundrie ministeris under his jurisdictioun remanit not at thair kirkis, visit not the seik in thair extremitie, and alsua that the zouth is not instructed. 5. That some ministeris come ouer lait to the kirkis wher they sould preach on the Lordis day, so that the peopill doe wearie staying upon thaim, and incontinent the sermon being ended, they depart. 6. That the ministeris resort not to the exercise, according to the order set down in the Book of Discipline.

Although the particular men making up the complement of the ministry of Angus and the Mearns at the end of 1562 is unknown, the similarity between the total stipends paid in 1562 and 1563 suggests that examination of the ministry of 1563 against these criticisms might be fruitful.

First, in the light of the suggestion that, 'manie popishe preistis' were appointed readers, how many of the eighty-eight had served in the pre-Reformation church? A total of thirty-three in all can be identified, which number — allowing for the unknown origins of many of the remaining readers — *might* approach half of those serving in 1563.[24] Of these thirty-three, some thirteen would appear to have been appointed to serve as readers (or, in two cases, exhorters) in their former parishes. The greater part of these were from the lesser clergy: curates and vicar-pensioners, four from the Mearns and the rest from Angus.[25] A further six readers had been in lesser orders in the Roman church; but either they had not held a specific benefice, or else they were not appointed to serve after 1560 in their own parish.[26] Although these lists together amount to nearly one in four of the ministry of 1563, it is less clear that the mere fact of service before 1560 would thereby make them 'unabill' in terms of the complaint of December 1562. The six graduates, if unwilling or unable to preach, would presumably be well qualified to read the public prayers and Scripture lessons on Sundays, and to do the various notarial tasks that fell to a reader. So, too, would those whose careers had included notarial duties: the books of Duncan Gray and Alexander Maxwell survive to this day. Still, the overall number certainly gives some support to the first charge against the superintendent.

If over half of the conforming clergy came from the ranks of those with lesser benefices, the remaining fourteen whose names are known came in the main from distinct groups. Four — Ninian Clement, Thomas Gormak, Thomas Lindsay, and Nicholas Howeson — had been monks of Arbroath Abbey. All four were probably fairly young. The first known appearances with the convent of Clement, Gormak and Lindsay are in 1554: they may have joined soon after Lord John Hamilton became commendator. The first known date for Nicholas Howeson is 1557. Ninian Clement had been one of two monks to matriculate at St Mary's College, St Andrews, in 1555: he became minister of Arbroath itself.[27] Three more of the new ministers were canons of the priory of St Andrews, presumably recommended to their new parishes by their prior, Lord James Stewart — the later regent. These men — Patrick Boncle, John Goodfellow and David Robertson — served in parishes appropriated to their priory.[28] A further two readers and a minister may be identified with former friars: John Christison at Glenbervie from the house of Montrose, John Blindscheill at Inverarity from that of Elgin and John Smith at Fordoun possibly from the Inverbervie Carmelites.[29] The reader of Glenbervie may have been the John Auchinleck who had had his parsonage of Cookston sequestrated on account of his association with the murder of Cardinal Beaton.[30] No complaint could have been laid against the admission of these men, whose conformity to the Reformation was apparently as a result of personal conviction or under the inspiration of known reformed leaders.[31]

The final three of the thirty-three of the reformed clergy known to have had associations with the Roman church before 1560 are best discussed under the second head of complaint against John Erskine of Dun: that of rashly admitting young men to the ministry without adequate trial. Mr James Fotheringham was a brother of Thomas Fotheringham of Powrie: by 1550, he had been presented to the parsonage of Ballumbie by Patrick, Lord Gray. Fotheringham was undoubtedly a young man at the time: he matriculated at St Leonard's College at St Andrews in 1556, and was to live to see the marriage of his grand-daughter in 1612. His service to the reformed kirk was curtailed, however, during the 1570s when he was accused of living in adultery; this episode may have been thought by contemporaries to justify criticism of his original acceptance for the ministry.[32] It may be that the superintendent was over-influenced by Fotheringham's patrons — Lord Gray, and the laird his brother: Powrie was himself a commissioner to the General Assembly.[33] The last two of the pre-1560 clergy should be considered special cases: Mr John Hepburn, treasurer and minister of Brechin, though as young and well-connected as Fotheringham, was accepted by the 1560 assembly of December, as has already been discussed. Finally, Mr Thomas Anderson was schoolmaster at Montrose and held the vicar-pensioner stipend from Barry. His active career can be traced back to the 1540s, however: he determined at St Leonard's in 1529 and so, though he lived until 1585, hardly qualifies as a 'young man' in 1562-3.[34]

Others of the supposedly unexamined young men may have been clients of the laird of Dun himself. Mr James Erskine, exhorter at Logie Montrose in 1563, had matriculated at St Leonard's only in 1557: of the six known exhorters, he alone fits the 1562 criticism — which explicitly referred to the intermediary post in this connection. This personal attack did not prevent Dun from elevating his kinsman to the post of minister of Dun by 1567.[35] Both Mr Andrew Milne and Mr William Gray (respectively ministers of Stracathro with Dunlappie and Dun with Logie-Montrose) were young men at the time of their first appointments. Milne was to serve the kirk for no less than fifty-one years: Gray completed forty-four years. Though Gray's university is unknown, Milne probably matriculated at St Leonard's in 1556. Their connection with the parishes and schools nearest to the barony of Dun suggests the superintendent's influence in their appointment.[36] Yet another young minister was Mr Gilbert Gardyne, brother to the laird of that ilk, who was appointed to the parishes of Monifieth with Monikie. The laird there, Durham of Grange, was a close associate of Erskine of Dun. Gardyne died as late as 1623: he may have determined at St Mary's College of St Andrews in 1558.[37] Finally, John Nevay, minister of Nevay with Eassie with Newtyle, must be mentioned. This young man served as minister continuously to 1591: at the time of his appointment, he was the heir of the laird of Nevay and succeeded his father around 1565.[38] It must be admitted that the superintendent of Angus and the Mearns does appear to have accepted some young, well-connected men for the ministry. In his defence, it might be said that (Fotheringham apart) they served the kirk well for many years, winning approval from others apart from their original sponsor.

Of the other criticisms of John Erskine of Dun's ministers made in December 1562, little can be said. That of non-residence with its corollaries, failing to visit the sick and teach the young, and that of late arrival for the Sunday service, seem an inevitable part of the system of linkage of several parishes under one minister. The shortage of ministers that made this necessary was, however, recognised by the Assembly of June 1563 when it petitioned the queen to authorise a full union of some parishes and hence allow for centralisation of services in one chosen church.[39] These complaints are at least good evidence of the difficulties and failings of the youthful system of ministry of the reformed kirk, if not of the young ministers themselves. In passing, it is interesting to speculate which of the superintendent's ministers brought these criticisms against him. It may be that complaint number six, that the ministers failed to attend the exercise, provides a clue. This institution, held to be expedient by the Book of Discipline, was intended to be a regular Bible-study for the mutual instruction and examination of ministers and others. Meetings were to be held at the 'chief towns' of the realm.[40] If such an exercise was intended for Dundee, as seems suitable, the minister there, William Christison, appears to be perhaps the sole minister in John Erskine's province who would have had the standing to criticise the superintendent and who could not himself be considered unqualified either by the taint of the priesthood or the inexperience of youth.[41]

It must be emphasised that the new ministry of 1563 had strong connections with Angus and the Mearns. These ministers and readers were predominantly 'local men', called to serve in or near their native parishes, or those in which they were living at the time of the Reformation. One such category of 'local man' has already been discussed: that of the curate or vicar pensioner who, on conforming, served the new church in his old parish. At a higher social level, a number of lairds served as ministers: John Erskine of Dun himself, Richard Melville of Baldovie, David Lindsay of Pitarlie, John Nevay of that ilk. In addition, Mr James Melville was the brother of Baldovie, Mr James Fotheringham the brother of the laird of Powrie, Mr William Gray the brother of the laird of Dunninald, Robert Maule the brother of Panmure.[42] Mr Thomas Anderson, Mr Andrew Milne and John Baty all had kin who were burgesses of Montrose.[43] Both Mr Alexander Auchinleck and Andrew Auchinleck served in the vicinity of Affleck Castle, seat of Auchinleck of that ilk. Other such local names abound: an Elder held land at the Stone of Benholm and Mr William Elder was reader there; an Arrat and several Fullertons, Erskines and Gardens were found serving in north and central Angus. James Lovell was reader at Monifieth: he was brother to Thomas Lovell in neighbouring Linlathen.[44] Besides being a notary practising in Dundee, Mr Alexander Maxwell was heir to the tacksman of the priestoun of Tealing and kin to Maxwell of Tealing. Robert Neilson had been baron officer of Arbuthnott before he became reader at Ecclesgreig. John Paton, reader at Dunnottar, was probably the natural son of Mr David Paton, former vicar pensioner of Fetteresso. Robert Rait, reader at Fetteresso, shared the same name as the laird of Hallgreen. Alexander Tyrie, minister of Auchterhouse, was kin to Tyrie of Drumkilbo and was occasionally described as 'in Nevay'.[45] The point need not be laboured further: the ministers, exhorters and readers of 1563 were 'local men' to a degree far exceeding that of the pre-Reformation clergy. This was the great strength of the new parish clergy. That these representatives of the Reformation were known, understood and accepted as a valid part of their localities must be attributed in large measure to the fact that John Erskine of Dun seems to have been content to approve local nominations, perhaps after only superficial examination; perhaps irrespective of their previous religious allegiance.[46]

In the light of this finding, new significance is shed upon the 1562 criticism of John Erskine of Dun that he assented to the choice of 'gentilmen of vitious lives' to be 'elderis in divers kirkis'. Although the role of the laity in the Roman church has in the past been unnecessarily minimised,[47] apart from the few remaining lay patrons, it lay almost entirely in the 'voluntary sector'. By contrast, the Reformed kirk offered (at least to the lairds) an important share in the governing of local congregations and in the imposing of moral discipline through the office of the eldership.[48] A creation of the period of the 'privy kirk', the office of eldership was fundamental to the 'erection of a public face of a reformed church'. In the circumstances of the late 1550s Knox was prepared to recognise as a church, a congregation in which elected elders maintained discipline even if no regular public preaching were possible.[49] The acceptance of discipline by *The Scots Confession* as one of three visible marks of a true church enshrined the office of the eldership as an institution as conceptually fundamental as the preaching ministry.[50] According to Book of Discipline, elders were hence to be:[51]

> Men of best knowledge in Gods word and cleanest life, men faithfull and of most honest conversation that can be found in the kirk . . . For it is not seemly that the servant of corruption shall have authoritie to judge in the kirk of God.

This 'unseemly' situation was precisely that alleged to exist in John Erskine of Dun's province in 1562. Unfortunately, the names of elders in the 1560s are even more elusive than those of ministers.

The records of only one kirk session or 'assembly' of the 1560s or 1570s survive from the sixteenth century from Angus and the Mearns: those of the parish of Monifieth. This register is missing pages for 1560-1-2 after the initial entry, if indeed they ever existed. When the record recommences in the winter of 1562/3, the kirk was equipped with a reformed ministry. The entry for 10 January 1562/3 ordained that the deacons were to inquire who of the congregation were sick, so that they could be visited and comforted by 'ye ministre, reidar or eldaris and diaconis'.[52] According to the Book of Discipline the office of a deacon was to 'receive the rents etc, gather the almes of the kirk, to keep and distribute the same, as by the ministers and kirk shall be appointed'.[53] On 16 January 1563/4, the Monifieth assembly instructed the 'diaconis to vesy and arrange distrib to ye puir against ye nixt Sonday . . .'[54] It would appear, then, that this rural parish had been equipped with a kirk reformed according to the Discipline by 1562/3 at the latest.

Between 1560 and 1590 the register gives only three complete lists of elders and deacons: those for 1573, 1575 and 1579. Thereafter the next list occurs in 1596. The first three lists are compared in table 5.2. Besides these three lists, individual entries in the register allow further insight into the careers of these elders and deacons. Six of the fourteen men named in the 1573 list can be shown to have been involved with the congregation from the 1560s. William Durham of Grange, Alexander Lauder of Omachie, Andrew Duncan and John Auchinleck appear as cautioners, taking it upon themselves to incur a financial penalty if their client failed to fulfil a promise made to the assembly, perhaps to learn the commandments or to compear to show repentance.[55] In addition, Alexander Lauder of Omachie instigated an important adultery case considered by the assembly of 1565,[56] and Henry Knight was mentioned as a deacon in 1563.[57] Further, John Auchinleck and John Gould had children baptised in 1566 and 1568 respectively.[58]

Table 5.2, showing Elders and Deacons of Monifieth.

f21r: (31) May 1573	f29v: 14 July 1575	f41v: 24 April 1579
ELDERS	**ELDERS**	**ELDERS**
William Durham	*Robert Durham*...............	Robert Durham
of Grange	*of Grange*	of Grange
John Lovell, fiar of		
Ballumbie		
Alex Lauder...............	Alex Lauder...............	Alex Lauder
of Omachie	of Omachie	of Omachie
James Ramsay	*Henry Ramsay*	*Alex Ramsay*
in Ardownie	*of Ardownie*	*of Ardownie*
	George Balfour	
	in Barnhill	
James Anderson in		
the North Ferry		
Mr William Durham...............	Mr William Durham	
in Linlathen	in Linlathen	
Robert Carmichael...............	Robert Carmichael...............	Robert Carmichael
in Ethiebeaton	in Ethiebeaton	in Ethiebeaton
Peter Nairn there...............	Peter Nairn there	
		Henry Lovell
		in Barnhill
		David Lindsay
		in Ethiebeaton
		...............Henry Knight
		in Monifieth
DEACONS	**DEACONS**	**DEACONS**
Thomas Quhittat		
Andrew Duncan...............	Andrew Duncan...............	...............Andrew Duncan
Henry Knight...............	Henry Knight...............	
John Gauld............>	*Thomas Gauld*	>...............John Gould
		Henry Lovell
John Auchinleck...............	John Auchinleck	
Henry Lorimer...............	Henry Lorimer...............	Henry Lorimer
		Walter Ireland
		John Kendall

Note: 1.   The list for each year is given in the original vertical order. Names are modernised, where possible.

2.   Personal continuity is indicated by ....

3.   In addition names are placed in parallel where surname or estate suggests continuity.

4.   New names are *in italic.*

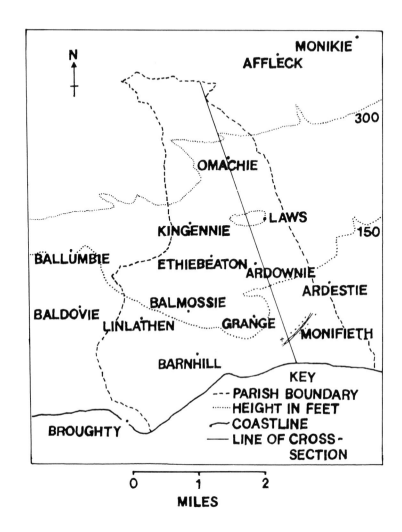

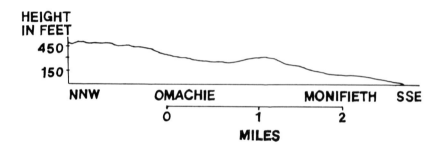

CROSS-SECTION OF MONIFIETH PARISH NNW-SSE

Taking the 1573 list of elders as probably not unrepresentative of the first decade of the congregation, it appears that the kirk of Monifieth was headed by lairds from most of the major estates that comprised the parish. Excluding Broughty Castle (an enclave of Caputh[59]), the bulk of the parish belonged to the earldom of Angus' regality of Kirriemuir. The Grange (of Monfieith), however, was held by a tenant-in-chief, and its laird William Durham headed the list of elders of the kirk. Linlathen's superior was Beaton of Melgund, from whom Anderson in North Ferry[60] and Mr William Durham held lands. Ethiebeaton was held from the earl of Angus by the earl of Crawford, two of whose sub-tenants were represented on the session. Ballumbie, though technically outside Monifieth, was one of those small parishes at first abandoned by the reformers: John Lovell, fiar of Ballumbie, also had several kin in Monifieth, whose reader was James Lovell. Alexander Lauder of Omachie had gained the feu of his lands from Lauder of Bass, who held before and after the forfeiture of the regality by James V.[61] James Ramsay in Ardownie was kin to Margaret Ramsay, wife of Alexander Durham of Grange.[62] Only Ninian Guthrie of Kingennie and Henry Ramsay of Laws played little part in the life of their parish church.[63]

The predominant influence of the Durhams of Grange in the kirk of Monifieth can be clearly seen from these lists of elders and deacons. Besides the seventh laird, another four of the remaining seven elders in 1573 had connections with his family. Mr William Durham in Linlathen is obviously of his name: James Ramsay in Ardownie was kin by marriage. Robert Carmichael and Peter Nairn, both 'in' Ethiebeaton, can also be shown to have had strong links with the Durhams of Grange. In particular it was these two alone of the session who on 31 July 1578 assisted in the distribution of the alms left by the seventh laird in his will.[64] Table 5.3 charts the connections between Carmichael and Nairn with four generations of Durhams and is based largely on the record in the register of choice of witnesses at the baptism of children. In a region where generations inherited Christian and surnames, the gift of a name expressed solidarity with the past and with, where appropriate, patrons. That Robert Carmichael, his son and the eighth laird of Grange should share the same Christian name, the laird standing as witness for the child's naming, was of considerable social significance. Though Peter Nairn's connection with the Durhams was less marked, his relationship to the leading elder seems to follow the same pattern as Carmichael — that is, until Nairn was charged with fornication and had the resulting baby baptised 'Robert' on 21 June 1584. Robert Carmichael was a sponsor.[65]

In William Durham, seventh laird of Grange, the parish of Monifieth had an elder positively committed to furthering the reformed kirk. During the wars of 'The Rough Wooing' he had supported the English occupation of Broughty. Present at the first recorded assembly of the kirk, he was also a commissioner in 1563, 1565, 1567 and, probably, at several other General Assemblies.[66] His links with the house of Dun extended from his obtaining protection as a client of Sir Thomas Erskine of Brechin in 1533/4 to his appointing John Erskine of Dun as overman to his executors in 1574. His will contained a classical account of a personal protestant faith, and left £100 to be distributed to the 'pure of this paroche and heirabout':[67]

> In the name of God, amen. I William Durehame of Grange seik in bodie bot haill in spreit and mynd makis my testam[ent] and latter will as eftir followis. First and aboue al thingis I com[m]it me to ye eternall god and to his mercie belevand w[i]t[h]out ony dout or mistrust y[a]t be yir grate meritis and passioun of Jesus and his resurrection of bodie and soule I haif and sall haif remissioun of my sy[n]nes as I am further p[er]swadit be his halie word . . . (He accepted that . . .) ony gudis that belangit to me of purpois be ye grace of god to bestow yame to be acceptit as ye fruittis of faith sua yat I no[ch]t suppois yat ony mereit is obtenit be bestowing of yame bot my mereit is in ye faith of Jesus Christ onlie.

Whether the *sola fide* phraseology of this testament was that of Durham himself, or that of Andrew Auchinleck, his minister, it seems unlikely that this laird could have been one of those described in 1562 as 'of vitious life'.

Evidence for the identities of the other elders of Angus and the Mearns during the first decade of the Reformation is scanty. Commissioners at General Assemblies were presumably also elders in their own congregations: thus William Durham of Grange attended the first assembly of December 1560 as a commissioner for Forfar(?-shire) together with Alexander Guthrie of Haulkerton. Montrose was represented by its provost and a bailie: John Erskine of Dun and Andrew Milne. The 'kirks of the Mernes' sent the lairds of 'Tullievaird' (?Dillavaird by Glenbervie) and Fettercairn. The identity of the first is unfortunately now unknown: the latter was probably Alexander Ogston.[68] A list of commissioners to the 1563 December meeting of the Assembly has been published by Professor Donaldson. Dundee sent its provost, Mr James Haliburton and two burgesses. From the shire of Angus came Lord Glamis, William Durham of Grange, Thomas Fotheringham of Powrie and Alexander Strachan of Brigton. Mr Walter Lyon represented Montrose: Alexander Ogston of Fettercairn, Archibald Douglas of Glenbervie and William his heir came from the Mearns, together with an Alexander Wishart.[69] Most of these men were of considerable standing in their shires, and would presumably have been as involved with their parish congregations as Durham of Grange was at Monifieth.[70]

Table 5.3, showing links between Robert Carmichael, Peter Nairn and the family and kin of Durham of Grange

References for this table are as follows, from OPR 310/1: 1. f38v: 31 July 1578. 2. f47r: 24 Apr. 1580. 3. f61v: 15 Aug. 1585. 4. f30r: 13 Nov. 1575. 5. f38r: 22 Jun. 1578.

WILLIAM DURHAM, SEVENTH LAIRD OF GRANGE
as an executor of his will,[1]
chose . . . .
    a)   ROBERT CARMICHAEL
        who chose as witnesses for his sons' baptisms . . . .

        for his son Robert:[2]   ROBERT DURHAM, EIGHTH LAIRD OF GRANGE
                          James Durham in Ardownie

        for his son James:[3]   James Durham in Ardestie
                          James Durham in Pitkerro
                          WILLIAM DURHAM, TENTH LAIRD OF GRANGE

        and stood as witness for the baptism of a child of . . . .

        Alexander Durham in Monikie
        who also chose as a witness . . . .[4]

    b)   PETER NAIRN
        who assisted in the execution of the will of . . . .[1]
                WILLIAM DURHAM, SEVENTH LAIRD OF GRANGE
        and chose as a witness . . . .[9]
        for his son William: WILLIAM DURHAM, NINTH LAIRD OF GRANGE

Angus and the Mearns were among the first areas of Scotland where the parochial reformation was to be generally implemented within a few years of 1560. Dr Haws considered the area one of the 'hot-beds of reform'.[71] John Erskine of Dun is generally credited with this success by historians — including Dr Haws. Yet Dun was publically rebuked in 1562, in effect for being over-ready to accept local candidates both for the ministry and the eldership. Many strands of evidence point to the critical importance of local — indeed, parochial — leadership in securing the implementation of a reformed order. That a significant number of the readers were appointed from the ranks of lesser clergy cannot be due to ecclesiastical leadership, such as was found in the diocese of Galloway and Orkney.[72] The postulant bishop of Brechin, abbot Donald Campbell, died during 1562, as did the canon of Glenbervie, Mr Robert Erskine in 1563; dean Cunningham had predeceased them.[73] Both the archbishop of St Andrews and the bishop of Dunkeld were hostile to the Reformation: an overwhelming majority of the Roman clergy of Angus and the Mearns failed to serve the reformed kirk.[74] The increasing conservatism of Lord Ogilvy and the earls of Marischal and

Crawford means that magnate-influence can be discounted. Leadership appears to have come from the lesser landholders, the lairds — whether as ministers themselves in some cases, or as elders and gentlemen of their parish kirks. 'The gentlemen of Angus and Mearns', having taken the lead in provoking the Reformation crisis in Scotland, then set an example in their establishment of a reformed parochial ministry.[75]

Local leadership was not necessarily moderate or compromising. The first entry in Monifieth's kirk session (or kirk 'assemblie'[76]) register echoed John Knox's apocalyptic language:[77]

> of yr holy g(damaged) in Apryll ye vi day of 1.5.6.0.
>
> The q[uhi]lk day it is appyntit y[a]t o[u]r assemblie of ye kyrk of (Monefut) . . . (damaged) . . . Sonday at twa efter noon at ye kyrk w[i]t prayar unto God for his assistans to do y[a]t may be fordrand to his gloir and subpressing of Satan . . . (damaged)
>
> ye q[uhi]lk day it is thoicht necessar be us yat ye hous of prayar (be mendit in) haist yat God may be glorifeit yair ye expensis to be tayn uquolie of (ye assemblie.)

It seems that the protestant lairds of Monifieth, encouraged by the arrival a few days earlier of an English army in Scotland contracted to support the Lords of the Congregation, planned during their Friday business meeting to commence public worship in their parish church, and were prepared to meet the necessary expenses for its repair. Both the talk of the 'subpressing of Satan' and the decision to share costs reflect Knox's radicalism. The reformer had insisted on an equal bearing of burdens in his tract *To the Commonalty of Scotland* in 1558, taking the Mosaic precedent of the erection of the Tabernacle as his text.[78] Knox's dynamic Biblicism was shared by at least some of the gentry of Angus.

In consequence, the continuing parochial reformation in Monifieth followed with some accuracy the guidelines of the Book of Discipline. From 29 August 1563, a regular weekly collection for the poor is recorded. Although the sums involved were never large, apart from communion days, they are the most regular item in the register. From these weekly collections, occasional aid was given to particular individuals in need.[79] Other regular entries reflect the concerns and priorities expressed in the Discipline. Children were expected to be taught the basics of the Christian faith as expressed in the Commandments and the catechism: 'without the knowledge whereof neither any man deserves to be called a Christian'. The Discipline enacted that none ought to be admitted to the Lord's Table without such knowledge; hence the Monifieth assembly used the occasions of baptism and marriage to examine and enforce knowledge of the reformed faith in adults. A common stipulation was to require of a child's father a promise to learn the Ten Commandments before the next communion as a condition of baptism: occasionally the Creed and Lord's Prayer were added.[80] Baptisms were frequent entries in the register, fulfilling the Discipline's requirement that it should be a public occasion, preferably restricted to Sundays. The Lord's Supper, or Communion, however, seems to have been celebrated only annually at Monifieth: the Discipline had recommended biannual administrations.[81] The terminology used by the clerk of the register was uniformly radical. In place of the banns of marriage, couples were 'proclaimed in marriage' and first publicly 'ratified their contract of marriage', to fulfil the Discipline's requirement that marriages be voluntary, adult public agreements. Similarly, godparents were now redefined as witnesses to baptism.[82] Finally, the Discipline's emphasis on the enforcement of moral discipline resulted in a scattering of references to sexual offenders compearing before the Monifieth assembly. The normal sanctions used against offenders were the imposition of fines and of one or more public appearances 'to show repentance'.[83]

How far the parish of Monifieth was typical of the other parishes of Angus and the Mearns is, of course, impossible to decide. Of those which originated in Scottish non-burghal parishes during the 1560s, its register has uniquely survived. In 1563 there were still many kirks in Angus and the Mearns where discipline was not practised and where no meetings of elders and deacons took place.[84] In 1565, John Erskine of Dun confessed to the Assembly (of which he was Moderator) that his visitations of congregations were less effective than they should have been because he had to seek hospitality from his 'friends', who were in most need of 'correction and discipline'.[85] Not all the lairds of this province were as devout as the laird of Grange. Several of John Erskine's ministers were held in esteem at the General Assembly, however. Mr John Hepburn of Brechin was appointed commissioner for planting kirks in Moray by the Assembly of December 1562: he had a similar commission to Banff in 1563.[86] On 4 September 1566, a group of the 'most qualified' ministers of Scotland wrote to Beza at Geneva to endorse the Helvetian Confession. Seven ministers from Angus subscribed, together with their superintendent.[87] Mr James Melville, William Christison and Nicholas Spittal were among the more select group who subscribed the letter sent by the Assembly in December 1566 'to there brethren the Bischops and pastours of Ingland'.[88] Both John Erskine and William Christison were to be Moderators of Assembly during the 1560s; Christison and the minister of Monifieth, Mr Gilbert Gardyne, were appointed to special commissions, or sub-committes, of Assembly.[89] The congregations of these ministers, at any rate, must have been conducted along lines that found approval with the kirk.

There was undoubtedly resistance to the imposition of reformed parochial discipline on the lines suggested by the Book of Discipline. That a substantial number of the parish of Monifieth hung back from adherence to the congregation is shown by a decree of the assembly in February 1562/3:[90]

> it is ordainit y[a]t so mony as dwellis in ye paroch off Monefurth y[a]t nocht communicatit at ye communion last ministrat ye vii of Jan(uary) that yair children be nocht baptist . . . .

The lairds of Laws and Kingennie may have been amongst those who failed to communicate. During the 1570s, the session engaged in a long process against Henry Ramsay of Laws in order to compel him to 'put aside' his 'harlot'. From public admonition through to citation before the synodical assembly at Dundee, the case was pursued from August 1578 to July 1580 when the laird 'maid his repentance'.[91] Laws, together with a new 'harlot' were, however, excluded from communion in April 1584. So too was Ninian Guthrie of Kingennie and his woman, 'becaus thay ar nocht reconcilit to y(i)r kirk'.[92] Outside Monifieth, Mr William Gray was attacked at Fern by Robert Lennox of Schandford while in the act of celebrating the Lord's Supper, because Gray had debarred the laird for persistent adultery and fornication.[93] Mr James Balfour was similarly attacked in November 1580 by Patrick Butter in Gormak while en route to Rescobie to preach.[94] Too rosy a picture of the reception of the Reformation by the lairds of Angus must not be painted.

One of the ways in which a recalcitrant, or simply less committed, laird could make difficulties for the new ministry was by failing to assist with provision of a manse and glebe for the reformed minister. In theory, each parish should have had the manse and glebe required by canon law for the benefice-holder. In practice, these had often fallen into decay or been alienated by tacks of lesser or greater length. The Book of Discipline claimed both manses and glebes for the ministers 'and failing thereof the readers' together with six acres of glebe, 'for else they cannot serve the flocke at all times as their dutie is'.[95] The Assembly of May 1561 reiterated this demand, and secured an act of parliament in June 1563 which passed possession of a manse or its equivalent in land to 'those who minister the charge' (i.e. either a minister or a reader) irrespective of existing feus. Enforcement of these provisions was delegated by the kirk to its superintendents. Little effective action seems to have been possible before parliament during Moray's regency agreed to a set of articles presented by the kirk, which again required a manse and glebe of six acres to be provided in each parish. This act and that of 1563 again needed interpretation by parliament in January 1572/3 by a measure which reduced glebes to four acres, but gave the superintendents statutory powers to designate manses and glebes, overriding existing tacks or feus.[96] Ministers and readers were to litigate for decades to enforce their rights under these acts, against both lairds and former benefice-holders. Requests for designation of suitable glebes must have provided John Erskine of Dun with one of his hardest tasks.

Twenty-three separate actions by ministers and readers of Angus and the Mearns to secure possession of manses and glebes have so far been discovered in the Registers of Acts and Decreets. Together with evidence from other sources, they provide many examples of the types of difficulty facing ministers for years after 1560. Some of these suits were, certainly, actions *pro forma:* undertaken as a matter of routine by newly-appointed ministers in order to obtain letters in four forms in case they needed to enforce their rights. Thus Archibald Douglas, newly presented by William of Glenbervie to be parson and minister of Glenbervie, brought an action on 14 December 1581 for his teinds, manse, glebe and kirklands. No defenders appeared: there was really little likelihood that the new parson, a son of the laird, would face opposition from his father's tenants.[97] Actions by Mr James Balfour of Guthrie with Idvies and Mr Gilbert Gardyne of Monifieth in March and July of 1569 were more serious. Balfour sued Patrick Gardyne of that ilk for 'wrangeous violent and maisterful spoilation awaytaking ressetting and withhalding' of various items from the glebe and kirklands of Idvies the previous summer. The minister of Monifieth complained that Henry Lovell of Ballumbie had ejected Gardyne's tenants from the glebe of Monifieth, cast down their houses, destroyed their trees and continued in occupation and cultivation of the ground, denying its profits since 1565 to the minister.[98] The result of the first case is unknown: but Lovell must have had some right on his side, for the Lords ordered him 'of his awin gude will and consent' to give up occupation.

Lairds as feuars and tacksmen were not the only ones to cause difficulties to ministers seeking their rights. Cases were brought against former Roman clergy who had retained possession of their own manses and glebes and against the widow of a minister's predecessor. The minister of Guthrie was successfully evicted from a manse he had occupied for seven years when it was claimed by the newly-appointed provost of Guthrie collegiate church. In 1588, the next minister of Guthrie even sued his own reader to evict him from a manse allocated to the minister by an arbitration of the presbytery of Montrose. Between 1573 and 1588 the reader at Alyth and the vicar-pensioner of Alyth fought over the manse and glebe there.[99] In 1586, Mr Alexander Norie, the new minister of Fern, was forced to appeal to the laird, Sir David Lindsay of Edzell, to intervene when John Erskine of Dun authorised Mr James Fullerton as a neighbouring minister to designate Norie a glebe of only two acres. Norie wrote to Edzell requesting that he order a full four-acre glebe that the minister could either tack or labour himself, in order to provide himself with a house in which to reside in his parish.[100] In the parishes, as well as in the burghs, 'the full-scale establishment of Protestantism' was delayed by the necessity to go to law against entrenched vested interests and to secure the resources necessary for a resident, preaching ministry.[101]

Similar legal difficulties had to be overcome in finding funds to repair church buildings. Responsibility before 1560 for such maintenance had been shared between parsons and parishioners, but the general system of appropriation had resulted in substantial decay. During the 1550s, the church authorities expressed concern at this neglect,[102] bishop John Hepburn explaining a feu of land in 1556/7 as intended to provide funds to repair Brechin Cathedral (described as lacking a roof and rooftiles) and to rebuild his palace ('destroyed utterly').[103] On inheriting these problems in 1560, the reformers obtained legislation from the privy council enabling taxation to be raised from parishioners to meet specific assessments, the resulting funds to be administered by kirkmasters. In addition, the superintendents were given general responsibilities to see to the repair of churches.[104] At Monifieth the local kirk assembly sought to raise funds amongst themselves for their 'house of prayer'. In 1569, £24 was allowed from the thirds to a slater for 'beitting of the kirk of Brechin at command of the kirk'.[105]

On 21 January 1572/3, parliament passed a further act to facilitate taxation to maintain parish churches. Considering that the 1563 act had fallen into disuse,

> because of the sleuth (and) vnwillingnes of the Parochinneiris quhilkis war slaw and refusit to cheis personis to taxt thair Nichtbouris and that alswa thair was not Kirkmaisteris or Deaconis appointit . . .

archbishops, bishops, superintendents and commissioners were given powers to issue adjudications which could be enforced by the normal processes of law, and to appoint local agents to oversee the tax where none had been elected. The act narrated that 'diuers Paroche Kirkis' had been 'demolischit cassin doun and destroyit' and that their stones and timbers had been appropriated to secular use.[106] The state of rural kirks in Angus and the Mearns around 1572 may be reflected in *The Lamentation of Lady Scotland,* whose author dedicated it to John Erskine of Dun.[107] The 'Lady' complained that, 'vpaland thay haue not dew seruice' for . . .

> The rowmis appointit pepill to considder,
> To heir Gods word, quhair thay suld pray togidder,
> Ar now conuertit to scheip Coits and Fauldis,
> Or ells ar fallin, becaus nane thame vphauldis;
> The Parische Kirkis, I mene, thay sa misgyde
> That nane for wynd and rane thairin may byde:
> Thairfoir na plesure tak thay of the tempill;
> Not zit to cum quhair nocht is to contempill
> Bot Crawis and Dowis cryand and makand beir,
> That nane throuchly the Minister may heir;
> Baith Fedders, Fylth, and Doung dois ly abrod,
> Quhair folk suld sit to heir the word of God.

Certainly the superintendent faced criticism in the March 1574/5 Assembly that quires within his diocese were ruinous. He replied that he had appointed tax-masters to every parish (presumably under the act of 1573), had raised summons for debt and generally done what he could, including the expenditure of his own resources on church buildings.[108] This may have been the occasion when the parishioners of Inchbrayock complained to the Assembly that their superintendent had pulled down their kirk. He replied that, during a visitation, he found the kirk 'largely in ruins', and had invited the congregation to meet in Maryton until it could be repaired, The Assembly supported the superintendent — but Inchbrayock remained linked with Maryton, without either a minister or a reader of its own, from 1572 to 1590.[109] The final victory may have been won by the 'Crawis and Dowis'.

Ultimately, strong and committed local influence was required to maintain the buildings of parish kirks. Hence it was to Sir David Lindsay of Edzell that Mr Alexander Norie looked in 1586. In his letter to the laird requesting his support to secure a four-acre glebe, he also asked that Sir David should command his tenants in Fern to compear at a forthcoming parish court to pay their tax 'for repairing off ye kirk . . . for ye sclaittor is w[o]rking in Brechine'. (Renewing Brechin cathedral's roof seems to have been the sixteenth century's equivalent of painting the Forth Railway Bridge.)[110] Assemblies and parliaments might fulminate and superintendents might visit; ministers might be appointed, but in the end they appear to have required the support of their local laird to obtain a manse in which to reside and a water tight church in which to preach.[111]

One area in which the ministry were — at least originally — less dependent on local support was in the provision of their stipends. From the crop of 1561, ministers and readers were paid their livings from the third of the revenues of the benefices which was granted by the pre-Reformation holders to the crown. Their payments came from the national collectory in

1561, 1562 and 1573, from local collectors between 1563 and 1572, and
from benefices and teinds specially assigned to each minister or reader
personally from 1574. In addition, from 1567 the reformed clergy were
entitled to succeed to the minor benefices as they fell vacant.[112] This process
was a slow one, however. By 1590, only fifty-three of the ninety ministers
and readers of Angus and the Mearns were receiving their stipends from
their own benefices.[113] The annual 'platt' during November established
from 1574 for the assignation and modification of stipends remained a
crucial feature in the ministry's year. This committee validated the current
roll of ministers and readers, allocated each to stipend bands, established
which had been presented to benefices during the preceding year, and
assigned particular local sources of teinds to top up vicarages or serve as
whole incomes. The fruits of these discussions are contained in the
Registers of Assignation and Modification of Stipends.[114] John Erskine of
Dun attended the 'platt' as superintendent of Angus and the Mearns, by
1584/5 assisted by ministers representing the three 'exercises' of his
province: Brechin, Montrose and the Mearns.[115] Mr Alexander Norie
sought a loan of £20 from Lindsay of Edzell in November 1586 to enable
him to 'pass to Edinburgh to the platt'.[116]

Thanks to the degree of control and stability introduced by this system, a
creation of the government of regent Morton, the financial rewards granted
to ministers drifted upwards. The number of ministers in receipt of incomes
of £100 and over, and the average incomes of this group, is shown in table
5.4. Not only did the number of better-paid ministers double between 1563
and 1590, but their average incomes also rose. By 1590, the top ten were
earning £200 or more, while the top three were awarded £300-plus. Nearly
£7,000 extra had had to be found to finance this generosity. This sum came
from a variety of sources. Most is explained by the continued succession of
ministers to benefices. For example, when the pre-Reformation parson of
Fettercairn died, his 'heirs', the ministers of Fettercairn, succeeded to a
parsonage worth £330 a year, thus transferring £220 from private hands to
the resources of the kirk. Similarly, Mr James Nicholson obtained an
income of £267 as dean of Brechin and minister of Farnell when he
succeeded Mr James Thornton in 1577.[117]

Ministers' stipends were also increased by the amalgamation of vicarage
revenues with their parsonages, an objective which became the policy of the
kirk from 1580, when, in conformity to the presbyterian polity of the
second Book of Discipline, the readers lost their status as members of an
'ordinar office within the Kirk of God'.[118] The seventh session of the July
Assembly decided that readers should in future not hold benefices, nor have
possession of manses or glebes where a minister was serving. While the

implementation of this policy was hampered by the kirk's controversy with King James VI, occasional examples of the union of parsonage and vicarage stipends did occur within Angus and Mearns.[119] The gradual reduction of the number of readers from their high-point of seventy-five in 1576 to thirty-one in 1590 also served to release funds to swell both the numbers of ministers employed and the stipends paid to them.[120]

The objective of the reformers of 1560 had been to create a ministry that would preach Christ throughout the parishes of Scotland. Provision of such

Table 5.4. Ministers' stipends

Year —	1563	67	69	72	74	76	78	79	80	85	86	88	89	90
	total number of ministers each year													
A	28	35	40	39	32	33	36	36	37	46	43	45	48	59
	no. of ministers with incomes of £100+ a year													
B	18	18	22	20	22	21	25	25	26	32	30	33	35	40
	average incomes of those in list B													
C	£121	121	117	133	132	131	147	147	156	168	157	163	164	175
	numbers in B expressed as a % of A													
D	64	51	55	51	69	64	69	69	70	70	70	73	73	68

  i. Figures from entries in RAMS, E 47.1 to E 47.5.

  ii. Where ministers were in possession of benefices, their whole income is included.

 iii. Figures are rounded to the nearest £1, and commuted from victual-income, where necessary, according to the price per piece current in Angus in 1574, as specified at the head of the Register of Assignations for that year; see NLS, ms.17.1.4.

a ministry, together with a climate of discipline within which it could operate, had been the goal of the parochial reformation. Financial, legal and other such difficulties had beset the way; disaffected lairds and the civil war of 1567 to 1573 had caused Knox to despair of his nation. A desire to strengthen the kirk's emphasis on preaching had lain behind the adoption of the second Book of Discipline (1578), with its declared aim of obtaining a minister for every parish — even at the cost of a further reduction in the number of parishes.[121] As a result, the total number of staff of the parishes of Angus and the Mearns increased from eighty-eight in 1563 to a high-point of 109 in 1578, only to decline again to ninety by 1590. The number of ministers, however, had doubled from twenty-eight to fifty-nine in 1590. Of these, forty-two were graduates, and twelve had served continuously since 1563 or before.

How comprehensively did these ministers serve the parishes of Angus and the Mearns? Although the Register of Assignation of Stipends was arranged by presbyteries from 1590, it is convenient to retain the tripartite division of the shires used previously. On Deeside, both Banchory-Devenick and Durris had their own ministers; Nigg and Maryculter shared a minister, and Strachan was linked (somewhat surprisingly) with Echt. Most of the rest of the Mearns kirks were single-minister parishes, Dunnottar and Arbuthnott having readers in addition to their ministers. Reader James Simpson still served at Catterline and Kinneff: Ecclesgreig and Aberlethnott were linked, as was Conveth with Pert and Logie-Montrose, and Newdosk with Edzell. These fifteen parishes therefore had the services (either *per se* or shared) of twelve ministers. The Mearns had moved towards single-minister parishes faster than Angus, perhaps reflecting a greater commitment by its ministers and lairds to the principles of the second Book of Discipline.[122]

The small Angus parishes vacant in 1563 were also vacant in 1590. Ecclesjohn had been united to Dun by act of parliament; St Skaa/Dunninald was linked with Lunan, and Ethie with Inverkeilor. Liff and Logie-Dundee were linked with Invergowrie; Longforgan was linked with Fowlis; Ballumbie, having been associated with Monifieth during the 1560s and linked with Dundee in the 1570s, was now linked with Murroes. Kirkbuddo had a reader of its own and was linked with Guthrie, of whose collegiate church it was a prebend. The highland parishes of the glens of Angus were linked with their mother churches in Strathmore: Lochlee with Lethnot, Clova with Cortachy, Glenisla with Alyth with Ruthven. The defunct prebends of Burghill and Kilmoir were still incorporated in Brechin. Inchbrayock still shared a minister and a reader with Maryton. Thirty years of struggle to find sufficient finance to pay the ministry and maintain existing buildings had left the reformed church no resources to rebuild and re-establish the smaller mediaeval parishes: from as early as the Assembly of June 1563, official policy had been to unite small parishes into larger units.[123]

In 1563, eight Angus parishes had ministers of their own.[124] By 1590, this number had increased three-fold to twenty-seven.[125] In addition, twenty-seven readers were still listed in the Register of Assignations, and more may well have been serving in the parishes. Montrose had had a new reader, Mr John Ogilvy, appointed in 1589 to assist the ageing veteran John Durie. Dundee called a minister to serve as associate to William Christison in 1590. Mr James Robertson was 'pait be the toun'.[126] Only three of the older-style three- or four-way groupings of parishes remained. Glamis was linked with Lintrathen, Eassie and Meathie; Ruthven with Alyth and Glenisla; Finavon with Aldbar and Aberlemno. The latter two groupings served baronies controlled by the earl of Crawford and Lord Ogilvy of Airlie — two of the leading members of the catholic earls' faction. Their conservatism seems to have held back the presbyterian trend to single-minister parishes. Only two parishes were vacant: Tannadice had been unlinked from Forfar, and awaited a minister of its own. The building at Cookston had been abandoned; the parish was to be re-erected as Kinnaird at the instigation and expense of Carnegy of Kinnaird in 1606.[127] In all, fifty-eight parish groupings were recognised in Angus and the Mearns (excluding Deeside) and these were served by fifty-four ministers.

The progress of the parochial reformation in Angus and the Mearns after the initial impetus of 1559-1563 had been slow and fraught with difficulty. In the first few years, much had been owed to those pre-Reformation clergy who had conformed and formed approximately half the staff of the new kirk. By 1574 the proportion of the ministry who had seen service before 1560 had declined to a quarter, though some who stayed the course were amongst the most valued — Mr John Hepburn, Patrick Boncle and Mr Andrew Elder: men who had been young reformers in the 1550s. A great deal of the credit for the provision of reformed services during the 1560s and 1570s must be given to the corps of readers, whose numbers were roughly double those of their ministers during the 1570s. The number of ministers who had university training, together with the number of those who held their own benefices, steadily increased in conformity with the 1561 Book of Discipline's programme of an educated ministry in possession of the revenues of the old church.[128] By 1590, the goal of a graduate reformed minister to each congregation was within sight. 'The face of a public church reformed' had been successfully created in Angus and the Mearns. When John Erskine of Dun died on 22 March 1589/90, having seen his eightieth birthday, he had good cause to be satisfied with his life's work.[129] His spiritually committed leadership, allied to his pragmatic preparedness to work with local society, had done much to establish the Reformation in his province.

NOTES

1. *The First Book of Discipline,* ed. J.K. Cameron (Edinburgh 1972), pp.115-6.
2. *The Scots Confession of 1560,* ed. G.D. Henderson (Edinburgh 1960), p.28 reprints the original (1561) title-page of the Confession of Faith and Doctrine, intended as a parallel to the Book of Discipline. The following verse from Matthew 24 was selected by the reformers to introduce the Confession: 'And this glad tydings of the kingdom shalbe preached throught the hole world for a witness to all nations *and then shall the end cum.' (Underlining* added for emphasis).
3. A considerable literature now exists discussing the origins of this office, its relationship

with systems of episcopacy, and how permanent it was intended to become in Scotland. *First Book*, pp.49-54; Donaldson, *Reformation*, cp.v; Cowan, *Reformation*, pp.129-131; *The Second Book of Discipline*, ed. J. Kirk (Edinburgh 1980), *passim* in the Introduction; D.G. Mullan, *Episcopacy in Scotland (1560-1638)* (Edinburgh 1986), Ch. 2.

4. *First Book*, p.119; the diocese or province was denominated 'Of Brechin' in the Book of Discipline, but thereafter as 'Of Angus and the Mearns'. Crockett, 'Life of John Erskine of Dun', pp.126-7.

5. M. Lynch, *International Calvinism*, ed. Prestwich 'the counting of ministers . . . has much in common with the counting of sheep and has . . . the same hallucinatory effects': p.248. The available sources are discussed by Donaldson, *Scottish Church History*, pp.99-110. C. Haws, *Scottish Parish Clergy at the Reformation* (SRS 1972) is indispensable but criticised by, *inter alia*, J. Kirk 'The Kirk and the Highlands at the Reformation': *Northern Scotland* vi (1986), 1f.

6. The original of this Register is available at the SRO as E.48.2 and was printed (not without occasional omissions) by the Maitland Club in 1830, retaining its original title; it is cited as *RM*. *Thirds of Benefices*, ed. G. Donaldson (SHS 1949) is cited *TB*. The information contained in these records concerning Angus and the Mearns is calendared in Bardgett, 'Faith, families and factions', ii, appendix A.2.

7. Bardgett, 'Faith, families and factions', ii, appendix A.c no. 060.

8. Bardgett, 'Faith, families and factions', ii, appendix A.c no. 209.

9. Bardgett, 'Faith, families and factions', ii, appendix A.a no. 324 and A.c no. 224.

10. This point is demonstrated with regard to Dunblane by J.R. Todd's thesis 'The Reformation in the diocese of Dunblane' (Edinburgh PhD 1973), cited Donaldson, *Scottish Church History*, p.110 and with regard to the Highlands by Kirk 'The Highlands', *Northern Scotland*, vi, p.16.

11. *TB*, pp.94, 152, 228: these figures exclude monies remitted to benefice-holders authorised to retain their own thirds. The bounds of the various provinces used by the collectory of thirds appear to be sets of shires, rather than the provinces suggested in the first Book of Discipline.

12. Crockett, 'Life of John Erskine of Dun', pp.130, 134.

13. Before 1563, the name of some ten of the new clergy are known from *ad hoc* sources. Besides John Erskine of Dun, the following were ministers: John Christison (Glenbervie), William Christison (Dundee), Mr John Hepburn (Brechin), Mr James Melville (? at Tannadice, Fern, Menmuir), Richard Melville of Baldovie (? at Maryton and Inchbrayock); see Bardgett, 'Faith, families and factions', ii, appendix A.c nos. 029, 030, 107, 143, 146. Mr Ninian Cook, Matthew Greiff and Mr David Meldrum had their vicars' thirds allowed for serving their parishes as readers from 1561; 'Faith, families and factions', ii, appendix A.c nos. 035, 088, 141. Matthew Moncur was reader at Nevay/Eassie in 1562, and Charles Michelson may have served as reader at Barry; see 'Faith, families and factions', ii, appendix A.c nos. 157, 151.

14. These figures and all that follow are from the appendices to Bardgett, 'Faith, families and factions', ii, as summarised in table 5.1. The parishes are those listed in appendix A.1.

15. Bardgett, 'Faith, families and factions', ii, appendix A.c no. 228.

16. Bardgett, 'Faith, families and factions', ii, appendix A.2 for linkages of parishes, 1563 to 1590.

17. Bardgett, 'Faith, families and factions', ii, appendix A.c nos. 250, 079, 199, 123, 203.

18. Bardgett, 'Faith, families and factions', ii, appendix A.c no. 216.

19. See above, n.9.

20. Bardgett, 'Faith, families and factions', ii, appendix A.a no. 098 and A.c no. 028.

21. WRH, NRA(S) 124: Jackson of Kirkbuddo Writs *passim*.

22. For Glamis: SRO, CH 1.1a; The Strathmore Writs, NRA(S) 885, box 9.201, SRO, Reg.Deeds RD 1.5 f.22r. The Chaseabout army: *RPC*, i, 379. Glamis' longest relationship was with Morton, a cautioner for his purchase of his own ward and marriage from Atholl in 1561 (RD 1.5 f.22r) and also part of the queen's forces in 1565.

23. *BUK*, i, p.25.

24. Cf. G. Donaldson, *Reformation*, p.85; C. Haws, *Scottish Parish Clergy*, p.vi, both suggesting 'well over half' had served before 1560.

25.

Name	parish	formerly	appendix A.c no:
The Mearns			
Mr Andrew Patrick	Arbuthnott	vic.pens.	176
Mr William Elder	Benholm	vic.pens.	050
Mr Alexander Wylie	Conveth	vic.pens.	248
sir James Symmer	Garvock	curate	233
Angus			
sir George Lyall	Aberlemno	curate	132
sir Duncan Gray	Auchterhouse	vic.pens.	085
James Sharp	Brechin	chaplain	212
sir Matthew Moncur	Eassie/Nevay	? vic.pens.	139
Mr David Meldrum	Maryton	vicar-perpetual	141
Walter Fairweather	Menmuir	curate	055
Matthew Greiff	Monikie	vic.pens.	088
sir James Fleming	Ruthven	vic.pens.	060
sir James Wight	Strathmartin	co-parson	244

26.

Name	new parish	formerly	appendix A.c no:
David Fowler	Aldbar	Montrose curate	066
sir John Smith	Glenisla	vic.pens.Airlie	219
Mr John Johnston	Idvies	Brechin clerk	113
John Baty	Lunan/Dun	Montrose priest	014
James Kinloch	Tannadice	Dundee chaplain	117
Mr Alexander Maxwell	Tealing	Dundee notary	139

These and subsequent identifications are subject to the qualifications expressed in the introduction to appendix A.

27. Bardgett, 'Faith, families and factions', ii, appendix A.c nos. 032, 083, 128, 109; also, M. Dilworth, 'Monks and Ministers', *RSCHS* xviii (1974), pp.209-10. Details given by Dr Dilworth are amended in the appendices in the light of further research.

28. Bardgett, 'Faith, families and factions', ii, appendix A.c nos. 109, 082, 204. Robertson's 1567 linkage of Rossie with Tealing may have originated before that date. To these canons can be added Nicholas Spittal (A.c.224); and John Smith, reader at Longforgan (A.c.218) from 1567. The patronage of the later earl of Moray was, by Scottish standards, considerable: M. Lynch in *International Calvinism*, ed. Prestwich, pp.243-5.

29. Bardgett, 'Faith, families and factions', ii, appendix A.c nos. 028, 018, 217.

30. Bardgett, 'Faith, families and factions', ii, appendix A.a no. 014 and A.c. no. 011.

31. Prof. Donaldson discusses the roles of conviction and leadership as motives for conformity in *Scottish Church History*, pp.76-79.

32. Bardgett, 'Faith, families and factions', ii, appendix A.a no. 123, A.c no. 065; *StA Recs*. p.263.

33. SRO, CH 1.1a (Extract register of the General Assembly).

34. Bardgett, 'Faith, families and factions', ii, appendix A.c nos. 107, 003.

35. Bardgett, 'Faith, families and factions', ii, appendix A.c no. 052.

36. Bardgett, 'Faith, families and factions', ii, appendix A.c nos. 152, 086; *StA Recs*. 263.

37. Bardgett, 'Faith, families and factions', ii, appendix A.c no.077. Durham of Grange was the son of a Jonet Erskine: *RMS*, iii, 304. He had been associated with Sir Thomas of Brechin: *ADCP*, p.420; and represented Forfar at the first assembly of the kirk: *BUK*, i, p.3.

38. Bardgett, 'Faith, families and factions', ii, appendix A.c no. 164 and appendix B no. 194.

39. *BUK*, i, p.33.

40. *First Book*, pp.43f, 187f.

41. Bardgett, 'Faith, families and factions', ii, appendix A.c no. 030. The procedure followed by the Assembly makes it clear that such complaints were brought against the superintendents in their absence by representatives of their own province; later, 'the ministers of Mernes and Angus wer removed and tryed' in their turn: *BUK*, i, pp.25, 26.

42. Bardgett, 'Faith, families and factions', ii, appendix A.c nos. 143, 065, 086, 138.

43. Bardgett, 'Faith, families and factions', ii, appendix A.c nos. 003, 152, 014.

44. Bardgett, 'Faith, families and factions', ii, appendix A.c *passim* and nos. 050, 131.

45. Bardgett, 'Faith, families and factions', ii, appendix A.c no. 139, 162, 174, 186, 236.

46. The same point is made with regard to Dunblane by Dr Todd, 'The Reformation in the diocese of Dunblane', p.329. Erskine confessed to having 'rubber-stamped' his Aberdeen colleagues' collation of Mr Robert Merser: Bardgett, 'Faith, families and factions', ii, appendix A.c no. 149.

47. I. Cowan, *Reformation,* Ch. 1 discusses this point. J.J. Scarisbrick, *The Reformation and the English People* (Oxford 1984), p.166 and elsewhere is more positive about the opportunities open to the English laity as church-wardens or members of confraternities and by participation in pilgrimages, support for altars etc. These aspects remained peripheral, however.

48. *First Book*, pp. 34-39; 174-179. J.K. Cameron summarises the duties imposed on elders by the Discipline as follows: '(a) determining and judging causes . . .; (b) admonishing the licentious liver; and (c) taking into consideration the 'manners and conversation' of everyone within their charge'.

49. *Knox's History,* i, 148; also, *ibid.,* ii, 277f. for Knox's order of the election of elders and deacons in the privy kirk of Edinburgh. The eldership preceded the office of the superintendent in the history of the Scots reformed church and was considered the more essential as an institution of government: *First Book*, p.37 demonstrates the way the Discipline was adapted to tack the superintendency onto the existing powers of the elders. J. Kirk and R. Greaves show that, in thus grounding the church in the eldership, the Scots Reformation followed the practice and theology of the European Reformed community of the French and Swiss: 'The Influence of Calvinism on the Scottish Reformation', *RSCHS,* xviii (1974), pp.163-7; *Theology & Revolution in the Scottish Reformation* (Grand Rapids 1980), pp.83-5. I. Cowan compares the office as it developed from the first to the second Discipline with evidence of later practice, perhaps unfortunately introducing an argument as to whether elders had a clerical or lay status. This distinction played no part in the terminology of the Scots reformers: see *Reformation,* pp.134-138; J. Kirk, *The Second Book of Discipline* (Edinburgh 1980), pp.88-97.

50. *The Scots Confession of 1560,* article xviii.

51. *First Book,* p.174.

52. NRH, OPR 310/1, f3v. The location of OPR 310/1 is not repeated in subsequent notes. The original ms. is available in addition to a microfilm of vols. 1 and 2 of the Monifieth Kirk Session Register.

53. *First Book,* p.178.

54. OPR 310/1 f6r.

55. OPR 310/1: f3v 3 Jan. 1562/3 (Durham); f11v 17 Nov. 1566 (Omachie); f13r 13 Jun. 1566 (Duncan); f5v 31 Oct. 1563 (Auchinleck).

56. OPR 310/1: f9v (blank) Apr. 1565.

57. OPR 310/1: f5v 5 Dec. 1563.

58. OPR 310/1: f11v 17 Nov. 1566; f13r 27 Jun. 1568.

59. *Broughty Castle,* p.10.

60. DAC, prot.bk.no.7 (Alexander Wedderburn), fs. 46v-47r: 13 May 1559; James Anderson in North Ferry and Grissell Wedderburn his wife had a precept of sasine from Beaton, directed to James and George Lovell, bailies.

61. See p. 10.

62. Bardgett, 'Faith, families and factions', ii, appendix B nos. 045, 046, 047.

63. Reasons for this are discussed n.92. The deacon Thomas Quhittat may be identical with a Thomas Quhittat in Balmossie, who was a surety for Henry Lovell of Ballumbie on 27 Jan.1564/5: SRO, Reg.Deeds, RD 1.7 f.102r: DAC, prot.bk.no.7 (Alex. Wedderburn), f.230v-231r.

64. OPR 310/1: f38v *ad loc.*

65. OPR 310/1 f61v, 15 Aug. 1585. J. Bossy discusses the 'kinship-creating capacities of the sacrament' (of baptism) in his chapter 'Godparenthood': *Religion and Society in Early Modern Europe*, ed. K. von Greyerz (The German Historical Institute, London 1984), pp.194-270.

66. *RSS*, iv, 87; *LHT*, ix, 13; Calderwood, *History*, ii, 45, 289, 382; SRO, CH 1.1a.

67. *ADCP*, p.420; SRO, Edin.tests. CC 8.8.3 f.172v-5r. Grange also witnessed a charter between David Lindsay of Edzell, ninth earl of Crawford, and Sir Thomas of Brechin in 1545/6: *RMS*, iii, 3219. He was to be one of the curators of the earl's heir in Edzell, Lindsay of Glenesk: SRO, Reg. Deeds RD 1.9 fs.353, 384-5. On 13 Apr. 1565, he witnessed the contract of marriage between John Erskine of Logie, grandson of the superintendent, and Agnes Ogilvy, daughter of Dame Katherine Campbell by her first husband James, master of Ogilvy: SRO, Erskine of Dun mss., GD.123.140.

68. *BUK*, i, p.3. The composition of General Assemblies has been hotly debated, and was probably ambiguous even in the first decade of the Reformation. The attendance of magnates was thought desirable by the kirk. When such as the earl of Huntly was present, he came in his own right or as a member of the privy council and not as a commissioner of shire, kirk or burgh: *BUK*, i, 33, 292-3; D. Shaw, *The General Assemblies of the Church of Scotland, 1560-1600* (Edinburgh 1975), pp.20, 42. G. Donaldson, *Reformation*, Ch. vi. I.B. Cowan, *Reformation* pp.124-128 for the general debate. Andrew Milne as a bailie of Montrose: Bardgett, 'Faith, families and factions', ii, appendix A.c no. 152.

69. G. Donaldson, *Scottish Church History*, Ch. 10 provides an introduction and transcription of a document in his own possession. A photocopy is available at the SRO, under the call-number CH 1.1a, which reference is generally used in this study.

70. Two more documents, available in Bardgett, 'Faith, families and factions', ii, appendix A.c, further illustrate the role of lairds in the new church. William Haitlie became minister of Abernyte in 1567 by the nomination and presentation of seven named gentlemen, headed by Lord Crichton of Sanquhar: A.c no. 098. Robert Graham of Morphie headed a list of seven gentlemen from Ecclesgrieg who in 1576 subscribed an agreement to provide finance for rebuilding the kirk, while attending a synodical assembly of the Mearns: A.c 001. These elders were of higher status than those studied by W. Makey, *The Church of the Covenant, 1637-1651* (Edinburgh 1979), Ch. 11.

71. C. Haws, *Scottish Parish Clergy*, p.xi.

72. Professor Donaldson summarises his research into these two dioceses in *Scottish Church History*, p.79.

73. Bardgett, 'Faith, families and factions', ii, appendix A.a nos. 050, 104, 079.

74. Although approximately half the reformed ministry of 1563 had served before 1560 in some capacity, consideration of the number of the catholic clergy alive in 1560 who confirmed presents a very different picture: some three-quarters of the known parochial clergy refused to join the reformed church. The personnel of the new kirk was markedly different from that of the old church:

	total	ministers	readers	total
parsons/prebendaries	55	5	2	7
perpetual vicars	33	1	7	8
vicars pensioner	23	2	8	10
curates, chaplains	35	—	11	11
TOTALS	146	8	28	36

This table allocates exhorters according to their designation in 1567. Service in the reformed kirk outside Angus and the Mearns is included in these figures.

75. This study therefore supports the conclusion of Dr M. Lynch in his chapter on

Scotland in *International Calvinism,* p.243: 'What the new church needed above all else was leadership, but as much in the localities as at the centre. This was provided in its first generation by a loose combination of a few nobles and a much larger collage of lairds, along with Knox, the five superintendents, and the handful of prominent Catholic churchmen who conformed in 1560'.

76. The term 'session' did not occur as a collective for the Monifieth eldership until an entry in 1581 — OPR 310/1 f.47v. Throughout the 1560s, the Monifieth kirk's court was known as the 'assembly'. This term relates to the Greek *ekklesia* (assembly, meeting, congregation, church) and was used in the *Book of Common Order* (ed. G.W. Sprott, Edinburgh 1901, p.17) to describe a court or consistory. The exact composition of the Monifieth body is unclear: it certainly included both elders and deacons in 1564 (f.7v: no assembly met one day because of the absence of some elders and deacons) and may have been open to the other gentlemen of the congregation: in July 1578, the elders, deacons and gentlemen were summoned to distribute alms (f.38v). Cf. the phrase 'ge[n]tlem[en] of the [con]gregat[ion] of the kirk of Eglisgreig': see note 70 above. The court at Perth's kirk used the term 'assembly' until roughly 1581: NLS, ms.31/1/1 (transcript of the Perth Kirk Session Register vol.1 1577-1620).

77. OPR 310/1 f2r. Material in brackets indicates words now missing from the page, but available to the author of Monifieth's entry in the *New Statistical Account* (Edinburgh 1845), xi, pp.542-4.

78. Knox, *Works,* iv, p. 528. I am indebted to Dr M. Lynch for this reference.

79. *The First Book,* p. 112, was insistent that the care of the poor was a prime duty of a true kirk; it left the means of fulfilling this obligation to local initiative. Cf. M. Lynch, *Edinburgh,* pp.20-21, 30-34 with regard to Edinburgh's various schemes. Examples from Monifieth's register read thus: fs. 16r, 18r, 30v:

'distrib. to Jhone Barnet ii d.'

'distrib. to Jhone R. cryppld chyld... '(amount missing)

'gatherit to ye puir xxi d. and wes gevin at y[i]r assemblie commandis to Jhone Valcar.' R. Mitchison, 'The Making of the Old Scottish Poor Law', *Past and Present,* lxiii (May 1974), p. 62 emphasises the kirk's concern to care for the poor.

80. *First Book,* p. 133-4 and p. 184. From OPR 310/1 f. 8r. 15 Oct. 1564: 'Andro Findlay and Elpit Hardye ratefeit thair contract of marriag and ye said Andro promisit to haid the believe befair the solenisation of his marriag under pane of v mk. and the commandments befoir the ministration of the Lordis supper under the pane of vther v mk'. Such requirements occurred roughly ten times a year in the 1560s and can be paralleled in other kirk session records. Cf. *The Buik of the Kirk of the Canagait 1564-1567,* ed. A.B. Calderwood (SRS 1961).

81. *First Book,* p. 182-4. J.K. Cameron discusses the reason for these recommendations and their Genevan counterparts in notes 13 and 14. Biannual celebration was recommended for rural areas; quarterly for burghs.

82. *First Book,* p. 191-199.

83. For example: 28 Nov. 1563: (blank), being accused of fornication, agreed to submit to the judgment of the assembly in fifteen days time; Durham of Grange offered surety that the accused would appear: f. 5v. On 15 Oct. 1564, Thomas Gould confessed to fornication and agreed to 'mak his repentance this day, this day viii dayis and this day xv dayis': f. 8r. Frequently the taking of 'caution' combined the effect of a 'suspended sentence' with 'community supervision': 'Janet Ramsay promisit to abstain in tyme cuming and to bring up hyr chyld in the fear of god, finds Jhone Affleck cautioner and has hyr chyld baptisit, callit Jhone'. The taking of financial caution or surety was a standard practice in Scots courts of the period.

84. *BUK,* i, 39. There is nevertheless occasional evidence for elders at a variety of kirks. Elders and deacons were appointed for the kirk of Arbroath during the 1560s, and exercised their office in tandem with the burgh council and court: Arbroath Public Library, Court

Book 1563-1575, fs.34v, 35r, 67r. Note 70 above refers to elders at Abernyte and Ecclesgreig. Sir John Wishart of Pittarrow and Mr James Wishart were elders at Fordoun in 1576: SRO, Acts and Decs., CS 7.55 f. 86v. John Livingston of Dunipace was probably the leading elder of Menmuir in 1586: see 'Faith, families and factions', ii, appendix A.c no. 049. David Straiton at the mill of Dalbog was an elder at Edzell in 1588: see appendix A.c no. 070. Richard Anderson, brother of minister Mr Thomas, was an active elder of Montrose: see appendix A.c no. 003.

85. *BUK,* i, p.65.
86. *BUK,* i, pp. 27,44.
87. William Christison, Mr John Hepburn, Mr Thomas Anderson, Ninian Clement, David Lindsay of Pitairlie, Mr James Melville and Mr James Balfour: *Knox's History,* ii, 190; *Correspondance de Theodore de Beze,* ed. H Aubert (Geneva 1960 x 1986), vi, pp. 346-349.
88. *BUK,* i, pp.85-6.
89. *BUK,* i, pp.65, 77, 82; 141, 157; 36, 145.
90. OPR 310/1 f.4v.
91. OPR 310/1 fs. 36r, 39r, 40r, 41r, 43v, 45v.
92. OPR 310/1 f. 57v. The persistent absenteeism of Laws and Kingennie may have resulted from more secular differences entertained between them and the lairds dominating Monifieth session. William Durham of Grange claimed half the lands of the Laws; Alexander Lauder of Omachie had slain William, heir of Ninian Guthrie of Kingennie. SRO, Edin. tests., CC 8.8.3 f. 172v-5r; SRO, Scrymgeour — Wedderburn mss. GD 137. 639 and SRO, Reg. Deeds RD 1.5.384 for Omachie's contract of assythment 10/15 December 1562.
93. *RPC,* iii, pp.197-8.
94. *RPC,* iii, p.264.
95. *First Book,* p. 162. M. Sanderson discusses the general position before and after 1560: 'Manse and Glebe in the Sixteenth Century', *RSCHS,* xi (1974), p.81f.
96. *APS,* ii, p.539, item 8; *ibid,* iii, p.38, item 13 and p.73, item 5. See *First Book,* p.162, note 41 and p.163, n. 42 for commentary on these acts; p.71 for the 1560/61 mandate to John Spottiswoode as superintendent of Lothian to secure manses and glebes for his ministry.
97. SRO, Acts and Decs., CS 7. 55 f. 180v; and Bardgett, 'Faith, families and factions', ii, appendix A.c no. 041.
98. SRO, Acts and Decs., CS 7. 42 f. 359v; *RPC,* i, 686.
99. SRO, Acts and Decs., CS 7. 42 f. 247r and 55 f. 39r; CS 7.55 f. 318v; CS 7.55 f. 117v; CS 7.57 f. 441r and 7.55 f. 329r; CS 7.55 f. 338v and 340v.
100. JRL, The Crawford mss., 4.2.120.
101. M. Lynch, 'From Privy Kirk to Burgh Church', *Church, Politics and Society,* ed. Macdougall, pp.90-1, on lack of finances in Edinburgh.
102. G. Donaldson, *Reformation,* pp. 22-3 explains the general position and cites the decree of the 1559 Provincial Council on repairs; also, D. McRoberts, 'Material Destruction', IR, x (1), p. 138 and n. 51.
103. *RMS,* v, 860.
104. G. Donaldson, *Reformation,* p. 99 cites the various national measures; p.226 for the mandate to superintendent Spottiswoode.
105. OPR 310/1 f. 2r; *TB,* p.230.
106. *APS,* iii, 76* item 15.
107. *Satirical Poems of the time of the Reformation,* ed. J. Cranstoun, (STS 1843), i, p.232 for the passage. The dedication of the 'Rurall veirse' referred to 'sum Schyre, thair is bot ane myre' — possibly a reference to the Mearns. The poem was anonymous.
108. *BUK,* i, p.314.
109. Petrie, *Compendious History,* p. 381; Bardgett, 'Faith, families and factions', appendix A.2.
110. JRL, The Crawford mss., 4.2.120. The Crawford muniments contain a manuscript copy of the 1573 act for repairing kirks, a fact which further suggests Edzell's interest in the

E

subject: box P bund. vi. Bishop Campbell raised a tax in 1580: D.B. Thoms, *The Council of Brechin* (SFBC 1977), p.32.

111. *The First Book*, p. 203 required that, in addition to waterproof doors and windows, each kirk should have a bell, a pulpit, a font and a communion table. Monifieth found the funds for repairing its table from its poor-box in 1582. Its assembly levied a local tax the next year for the provision of a new bell and to repair the kirk's windows: 4s per plough and specific sums per mill. Provision of water for each baptism was a duty of its kirkofficer, who had 6d. for his services per occasion; OPR 310/1 fs. 51v, 54v, 45r. Little came free in the sixteenth century!

112. G. Donaldson, *The Thirds of Benefices* (SHS 1949)provides a detailed explanation of the shifting politics and administration of this system from 1561 to 1574: 'Introduction'.

113. See Table 5.1.

114. See the introduction to Bardgett, 'Faith, families and factions', ii, appendix A. 2.

115. *Spald. Misc.*, iv, p.72.

116. JRL, The Crawford mss., 4.2.120.

117. Bardgett, 'Faith, families and factions', ii, appendix A.1 for successions in benefices. Figures for these stipends from SRO, RAMS, E 47.1 f. 22v, 23v. Increases in stipend were eroded by inflation, however.

118. *BUK,* i, 455; *The Second Book of Discipline,* ed. J. Kirk (Edinburgh 1980), pp.82-3. Readers' stipends never increased from the 1563 levels of £16-20.

119. Bardgett, 'Faith, families and factions', ii, appendix A.1: Dun, Fetteresso, Fowlis, Idvies, Kinnettles, Stracathro.

120. Unfortunately the registers of assignations become less reliable after 1585 in their recording of the existence and stipends of readers, as increasingly readers were paid directly by their ministers to whom the combined stipend was assigned. See Bardgett, 'Faith, families and factions', ii, appendix A.c no. 033, 091: and especially 099 (George Halden).

121. F. Bardgett, 'Four Parische Kirkis to Ane Preicheir', RSCHS, xxii (1986), pp.195-211; M. Lynch, *International Calvinism,* p.250.

122. These figures and the final assessment from Bardgett, 'Faith, families and factions', ii, appendix A.2.

123. *BUK,* i, p. 33: 'Ordainit that suplicatioune be made to the Queens Majestie and Secreit Cousell for unioun of Kirks, that wher two or thrie are within two or thrie myles distant, the same to unite, and cause the inhabitants to resort to ane of the saids kirks, to heir the word and receive the sacraments; because the scarcenes of ministers permitts not every kirk to have a severall minister, and also the small number of sick parochines requyres not the samein'.

124. Dundee, Brechin (ignoring its link with Panbride), Montrose, Arbroath, Auchterhouse, Tealing, Dunnichen and Rescobie.

125. Dundee, Brechin (with Kilmoir + Burghill), Montrose, Arbroath, Auchterhouse, Dunnichen, Rescobie, Kettins, Lundie, Benvie, Strathmartin, Mains, Monifieth, Panbride, Monikie, Arbirlot, Newtyle, Nevay, Airlie, Kingoldrum, Kirriemuir, Forfar (with Restenneth), Farnell, Fern, Navar, Lethnot; also Dun and Ecclesjohn — counted here as one parish, though as two in 1563.

126. Bardgett, 'Faith, families and faction', ii, appendix A.c nos. 172, 048, 205.

127. See entry 'Cookston' in Bardgett, 'Faith, families and factions', ii, appendix A.1.

128. Table 5.1; Bardgett, 'Faith, families and factions', i, p. 192 for figures of graduates, pre-Reformation clergy and benefice-holders.

129. *Spald.Misc.,* iv, 'The obits of the lairdis and Ladeis of Dwne' (appendix to preface), p.lxxvii.

CHAPTER 6

Factions and Fighting, 1565-1574

Both the speed and the direction of the Reformation in Angus and the Mearns were limited — not to say, determined — by political and even military conflicts. A parish system reliant upon the support of local lairds could not be otherwise than strongly influenced by the other priorities of the gentry. Their various factions did not, however, divide on simple religious lines. Even during the period of civil war between those lords supporting Mary and those adhering to the regents ruling in the name of her infant son James, protestants and catholics were to be found on both sides of the political divide.[1] Before 1567, despite the series of crises that followed after Queen Mary's marriage to Darnley, she continued to deny, as she had from her return to Scotland, that she 'intendit to impede or molest ony trew subiectis in the using of their religioun and conscience . . . bot innovacioun or alteration of ony sorte'.[2] Nevertheless, the Reformation parliament of 1560 appears the decisive revolutionary event only in retrospect; men of the time were less than certain that the kirk had a secure future. After 1560, the pattern of reformed religion achieved in Angus and the Mearns, as in Scotland as a whole, developed out of the interaction between the reformers' aspirations and the political circumstances which provided the kirk with support, finance and freedom of manoeuvre. An examination of the impact of the various political factions is therefore needed to complement an account of the success of the Reformed Church.

The first observable test of opinion after 1560 came in the summer of 1565, when the earl of Moray took his opposition to Mary's marriage to Darnley to the lengths of armed resistance to the new king and queen. Although Moray claimed to be acting in defence of the reformed faith and had the support of Argyll and the Hamiltons, Angus and the Mearns remined loyal to the crown.[3] During the crisis, Mary maintained the correspondence with Patrick, Lord Gray, that had commenced before she returned to Scotland. In May she summoned him with others to Stirling 'quhare we may haue zoure advise and opinion in sic affairis as ye sall knaw at yir coming'. July 15, she wrote to Gray to counter Moray's propaganda — 'this euill brut and untrew report spred be seditious persounis amangis oure leigis'. The queen assured Gray (in the words cited above) that she had no intention to disturb the existing religious balance. In a postscript, she summoned him to attend the host with his men, prepared for fifteen days' service.[4] Assuming that Gray obeyed this summons, all of the Angus magnates served against Moray. Atholl was appointed lieutenant in the north and given authority to raise the levies of Forfar and Kincardine. With Huntly and Crawford, his colleagues from the 1560 parliament, he was appointed to command the rearguard of the army. Lords Glamis and Innermeath also served in that division, as did the forces brought by the commendator of Deer on behalf of the earl Marischal. James Lord Ogilvy served in the main battle, nominally under Darnley; presumably his dispute against Atholl over rights in the abbey of Coupar made it inexpedient to subordinate Ogilvy to Atholl. In October, Randolph reported that 'The whole force of the north is come' to support the queen.[5]

From Angus, only Mr James Haliburton, the provost of Dundee, supported Moray. Together with the earl of Rothes and Kirkcaldy of Grange, he was ordered into ward at the beginning of August, and horned and escheated for disobedience on the fourteenth.[6] The Comptroller and Collector of Thirds, John Wishart of Pittarrow, was the sole laird of the Mearns to join the rebellion.[7] Both Haliburton and Wishart had been active during the rising of the Congregation in 1559-60. Their colleague from that period, John Erskine of Dun, was ordered into ward by the queen as a preventative measure, though he 'never stirred against her'. Erskine had in fact been used as a messenger from Mar to Moray in July, in a final attempt to prevent an appeal to force.[9] Moray's close friend and brother-in-law, the master of Marischal, also appears to have remained inactive in 1565, though it was his younger brother, Deer, who led the Keith troops sent to Mary. The key protestant leadership of the province, in fact, was completely split in its attitude to the crisis. Dun and the master of Marischal may well have held the view, cited disapprovingly by Knox, that the rebellion was motivated by 'hatred envy of sudden promotion or dignity, or such worldly causes'.[9]

One consequence of Haliburton's accession to Moray's revolt was his replacement as provost of Dundee by the earl of Crawford. The earl had a hereditary interest in Dundee. The barony of Finhaven/Finavon included within it the earl's 'Great Lodging' in Dundee, a tenement contiguous with it and the patronage of the lodging's chapel. Five further chaplaincies at altars in Dundee parish church were also claimed by Crawford, who inherited rights under royal charter to £66 13s 4d annually from the Dundee customs. The earl's predecessors had been patrons of the Dundee grey friars, and the tenth earl maintained against the burgh council his claim to a feu of the friars' lands. Pre-1560 investment in the catholic aspects of burgh life led to a conflict of interests between the conservative earl and the protestant council, who were compelled by Mary to elect Crawford as provost. Relations between the shire magnate and the burgh cannot have been helped by the fine of £2,000 Scots that Mary imposed for its assistance to Moray, nor by the lavish hospitality for her that the new provost authorised.[11] Crawford was not re-elected in 1566.

Apart from Dundee's grudging welcome, support for Mary was general throughout Angus in 1565. A list of guardians of ports against possible English attack, dated 19th October, demonstrates this.[12] Dundee was entrusted by the Council to its provost (Crawford) and bailies. Lord Gray held Broughty; Lord Innermeath, Redhall. John Carnegy of Ethie, Kinnaird's able illegitimate son, held Ethie while the chamberlain of Arbroath was entrusted with that port. Crawford, Gray, Kinnaird and Innermeath had all opposed Moray.[13] Given John Erskine's predominant position in Montrose, no option existed but to entrust its defence to him as its provost and to its bailies; however, David Wood of Craig and Leighton of Usan were named for Ferryden and Usan, havens immediately adjoining the royal burgh. Craig, James V's Comptroller, had served Mary of Guise and had no associations with the reformed camp in Angus. Usan's predecessor and Craig had shared with Dun responsibility for defence of Montrose in 1544.[14] Further north, Inverbervie was committed to the laird of Benholm — Robert Keith, commendator of Deer, who was to marry Elizabeth Lundie, the heiress of Benholm, in 1566.[15] From Bervie to Cowie was the responsibility of the earl Marischal; from Cowie to Aberdeen, the provost and council of Aberdeen. Evidently the queen preferred to trust only the Keiths among the lairds of the strongly protestant Mearns, passing over both Glenbervie and Arbuthnott.

On the same day that the list of guardians of ports was approved, David Lindsay, tenth earl of Crawford, took his oath as a member of Mary's privy council.[16] The potential support for Crawford within Angus and elsewhere was large. Among the tenants of the earldom in 1532 were Bonar of Rossie, Maule of Panmure, Meldrum of Segy, Blair of Balthiok, Crawmond of Aldbar, Lovell of Ballumbie, Ogilvy of Clova and Scott of Balwearie: all men of some substance.[17] Additionally the number of Lindsay lairds in Angus was considerable.[18] The earldom comprised, beyond the barony of Finavon, superiority of the baronies of Inverarity, Clova, Downie, the forest of Plantane, Alyth, Meigle, Megginch, Ballindoch and other lands in north-eastern Forfarshire and Perth.[19] In south Angus, Crawford held Ethiebeaton in feu from the earldom of Angus, and was kin to the Grahams of Fintry and Claverhouse by virtue of their marriages to daughters of cardinal David Beaton. The tenth earl also had long-standing ties of friendship with James Lord Ogilvy of Airlie, whose house had supported his youthful claim to the earldom as heir of the disinherited 'Wicked Master'. If properly managed, these were sufficient resources to give Crawford a formidably strong position in Angus: a position which his accession to the privy council and the queen's favour could not but have assisted. The subsequent history of events after 1565 was to demonstrate that ties of feudal tenancy and of kin were not by themselves to be relied upon: the tenth earl was not, in fact, a good manager of men.[20]

If the earl of Crawford's strength was not as great as it might have been, the influence of the Campbell earldom of Argyll also suffered diminution in Angus during the 'Chaseabout' crisis. The young earl, an early protestant, had been in favour in court in the first year of Mary's return. Argyll had had a royal gift of the goods, 'geir', profits and debts of abbot Donald Campbell on the latter's death and had expectations of the commend of Coupar abbey itself. On 31 July 1565, however, when the earl supported Moray's rebellion, the queen revoked his rights and granted them instead to John, earl of Atholl — who also obtained the right to appoint a commendator of Coupar.[21] During the autumn of 1565, Argyll also lost his gift of the temporalities of the see of Brechin — which he had held since the pre-Reformation death of bishop John Hepburn. Mary nominated John Sinclair to the Pope as candidate for the bishopric in September 1565, and Sinclair obtained provision. By February 1565/6, Sinclair was attempting to gain possession of the lands 'allegeand hym to be lauchfullie providit'. However, he died in April 1566, probably never having exercised effective control as bishop.[22] In any case, the queen had used her rights during the vacancy to grant David, brother of Sir Andrew Murray of Arngask, a pension of 500 merks annually for life from Brechin's rents and fruits — little was left of the temporal revenues of the see once this pension had been abstracted.[23]

With the rehabilitation of Moray and his followers in the spring of 1566, Argyll obtained compensation for his loss of Coupar to Atholl. Alexander Campbell, brother of Campbell of Ardkinglas, was only sixteen when he was presented to the see of Brechin on 6 May 1566, with powers to alienate its lands at his own discretion. On 10 December, he granted Argyll the lands of Farnell and the office of bailie for life.[24] Argyll's policy appears to have been to feu as many lands as possible: recipients were the main neighbouring lairds or the existing tenants of the lands. In effect, the bishopric kept its own teinds (less the third); Murray took its cash income. By the time Argyll's chamberlain, Mr John Hutton, submitted an entry for the Book of Assumption, the feu duties for temporal lands amounted to over £300 — all of which was assigned to pay 'David Murrayis portoun'.[25] The earl's new rights in Farnell were to bring him into renewed conflict with his aunt, Dame Katherine — who illegally retained possession of the increasingly dilapidated property from 1564 to 1570, maintaining her claim against both Bishop Sinclair and the earl of Argyll.

By contrast with both Argyll and Crawford, Patrick Lord Gray built up a compact following in southern Angus during the 1560s. By remaining strictly loyal to Mary queen of Scots while she remained a power in the state, Gray preserved his offices of sheriff of Angus and constable of Forfar — thus preventing Crawford from recovering the former.[26] Lord Gray had barely survived 'The Rough Wooing' wars with his life and had lost his struggle against Lord Ruthven for influence in Perth. He had also suffered a lengthy imprisonment in England. He set about restoring his fortunes by marrying off his large family of daughters.[27] The feud against Ruthven was settled by a double marriage contract in 1556.[28] Patrick, master of Gray, married Barbara Ruthven, and Patrick, master of Ruthven, had his own choice from among Gray's daughters. He in fact died soon after his marriage to Marion Gray. Thereafter, Gray's daughters made a series of matches that were politically most expedient. Marion remarried Ogilvy of Inchmartine (April 1561); Helen married David Maxwell of Tealing (1561x1566); Isobel married Thomas Strachan of Carmyllie (pre-1564); Mary married Seton of Parbroath, the comptroller, in 1568; Margaret married Ogilvy of Balfour by 1576.[29]

The harmonious operation of Gray's circle of friends can be seen in a series of documents. On 4 February 1562/3, Ogilvy of Balfour agreed to stand surety for Gray; one of the witnesses to the deed was Gray's principal deputy-sheriff, Ninian Guthrie of Kingennie.[30] On 6 November 1566, Gray took the side of Henry Lovell of Ballumbie in the latter's dispute with his eldest son, John. The two Lovells agreed to arbitration and nominated as cautioners friends who would guarantee their acceptance of the final result. The elder laird chose, besides Gray, Ogilvy of Inchmartine, Strachan of Carmyllie, Maxwell of Tealing, Fotheringham of Powrie, Auchinleck of that ilk and two further lairds from outside Angus.[31] The next year, Henry Lovell of Ballumbie and Guthrie of Kingennie were among the witnesses to a contract implementing the marriage of David, fiar of Tealing, to Helen Gray.[32] Gray's ties stretched beyond south Angus: on one occasion at least he was reported as using his power as sheriff to support the claims of John Lord Glamis and his curators (Morton, Mr James McGill and Bellenden of Auchnoule) against the minor laird Lyall of Murthill. Lyall complained to the Lords that he could not get justice as Gray, being a tenant of Glamis in the Mains of Huntly, was not an impartial judge.[33] Trimming carefully between links with such as Morton and his loyalty to the crown, Gray built up a following with lands on both sides of Dundee and maintained his grip on the strategic fort of Broughty, which had been recovered from the French during the campaigns of 1559-60.[34]

One further set of Angus lairds should be discussed. Since the death of abbot Donald Campbell of Coupar, Dame Katherine Campbell's relationship with Archibald, earl of Argyll, had steadily deteriorated. She had been forced to surrender to him the spoils of Coupar abbey, and had to litigate from 1562 to 1566 to recover a purse of rings and gold coins bequeathed by the abbot to her. The earl was also to force her out of the tenancy of Farnell.[35] Nor were Dame Katherine's relations with the tenth earl of Crawford amicable. She had inherited his hostility to her husband, David Lindsay of Edzell, the usurping ninth earl of Crawford: in consequence, she had to sue to obtain her widow's terce rights.[36] Dame Katherine also successfully expelled the hereditary keeper of Crawford's castle of Finavon, Lindsay of the Haugh, from his lands and infeft her younger son Walter there.[37] As tutrix to Lindsay of Glenesk, the ninth earl's heir in his personal lands of Edzell, Glenesk, Fern and Newdosk, Dame Katherine was sufficiently influential to host Mary, queen of Scots, and her entourage during the northern progress of 1562 that culminated in the battle of Corrichie.[38] To compensate for her increasingly isolated position, she appears to have attempted to draw together her eldest son, James Lord Ogilvy, with John Erskine of Dun and William Durham of Grange.

Ties between the houses of Airlie, Edzell and Dun were long standing. Walter, third laird of Edzell, had married a daughter of the house of Dun: John Erskine the superintendent and David Lindsay the ninth earl were therefore kin by marriage.[39] Edzell had been part of Sir Thomas Erskine of Brechin's faction in the 1530s. In the 1540s, a Thomas Erskine was bailie in Edzell: Sir Thomas attempted to protect Edzell from his financial liabilities to Arran in 1543. A fragment of a letter from Sir Thomas to the ninth earl survives, commencing: 'y[air] is no freind or s[er]vand y[a]t zou haue y[a]t would be gladder on zour behalf . . .' Sir Thomas and Lindsay had a joint licence to remain from the host in 1547. After the spulzie of Finavon, it was John Erskine of Dun who had negotiated on the earl's behalf. On the other hand, Sir Thomas's son Thomas had married into the house of Airlie during the 1540s.[40]

Bonds of marriage could, of course, be overlooked — or else they could serve as foundations for an alliance. In April 1565, an attempt was made to pull together the different interests of Dame Katherine's children's houses. She entered into a contract with Lord Ogilvy, her eldest son, whereby his sister Agnes was to marry John Erskine, the superintendent's grandson. Agnes's tocher was set at 1,500 merks and was to be paid to Dame Katherine by Ogilvy. She was to keep 500 of this and pass on 1000 to the laird of Dun. The witnesses to this arrangement were Robert Erskine, fiar of Dun, John Ogilvy of Inverquharity, Alexander Lindsay of Vane and Mr

Nicol Campbell, besides the lawyers. Both Robert Erskine and his son John had been in Dame Katherine's company the previous year.[41] Inverquharity's son John had married Helen, another of Dame Katherine's daughters by the master of Ogilvy, in 1559.[42] Besides Dun and Inverquharity, another protestant closely associated with the house of Edzell was Durham of Grange, who is known to have witnessed transactions of the ninth earl in 1546 and 1552, and of Dame Katherine in 1561. William Durham, with Lindsay of Vane himself a cadet of Edzell, and Lord Ogilvy were curators for David Lindsay of Glenesk. In June 1566, Dame Katherine found as witnesses and sureties for her fulfilling an obligation, Lord Ogilvy, Robert fiar of Dun, Durham of Grange and Lindsay of Vane.[43] Dame Katherine had succeeded in binding to her as protectors for her heirs in Edzell the houses of Vane, Dun, Grange and Inverquharity — the latter three lairds strongly protestant. Through her, they in turn were associated with James Lord Ogilvy.

Dame Katherine's family ties to the protestant camp in Angus were not her only connections, however. The complex deal between the houses of Cunningham, Campbell and Hamilton whereby the Hamiltons exchanged the deanery of Brechin for the bishopric of Argyll in the 1550s has been dicussed.[44] A Hamilton link with Dame Katherine Campbell persisted. Archbishop John presented John Lindsay, Dame Katherine's second son, to the parsonage of Lethnot in 1560.[45] In 1566 she also acquired for John, who was to become the celebrated lawyer Lord Menmuir, the parsonage of Menmuir by which title he was to be known. Mr James Hamilton, a natural son of the Duke, had held Menmuir from the 1550s, but from 1559 had increasing difficulties with his tacksman, the local laird (and client of Edzell), George Symmer of Balzeordie. In 1562, he tacked the parish to Dame Katherine, and in 1566 agreed to resign in favour of her son in exchange for an annual rent of 240 merks. The recusant bishop of Dunkeld agreed to collate Lindsay, who was still a youth, on condition that he was educated at a catholic university. In consequence, after collation at the hands of Mr James Strachan and friar Andrew Abercromby, John Lindsay with his elder brother David of Glenesk and his younger brother Walter (later of Balgavies), and David Borthwick (son of Dame Katherine's lawyer) travelled to Paris under the tuition of David Lawson, newly graduated from St Mary's college at St Andrews university, where his regent may have been Archibald Hamilton.[46]

Dr John Durkan has implied from these circumstances that Dame Katherine retained a catholic faith to the mid-1560s and, indeed, she may have done — despite her newly acquired protestant kin.[47] Paris university, however, was by that date not as strictly catholic as it was to become after the St Bartholomew massacres. John Lindsay's collation in 1566 by the recusant commissioners of the bishop of Dunkeld was a matter of correct form and may have meant no more than that the bishop sought to maintain links with his Angus parishes. Similarly, a Paris education was 'good form' for the Scots gentry. Nor does Dr Durkan take into account Dame Katherine's links with key protestants, which in some cases pre-dated 1560. Yet she had received from abbot Donald the treasures of his abbey when it was 'cast doun' — an act fraught with ambiguity: perhaps undertaken with pious motives, perhaps from a love of beautiful things, perhaps from sheer avarice, perhaps to please her kinsman.[48] Nor was a minister appointed to Edzell until 1574, by which time she had left there; until then a Mr Thomas Ramsay served as reader at Edzell, while Mr James Melville was appointed minister of Fern, Menmuir and Tannadice — the first two outlying estates of Edzell. A sir Thomas Ramsay had been Dame Katherine's chaplain in 1559.[49] Clearly the dowager countess of Crawford was not a convinced protestant like her 'in-laws' at Dun. Her latter husband, the earl, however, had been associated with the English alliance during the 1540s; her Campbell kin, besides the houses of Dun, Grange and Inverquharity, were protestants. Most likely the ambiguity was deliberate: a twice-widowed tutrix of a major house could not afford the luxury of alienating potential friends.

The outbreak of civil war that followed Mary's marriage to Bothwell in 1567 and lasted spasmodically to 1573 was a severe test of the various loyalties of the lairds of Angus and the Mearns, as for others in Scotland. The issues at stake were far from clear. For some, it was a question of loyalty to the queen as to the lawful monarch and hence to those appointed to govern as her lieutenants. Others saw the dynastic ambition, whether of the Hamiltons, the earl of Moray or the Lennox Stewarts, underlying such honourable claims. Those that supported the claims of infant King James — and hence the authority of 'his' regents — advocated a rule of law according to which Mary, accused of murder and adultery, had abdicated. Radicals like Knox believed the future of the reformed kirk was at stake and prayed for the victory of the king's men: yet Argyll and Châtelherault, whose adherence to the Congregation in 1559 had been decisive, were among the queen's lords.[50] Militarily, the factions sought to subdue the strengths held by their opponents and to extend their authority over the debateable areas between their heartlands. As in the English wars of the 1540s, Angus and the Mearns were pivotal shires. With the queen's lords based in both the Gordon territories of the north and the Hamilton/Campbell alliance of the west, it was essential that they should hold Angus to maintain their unity and offer opportunities of advance into central Scotland.

On 2 May 1568, Mary escaped from her imprisonment at Lochleven and subsequently repudiated her abdication, challenging the authority of Moray's government. The northern lords rallied to her: the bond of her adherents subscribed at Hamilton included the names of the earls of Huntly, Crawford, Errol and Montrose and the lords Ogilvy and Oliphant.[51] Crawford and Ogilvy were to be persistently faithful to Mary — and also to each other. As their lands were intermingled along the Braes of Angus, it would in fact have been folly for them to support opposite sides. Crawford was considered one of the leaders of Mary's faction: he had been part of the conspiracy to challenge Moray's claim to the regency after Carberry, his promise of 1000 troops (September 1567) equalling the offer of both the Hamiltons and Huntly.[52] In May 1568, he sought to raise a force to go to Mary's aid. A letter dated 8 May sent in the names of both Crawford and Ogilvy to John Ogilvy of Inverquharity, summoning him to bring troops to Cupar in Fife, still survives in the Inverquharity muniments.[53]

Inverquharity, however, opted to remain loyal to the king's party and the house of Angus, for whom he was bailie of the regality of Kirriemuir.[54] In July 1568, Moray was writing to him to seek support for an enterprise to be attempted 'in thay boundis' by the earl of Buchan.[55] Nevertheless, it took Moray until 1569 to obtain obedience to his government from the conservative magnates of Angus. The weakness of the king's government beyond the Tay was clearly shown on 27 July 1568. On that date, David Graham of Fintry was due to be tried by the justiciary court of Kirriemuir for wrongfully imprisoning John Piggot of Balnaboth. Morton himself arrived, staying with Lord Glamis at Glamis. Fearing that Ogilvy would bring a force to support Fintry, Morton sent his deputies to continue the case. While Inverquharity and Scrymgeour of Glasswell were holding the court, Dame Katherine Campbell sent warning from Edzell that Huntly and a force of 700 to 1000 horsemen were approaching, 'causing the saidis bailzeis, thair clerk and vtheris memberis of Court, for feir of thair lyvis, to ryse and depairt thairfra, the samin Court being dewlie fenceit of befoir . . .' Morton, who had left Glamis, fled in the direction of Dundee, summoning aid from Lord Gray by means of a servant of Fotheringham of Powrie. Gray the next day provided a convoy of 300 men to see the Douglas safely to Stirling. Huntly, meantime, stayed with Crawford at Finavon 'and drank with him', receiving Ogilvy while he was there. Crawford, it was reported, returned north with Huntly, staying at Balbegno in the Mearns en route.[56]

Further evidence of military activity by the queen's lords in Angus and Perthshire can be found in the accusations levied against David Ramsay of Jordonstone in 1570. Ramsay was said to have 'fortified Crawford and

Huntly in their usurpation of authority' in 1568, especially by assisting them at Meikleour in August.[57] This appears to relate to the charges against John Ogilvy of Inverkeilor and his son, John of Balgro, said to have assisted Huntly in forcibly dispersing an exercise of arms at Kinclaven the same month. Kinclaven and Meikleour are on opposite sides of an old ford of the river Tay above Perth.[58] The northern magnates were clearly able to impose their will along the entire length of Strathmore, from the Tay across the Mearns to the Dee. Nor were they without support in mid- and south Angus. Ogilvy of Inverkeilor, uncle of James Lord Ogilvy, was also involved in the killing in Dundee in September 1568 of James Ramsay, tutor of Laws, and Alexander Auchinleck, brother of Gilbert of that ilk. Also charged were Robert Beaton of Westhall, David and Alexander Guthrie in Tulloes, William Cockburn in the Grange of Barry and Robert Wedderburn, a Dundee burgess.[59] Though this was probably as the result of a private quarrel, the parties involved took opposite sides of the political divide. Queen's men were to be found, not only on the Braes of Angus and in Perthshire, but also throughout the shires and in Dundee itself. During Moray's absence in England, Crawford, with Ogilvy and Huntly, appears to have controlled Angus.

Once Moray returned, supporters rallied to him. On 16 February 1568/9 a number of influential lairds presented the council with a written petition declaring that they had been attacked by Huntly 'by fire and sword', that they were loyal subjects of the king, and requested protection. Subscribers included, from the Mearns, Wishart of Pittarrow and the master of Marischal; from Angus, lords Glamis and Innermeath, Ogilvy of Inverquharity, the earl of Buchan and the provost of Dundee. Significantly, several Forbes subscribed the request: the northern feud between the Forbes and the Gordons was taking its place within the context of the civil war.[60] This initiative was followed up locally by Lord Glamis, whose name headed the list on a bond of thirty-two king's men in Angus subscribed on 23 February.[61] These names included many of the most influential lairds in Angus below the nobility and provided a thorough base for Moray to advance to Brechin in person within the week, to forfeit his key opponents Crawford, Ogilvy and Carnegy of Kinnaird and order the seizure of their homes.[62] Moray's new-found authority had its reward: Huntly, Crawford, Ogilvy, Deer, Fintry, John Carnegy of Kinnaird and others submitted to the king's rule in April, and appeared to register their formal submissions at the privy council in May.[63]

The composition of the group who subscribed as king's men in Angus is of some interest. The band was explicitly military, concerned with mutual defence. No justification for the band beyond the upholding of the king's authority was specified:

We ye barronis and gentilmen und[er]subscrivand bindis and oblissis us be ye fayt[h] and truthe of o[ur]e bodiis upoun o[ur]e hono[u]r and loute to ma[n]tene and set furthe ye kingis g[race] authoritie and service to ye uttermaist of o[ur]e pouer . . .

Those who subscribed were, in fact, mainly those who were associated either with Lord Glamis or with the earldom of Angus. Morton's bailies, Inverquharity and Scrymgeour of Glasswell, subscribed; so too did others of those who had previously given bonds of manrent to the house of Angus — Fotheringham of Powrie and Maule of Panmure, as well as other tenants of the regality of Kirriemuir like Lauder of Omachie. Others from southern Angus included Gilbert Ogilvy of that ilk and Auchinleck of that ilk, who had both suffered from the attack of the lairds of Inverkeilor and Westhall. Significant subscriptions were those of Scrymgeour of Dudhope, constable of Dundee, and of the lairds of Guthrie and Gardyne of that ilk. The kin of these lairds were numerous in southern and central Angus. Some more landward lairds were also among the king's men: Ogilvy of Balfour, Lamby of Dunkenny and Strachan of Brighton were neighbours of Lord Glamis. George Symmer of Balzeordie also attended, possibly as proxy for his neighbour, Dame Katherine Campbell. It should also be noted that most of these king's men came from houses that supported the reformed church.[64]

In the Mearns, too, a group of lairds subscribed a similar king's men bond on 16 March 1568/9, for mutual defence against Huntly. The master of Marischal, described as 'lieutenant of our sovereign lord within the Mearns', headed the list of names. Barclay of Mathers, Wishart of Pittarrow, Strachan of Thornton, Douglas of Glenbervie, Straiton of that ilk, Hay of Ury and Ogston of Fettercairn comprised the major lairds promising to meet Huntly in battle.[65] The close-knit nature of Mearns society once again demonstrated itself. Ury's presence signified that, although his chief the earl of Errol supported Mary, the master of Errol was a king's man and a brother-in-law of the master of Marischal.[66] Both the houses of Hay and Keith, in fact, had representatives on each side of the divide: for William Keith's younger brother the commendator of Deer — whose lands lay across the Dee — was allied to Huntly.[67]

Between January and April of 1569, Crawford and Ogilvy had lost control of Angus. Only one Lindsay is known to have supported Crawford — John of Evelick, whose house stemmed from a younger son of the third earl. Evelick had been forfeited after Langside.[68] Three key Ogilvies actually opposed the lord of Airlie: Inverquharity (despite ties of name and marriage), Balfour and Gilbert Ogilvy of that ilk. Forced to choose between outside forces, the lairds of Angus overwhelmingly chose the Douglas interest before the Gordons — whose occasional display of naked force cannot have been popular and yet proved itself too transient to compel. The support given by Morton, Glamis and the master of Marischal was decisive and enabled these two large coalitions of lairds successfully to challenge two of the native magnates of Angus. Again, it must also be emphasised that many of the lairds subscribing these bonds of 1569 can be shown to have been active in their support of the reformed church — Crawford and Ogilvy, by their pronounced religious conservatism, placed a gulf of mistrust between themselves and potential friends. Good management might have overcome religious differences, but failure even to maintain support from their local kin shows that such management was patently lacking.[69]

Patrick Lord Gray was perhaps the most conspicuous of those who had failed to subscribe the bond of 1569; nor had his clients Maxwell of Tealing, Strachan of Carmyllie, Guthrie of Kingennie, Henry Lovell of Ballumbie or Ogilvy of Inchmartine. The sheriff of Forfar appears to have decided to give no hostages to fortune by giving active support to neither side. He had retained links with Morton. Before Carberry, Morton had been given responsibility for bringing the lairds of Fife, Angus and the Mearns to aid the confederate lords, and Gray's copy of the circular letter sent appealing for support has survived. Gray had been addressed as one who 'tenders the commonwealth and establishment of the religion'. After Mary had been taken and imprisoned, Gray had approved the act justifying those who thus restrained their sovereign. Hence he could keep company with Moray, Glamis, Erskine of Dun, Pittarrow and the provost of Dundee.[70] On the other hand, he had protected Beaton of Westhall and the Ogilvies of Inverkeilor and Balgro after the affray at Dundee,[71] and was to show an increasing tendency to vote with Huntly and the conservative faction whenever it was legally possible to do so. For example, Gray was part of the minority at the Convention of Perth of July 1569 who voted for the proposed divorce between Queen Mary and Bothwell.[72]

Dame Katherine Campbell's position during the civil wars was an invidious one. Her eldest son, James Lord Ogilvy, was a leading participant on the queen's side. Her daughters Agnes and Helen, however, had married into houses that took the opposite position. The interests of her children by David Lindsay of Edzell were opposed to those of the tenth earl of Crawford; however, her own clan the Campbells supported the queen. Further, her sister was married to Forbes of Towie — an inveterate enemy of Huntly. From the available evidence, it seems that her tenants and Edzell's cadet houses, Pitairlie and Vane, took no direct part in the first campaigns of the wars. However, Dame Katherine has been noted sending a man on a fast horse, riding bareback in his haste, to warn Morton of

Huntly's approach in 1568. Edzell was in a strategic position to obtain early warning of troops crossing the Mounth into Angus. An undated letter survives in which Ogilvy of Inverquharity, in addition to asking for a loan of £50 cash, requested her to act as the eyes of the king's party:[73]

> Prais your l(adyship) adwertise me of the erll of Hwntleis dyet quhat way hi cwmmis baith horse mene and fit mene his nwmmer. Gif ye cane nocht woth this bearer prais your l(adyship) gar swm trutfal mane meit yame the morne at ye fit the mwnth qwha nwmmer thame and haist adwetisment efter me til Dunde woth ane trutfwl hand wotht ane tikket on (ie not) swp[er]scrywet for takkine that I may mak thame that is affor ws forseine of thair dyet and thair nwmmer.

In 1571, after Adam Gordon burnt the house of Towie with its mistress in it, the dowager countess of Crawford sent bowmen from the lands of Edzell to assist the master of Forbes' unsuccessful assault on Aberdeen and to avenge her sister.[74]

Dame Katherine's favouring of the king's men may have been responsible for her loss of Farnell at the hands of her chief Argyll and her son Lord Ogilvy, both of whom were said by her agent to have acted 'unkindly' towards her. After 1566, she had remained in possession of Farnell, and negotiated with Argyll and his chamberlain for a new charter of tack to regularise her position. By 27 May 1568, however, Argyll was noticeably cooler towards Dame Katherine; after further correspondence a rapid series of deals took place in March and April of 1569/70. Dame Katherine was formally warned to 'flit and quit' by an officer reading the precept both at Edzell and at the parish kirk of Farnell, 'at time of preiching and com(m)un(ion)'. At the end of March, Argyll tacked the property to Lord Ogilvy, who in April found funds for a company of footmen to serve under Argyll. In May, Ogilvy secured a feu-charter to the Place and Mains of Farnell, under reversion for 4,000 merks. Dame Katherine's claims had been overridden. Her lawyer wrote to her around this time:[75]

> . . . anet ye mater of Farnwell ye ar verra vnkyndlie and vncourteslie handelit thairintill bayth be your cheiff and your sone . . . for ye remeid yairof I ca[n] say na thing yairto becaus I knaw nocht quhat . . . titill zo haif yairto.

The civil wars against the king's regents were a heavy expense on Argyll's pocket. Moreover, he had been under pressure to part with Farnell to that other supporter of Mary, Dame Katherine Campbell's eldest son, James Lord Ogilvy of Airlie, to whom the queen had promised the estate in 1565.[76]

John Erskine of Dun and Robert his heir were also missing from the list of Angus king's men, despite the laird of Dun's leading role in the coronation of the infant king.[77] He had, after all, recently married his grandson to Lord Ogilvy's daughter. As late as April 1568, Erskine had shared the justiciary commission from Argyll to try witches in Arbroath with Ogilvy, Inverquharity and Fintry. Two further pieces of evidence suggest that Dun was initially reluctant to engage in military activity in the civil war. First, it was to Montrose that John Craig came when he was transferred from Edinburgh in 1572. Craig had attempted to mediate between the factions, and had gravely offended the radicals by affirming that blame lay on both sides. It could be suggested that he sought protection from one like-minded.[78] Second, the anonymous tract *The Lamentation of Lady Scotland* was dedicated to John Erskine and took a moderately impartial line:[79]

> Nane I excuse on ather syde; for quhy
> Ilk ane his awin hous seikis to edify,
> And nane dois cair for Commoun-weill ane prene.

'P.R.' took a more objective view than Buchanan, who blamed the wars solely on Hamilton ambition. His tract, however, came from Levprevik's press at St Andrews: 'Lady Scotland' looked forward in hope to the day when 'That fair zoung Prince in Stirling, my richt hand . . . sall purge thir foull humouris away'.[80] If the *Lamentation* does reflect the superintendent's attitudes — and certainly it contains an appeal to fraternal love as the mark of 'God's children' — his favourite theme, then he combined allegiance to the king with grief at the disturbance and distress caused by war.[81] In May 1569, John Erskine of Dun was acceptable as an assessor appointed with Wishart of Pittarrow and Thomas Menzies, provost of Aberdeen, to agree any claims for damages to be brought against Huntly.[82]

With the assassination of Moray in January 1569/70, the civil war began a new phase. Several Angus king's men attended the convention of February that agreed to elect a new regent: those present at Edinburgh included Erskine of Dun and James Haliburton, provosts of Montrose and Dundee, Ogilvy of Inverquharity, Ogilvy of Clova and Gilbert Ogilvy of that ilk, and Alexander Guthrie, fiar of that ilk. The faction of Lord Gray was represented by the master of Gray. Lord Glamis' continued support of Morton, his former curator, ensured that the majority of the shire would continue to decline to follow the lead of Crawford and Ogilvy, who attended the queen's lords' rally at Linlithgow.[83] There had been some defections from the king's men: when in May Levprevik published a broadsheet accusing Huntly, Crawford, Ogilvy and others of breaking their solemn oaths to support King James, Ogilvy of Balfour and Garden of Leys had switched sides since February 1568/9. Fintry, Kinnaird and the commendator of Deer continued in their allegiance to Mary and were joined by Ogilvy of Lawton and William Rait of Hallgreen, by Inverbervie in the Mearns.[84] It was this faction that began the 1570 campaign by proclaiming Huntly as Mary's lieutenant at Forfar and Brechin.[85]

The queen's party had by no means been wholly removed from Angus by Moray. An entry in the Arbroath court book for November 1569 refers to the collector of the *queen's* third. In October, John Aikman and others had sought recompense from 'the whole neighbours' for 'ye skaith cum apoun yaim fra ye ryde w[i]t my lord Ogilby'. The abbey had been gifted to George Douglas by the regent in August 1568: Ogilvy had paid him dues in September 1569.[86] Lord John Hamilton was again in control by March 1569/70, however. He, with Huntly, Ogilvy, Sir John Carnegy of Kinnaird and Ogilvy of Lawton were at Arbroath at the end of the month to grant — with the consent of six of the convent, including the minister and reader of the burgh — pensions to two of Ogilvy's sons, for[87]

> defens of us o[ur]e convent ten[n]antis and servandis and o[ur]e special place (and) for resisting o[ur]e nonfreindis and innemeis in manifest assultis and attemptis of yame attemptit till o[ur]e apeirand hurt and damnage and skaith.

Ogilvy had also provided the sum of 400 merks towards the earl of Argyll's contribution for raising companies of foot-soldiers, in exchange for possession of Farnell from which he was evicting Dame Katherine Campbell.[88] The queen's lords' attempt to establish their authority both in Scotland and in Angus was determined, organised with both finance and troops, their morale bolstered by personal letters from Queen Mary to their leaders. One such still survives at Kinnaird Castle, sent to Sir John Carnegy of Kinnaird, noting that the exiled queen had been informed 'of zour greit constancie towarde the advauncement of oure auctoritie' and 'assuringe zou that whensoeuer it sall ples God we returne . . . we sall haue the samin in good remembraunce . . .[89]

Nevertheless, with Lennox elected regent in June, the king's men rapidly enforced their authority north of the Tay. By June, the *king's* collector of thirds (John Erskine's agent, William Fullerton of Ardoch) was dealing with the burgh of Arbroath, and Douglas was again commendator. He reinforced his hold on the burgh by seizing Seaton from John Carnegie of that ilk.[90] An attempt by Kirkcaldy of Grange to fortify Broughty for Mary came to nothing.[91] By the end of July, Randolph was able to report that Huntly 'finds great disobedience in the north'.[92] Despite the number of earls who supported Mary in the first half of 1570, they could only obtain obedience in Angus by demanding it in person and with a display of force.

In August, the queen's lords gathered at Aberdeen and planned a campaign to commence with a muster at Brechin, where Crawford and Ogilvy had fortified the cathedral's steeple and acted as an advance guard for the occupation force, garrisoning Brechin castle with 400 harquebusiers. (The castle and lordship of Brechin had been held by Mar since he obtained the feu from Sir Thomas Erskine of Brechin.) Lennox took decisive action. He proscribed the parliament Huntly had summoned to Linlithgow and ordered the seizure of Crawford's castles of Finavon and Inverquiech, and Ogilvy's castle of Airlie. Morton raised a task force of cavalry and, accompanied by Glamis, Ruthven, Lindsay and Methven, and with the lairds of the shire flocking to support him, seized Brechin before Huntly could arrive. More than thirty of the garrison were hanged; Mr John Cockburn, one of the burgh's bailies and Lord Ogilvy's agent, was escheated.[93] Crawford and Ogilvy fled. Huntly reached no further than Fettercairn, where he pillaged some horses and victuals before withdrawing.

Morton's seizure of Brechin was the decisive campaign of the civil war in the east of Scotland. Crawford surrendered to the regent, finding that his crops were at the mercy of the king's men.[94] Lennox was able to write to Cecil that he had thwarted his adversaries' purposes and that he now held their houses. Ogilvy of Clova was placed in Airlie: a Haliburton in Inverquiech. Interestingly, Lennox also claimed to hold Broughty, 'a place to have been suspectit in many respects', not least, no doubt, because of the dubious loyalties of its owner, Patrick Lord Gray.[95] The master of Marischal's brother-in-law, Lord Saltoun, remained at Glenbervie to watch Huntly. He reported that opposition to the Gordons was increasing, with the master of Errol and the Forbeses actively seeking support:[96]

> I assure your lordship I saw never this country so cold to the earl of Huntly and if they see any appearance of help or rescue, he will find part (i.e. opposition) at his door . . .

By October, the Arbroath burgh court were stenting the neighbours to furnish eight men to ride with their commendator, George Douglas, to the regent. In the same month, seventeen men from the Mearns, led by the brother of Marian laird of Hallgreen, were tried for treason for contravening the acts prohibiting the Feast of Unreason.[97] Once again, the queen's supporters had been humiliated in Angus, their campaign for the year destroyed. Once again, they submitted to the king's authority, seeking arbiters to plead their cause and find favourable terms. David Lindsay, earl of Crawford, turned to Lord Lindsay of the Byres; James Lord Ogilvy sought the aid of his mother Dame Katherine Campbell in negotiations with Morton. John Erskine of Dun and the earl of Mar were the hope of Lord Home; Lord Glamis, that of his kinsman by marriage, the earl of Cassillis. Finally, Queen Elizabeth of England used her influence to impose a national abstinence (or truce) that lasted seven months.[98]

The attempt of Huntly, Crawford and Ogilvy to dominate Angus and the Mearns had failed and was not to be renewed in any form that promised success. Crawford, having spent his entire adult life since his teens in opposition to the house of Edzell, finally came to terms with Dame Katherine. Towards the end of 1570, he agreed to the marriage of his daughter Helen to David Lindsay of Glenesk. No tocher was provided; instead, Crawford recognised the claims of Edzell to the superiorities of Edzell, Fern, Dalbog and Newdosk that it had won from the earldom at the time of the ninth earl. Dame Katherine agreed to restore Lindsay of the Haugh to his hereditary lands, and the earl confirmed her terce rights.[99] The settlement was judicious on both sides: David Lindsay of Edzell came of age and into his inheritance in 1573 and was to prove a loyal supporter of his brother-in-law and chief, the eleventh earl of Crawford who also succeeded on his father's death c.1574. The long, draining division of the Lindsays of Angus had been overcome — but too late to secure any advantage for the cause of Mary queen of Scots. When Kirkcaldy of Grange renewed hostilities in the spring of 1571, both Ogilvy and Crawford remained with the king's party.[100] The latter's loyalty may have wavered when Adam Gordon of Auchendoun raided Brechin and Angus in July 1572, taking a somewhat lax defence by surprise,[101] but by this time even Adam Gordon's military prowess could not turn the tide in Angus. Crawford attended Morton's first parliament as regent in January 1572/3, but was reported as 'deadly sick' and appears to have died soon after.[102] Ogilvy left Scotland for France sometime in 1572, leaving his affairs in the hands of his wife Dame Jane Forbes, his mother Dame Katherine Campbell, and his kinsmen Ogilvy of Balfour and Ogilvy of Clova.[103]

One lacuna remains to be filled to complete an account of the civil wars in Angus. Lennox wrote to Patrick Lord Gray in August 1571 to request the use of artillery from Broughty Castle for use at Leith in the siege of Edinburgh, 'as ye will declar yir gude affection to the furthsetting of the kingis actoritie'.[104] The regents remained nervous that Broughty might fall (or be given?) into the wrong hands. In December, Mar wrote to Gray assuring him that he had no desire to remove him or any of the king's nobles from their 'rooms' and especially from his fort of Broughty, but that it was considered better not to run the risk of losing it.[105] By April, it was reported that Gray had surrendered Broughty into the keeping of the earl of Buchan, whose main residence was at nearby Auchterhouse.[106] When Adam Gordon seized Brechin in 1572, it was considered suspicious that Gray had left the day before; the question of his foreknowledge was raised.[107] Certainly members of his family were openly supporting the queen's cause. Gilbert Gray, one of his sons, was part of the garrison of Edinburgh castle: Seton of Parbroath, one of Lord Gray's sons-in-law, assisted in Kirkcaldy of Grange's raid on Stirling castle when regent Lennox was killed.[100] Morton appears to have decided to clip the wings of the sheriff of Forfar. The council resurrected an old grievance against the Grays that, in the time of Moray's regency, they had violently removed John Lovell of Ballumbie's tenants from disputed fishing grounds off Broughty. Both the Lord and master of Gray were put to the horn for this offence in February 1572/3.[109] By then, the civil war was in its last stages: the Hamiltons came to terms at Perth the same month, leaving only Grange and Maitland to their respective fates still withholding Edinburgh castle from the king.

At first sight, the course of the civil wars had little impact on the development of the reformed kirk in Angus and the Mearns. There was considerable stability of both ministers and readers, who in the main continued to serve in the same parishes between 1567 and 1574.[110] Two changes probably had some relation to the course of political and military events. Ninian Clement, the former monk and minister of Arbroath, was transferred to Forfar in 1574. It may be that he had given support to the queen's faction: certainly he had subscribed the charter granting pensions to Ogilvy's sons for defence of the abbey. In his place was appointed Mr James Melville — a man much closer to John Erskine of Dun, and likely to be reliable from the point of view of the authorities of church and state.[111] Second, it should be noted that in 1574 a minister was for the first time appointed to Finavon, seat of the earl of Crawford. David Lindsay of Pitairlie, a cadet of Edzell, was transferred from Forfar to Aberlemno with Finavon with Inverarity with Kirkbuddo. No reader was yet resident at Finavon, however.[112]

If the structure of the kirk remained intact during the period of conflict, nevertheless political insecurity affected the operations of its institutions. The Monifieth Kirk Register is lacking pages and entries from May 1565 to February 1565/6 — the period of the Chaseabout raid and its aftermath.[113] When the record resumes, the assembly was less concerned with disciplinary matters than earlier. The routine of collections for the poor, baptisms and marriages with their associated taking of cautions to learn the 'belief' and the commandments continued.[114] The Lord's Supper occurred ('the qu[hil]k day commun[iou]n wes ministrated') on 17 October 1568; on 19 August 1570 the assembly authorised the distribution to the poor of twenty-seven shillings from a poor-fund of three pounds twenty-two pence.[115] From August 1572, however, occasional entries are found whereby parishioners promised 'to observe the order of the kirk in time coming' as a new start was attempted. In May 1573 the register records its first full list of elders and deacons, together with instructions for deacons, and regulations concerning the kirkyard and its dykes. Thereafter, the assembly began its lengthy campaign against sexual offenders and the parish's dissident lairds, again exercising an authority that had diminished during the civil strife.[116]

In Arbroath, a new start was made on 9 October 1573, by which time the transfer of the commendatorship from George Douglas to Lord John Hamilton had been effected. The basic relationship between the burgh court and the kirk authorities was laid down:[117]

> It is concludit be ye co[un]sall anent ye ordour of ye kyrk that qu[hat]soeuer be decernit be ye minister elderis and deconis for observing of gud order salbe put to executioun be ye bailzeis and co[un]sall in dylygnce.

Thus co-operation between the burgh's two courts was re-established, with the kirk's court obtaining perhaps a greater independence than it had enjoyed before. In 1567, it had been possible to appeal from the judgment of the elders and deacons to the burgh court — whose authority was also exercised to enforce decrees of the kirk.[118] 9 October 1573 also saw a new attempt to endow the burgh school with a master's stipend from the old altarage annuals:[119]

> The q[uhi]lk day it is thowth expedient for ye co[m]on weill becaus of inlaik of ane maister of schwell for ye suppurt y[air] of it is co[n]cludit y[a]t O[u]r Lady benyfes w[a]t ye haill a[n]wellis pertenand to ye deirygeis be collectit and tayn op and xx lib. yairof to be giffy[n] to ane maister and ye rest yairof to be disponit at ye sicht of ye bailzeis and co[un]sall to ye puyr or co[m]on werkis.

Once this principle was settled, the court offered the post to one David Nichol on 27 October, and he agreed to begin from the forthcoming New Year.[120] The head court of October 1574 continued the process of re-establishing reformed discipline:[121]

> . . . certan of ye actis of Assemblie conform to their form be observit and put to execution and ye bailzies and counsall gave yair aithis yairto; and for punishing of transgressoris yairof certan to be appointit to every quarter to await yairon.

With James Lord Ogilvy as bailie of the abbey and Lord John Hamilton as commendator, Arbroath had been a focus for the activity of the queen's lords during the wars. By 1574, the burgh once again approximated to the pattern of reformed religion expected by the General Assembly.[122]

If the available evidence from Monifieth and Arbroath, scarce though it is, suggests that the victory of the king's regents encouraged the kirk in microcosm, so to speak, it also did so macrocosmically both in Angus and in Scotland. The deaths of first the earl of Moray and then the earl of Lennox brought to the fore the houses of Mar and Morton — Erskine and Douglas — as the leaders of the king's party. Even from 1570, Morton was perceived as the man with authority in the government.[123] Although calculating, grasping and where necessary devious, he appears to have had a genuine commitment to the protestant faith and was prepared to spend considerable time and effort in unproductive negotiations with a frustratingly principled General Assembly. It is at least arguable that his 'platt' of 1573-4 gave the kirk a financial stability that was fundamental in achieving the restoration of its discipline and parochial structure on a national basis after the civil wars. Although they preached at him and prophesied against him, the kirk's radicals in the end concluded that Morton was a 'man ever cast upon the best syde' — their own.[124] Though insufficiently recognised at the time, it was the king's party's victory in the civil war that guaranteed that the kirk would be able to continue to develop along the lines laid down during the 1560s — as least as far as parochial reformation was concerned. Morton's military skill and forceful leadership, as exemplified in his capture of Brechin in 1570, had had a great deal to do with that victory.

As Morton's power grew in Scotland, it also grew within Angus. As tutor to the young earl of Angus, he had succeeded in enforcing his personal control over the regality of Kirriemuir both by the series of bonds signed with its tenants in 1558 and by winning the active and committed support of his bailie in Angus, Sir John Ogilvy of Inverquharity. Like Morton, Inverquharity's protestant allegiance dated from before 1560. He had subscribed the bond 'to the house of Angus' in 1558, and had his bailiery recognised by charter in 1562 and 1571.[125] Sir John's role in the civil war in Angus itself has been described. He was also called upon by the regents to supply troops (horse and foot) at Kinghorn in 1571 and for the siege of Leith in June 1572.[126] To reward Inverquharity for his service in the key shire of Angus, Morton helped him to extort tacks of teinds out of James Lord Ogilvy of Airlie. While Lord Ogilvy was held in ward on his return to Scotland, he was compelled to sign away to Inverquharity (and three of the latter's kin) tacks of teinds from Kirriemuir and Lintrathen, and other lands held by Inverquharity. Morton wrote to Patrick Adamson as archbishop of St Andrews, urging him to facilitate confirmation of the transfer of these revenues.[127] He also wrote to Inverquharity, asking him not to enforce his new rights too harshly against Lord Ogilvy's assignee of the teinds of Shielhill, one Janet Ogilvy:[128]

> that pure gentilwoman is in greit doubt fearing hard handilling at zour handis Off quhome cheiflie sche mon lippin for ma[n]tenance and [con]fort. And albeit we think our request be all litlie newis to zow this matter tuching ane of zour awn, But the guidwill that we bear baith to zow and all ouris muvis us at this tyme to request and desire zow effectuously y[a]t ye will suffer the said y[i]r kyniswoman to bruike hir tyndis . . .

Morton obviously took very seriously his interests in Forfarshire: by 1577, Angus was of age and managing his own affairs. The regent, however, sought to keep his hands on the reins of power via his contacts in a shire favourable to the Douglases.[129]

More important yet to Morton among the gentry of Angus was John, Lord Glamis. Glamis' relationship to Morton extended back to his minority, when Morton had been one of his curators.[130] They worked together throughout the 1560s: both supported Mary in 1565, both supported the regents Moray, Lennox and Mar in the critical events after 1566.[131] His role in heading the alliance of king's men in Angus in 1569 has already been described. Like Morton, Glamis appears to have been a convinced protestant, being described as such in reports by English agents.[132] When Morton gained the regency, he handed on his own previous post as chancellor to Lord Glamis, who was thus as involved as the regent in attempting to find a settlement with the General Assembly of the question of the future polity or government of the kirk. Glamis' letter to Beza, which raised the questions of the validity of bishops in the kirk and of the power of the crown to summon ecclesiastical assemblies and dispose of the wealth of the bishoprics, shows a balanced appreciation of both theological principle and political necessity: a more balanced view, it might be said, than that of the reply he received.[133] Glamis, like Morton, appears to have favoured a form of episcopacy for Scotland, perhaps on Anglican lines.

Glamis' leading role in the civil war had substantial significance for the future development of both politics and religion in Angus. The sheer size of his following was indicated in 1577 when he and his tenants obtained licence to remain away from a raid summoned for Dumfries. Besides Lyons, thirty-seven of the important lairds of Forfarshire and two from Perthshire shared in Glamis' licence.[134] Considerable similarity exists between this list, and those who subscribed the 1569 bond to the king. Well-known names recur: Maule of Panmure, Ogilvy of that ilk, Fotheringham of Powrie, Strachan of Brigton, Symmer of Balzeordie, Lamby of Dunkenny, Scrymgeour of Glasswell, Auchinleck of that ilk, Gardyne of that ilk, Robert

Durham of Grange, Scrymgeour of Dudhope, Lauder of Omachie, Guthrie of that ilk. Glamis was said by the English agents in 1577 to be 'of no party or faction'.[135] With this volume of support in his home shire, as one of the wealthiest lords in the kingdom and as Chancellor of Scotland, Glamis had little need to seek the patronage of others. His sole weakness lay in the fact that in his rise, he had humiliated David, tenth earl of Crawford. The consequent Lyon/Lindsay feud was to lead to Glamis' death on 17 March 1577/8 at the hands of servants to the eleventh earl,[136] after which Thomas Lyon, master of Glamis, succeeded to the leadership of the eighth lord's friends.

The third side of the triangle of forces by which Morton retained power in Angus was his relationship with the house of Erskine. Mar and Morton had both been involved with Congregation before 1560 and had equivocated during the Reformation crisis,[137] Mar (then Lord Erskine) especially, attempting to present himself as an impartial national servant, holding Edinburgh castle above faction.[138] Mar's similar role from 1567 as keeper of the castle of Stirling came to have crucial significance when Stirling became the home of the young King James: the earl and countess of Mar were responsible to parliament for his upbringing there and won the Erskines the compliment of being 'ane race of men to me maist kynd' from the author of *The Lamentation of Lady Scotland.*[139] In 1572, when Morton became regent, new arrangements were made for the king's house at Stirling. Alexander master of Mar became responsible in the name of the young earl, assisted by the dowager countess. A bond of the friends of the house of Erskine was subscribed at that time in order to provide sureties for the master on undertaking his new responsibilities to the nation. Heading the list was the name of John Erskine of Dun; his son Robert also subscribed, as did David Erskine, commendator of Dryburgh, and Adam Erskine, commendator of Cambuskenneth, and William Douglas of Lochleven.[140] Cambuskenneth was to be Collector-General of Thirds for Morton and both Erskine commendators were to play important roles in national politics as allies of the regent. The alliance between the houses of Erskine and Douglas was sealed in 1573 by the marriage of the young earl of Angus (with consent of his curators Morton and Glamis) to Mary Erskine, sister to the young earl of Mar. An English agent reported thereafter: 'The Earl of Angus's marriage confirms the devotion of the house of Erskine to the Regent'.[141]

With the accession of first Mar and then Morton to the regency, John Erskine of Dun as an elder statesmen of the name of Erskine was brought closer to the centre of the government of the king's party. John Erskine had in any case maintained his political support for the king by attending the

'Creeping Parliament' of 1571 in his capacity as provost of Montrose.[142] The superintendent's role as intermediary between the government and the kirk at the time of the Leith agreement in January 1571/2 seems therefore somewhat suspect in the light of his political alignments. The privy council sederunt for the meeting at Leith 2 December 1571 included, besides Mar and Morton, the newly reconciled earl of Crawford and the master of Marischal, the commendator of Dryburgh (David Erskine) and Douglas of Lochleven, John Erskine of Dun, James Haliburton, provost of Dundee, and the officers of state. Apart from Crawford, the council was dominated by a Douglas/Erskine protestant alliance.[143] It is hardly surprising to find, therefore, that in January the commissioners of the kirk granted supply from the thirds for the support of the king's house and the regent's house and expenses, and for Mr James Haliburton's pension.[144] These commissioners included the laird of Dun, his agent William Fullerton of Ardoch, collector of Angus and the Mearns, and David Lindsay, minister of Leith, Dun's protégé. At this time, John Erskine of Dun himself had a payment of £666 13s 4d from the treasury supposedly for previous assignations made by the deceased earl of Moray.[145] In the light of these evidences of the closeness of John Erskine to the government, the proposals at Leith to institute an episcopate reformed according to the model of the superintendency look somewhat less like a negotiation and more like a *coup* by Morton, who headed the team on behalf of the secular authorities.[146]

By 1574, John Erskine of Dun as superintendent of the diocese of Brechin with the kirks of Dunkeld and St Andrews between Tay and Dee was responsible for the continued parochial reformation of his province. His position was unassailable, being backed by the General Assembly of the Kirk on the one hand, and by the support of such as regent Morton and chancellor Glamis on the other, who not only controlled the government but also headed the major coalition of lairds in Angus. The dissident magnates of Angus had been cowed: the support of the lairds of both Angus and the Mearns had been won for the cause of the king, and hence of his regents and the reformed kirk. Whereas John Erskine and his immediate supporters had, however, been the leading protestant military force in their shires at the time of the Reformation, that role had now passed to the Lyons of Glamis. Both Morton and Glamis opposed the newer, presbyterian, faction in the kirk: Erskine of Dun had been associated with the episcopalian proposals of 1571/2, and organised his province during the 1570s firmly along the lines of the 'platt' of 1574 whereby one minister was allocated four kirks. The civil wars of 1567-74 had resulted in the victory of the king's men, both nationally and in Angus. The parochial reformation of the 1560s, with its emphasis on preaching and collegiate discipline, was thereby enabled to recover its lost ground and make further progress. As far as the debate on polity was concerned, however, Angus began to reflect, rather than lead, the thinking of the kirk. The increasing ecclesiological conservatism of this province north of the Tay was also a result of Morton's victory.

NOTES

1. G. Donaldson, *All the Queen's Men* (London 1983), p.115.
2. BL, Egerton ms.1819 f.52r: Mary to Lord Gray, 15 July 1565.
3. As did lairds from that other protestant 'hot bed', Ayrshire. G. Donaldson, *All the Queen's Men*, pp.71-76 discusses allegiances in 1565.
4. *CSP(S)*, i, 912 (8 Oct. 1560); BL: Egerton ms. 1819 f.19 (10 Apr. 1561); ibid., fs.51, 52. The summons in f.52 is substantially that reported in *Knox's History*, ii, p.155 as sent to 'a great number of Lords' of Fife, Angus, Lothian etc.
5. *RPC*, i, 362, 379, 380; *CSP(S)*, ii, 278.
6. *RPC*, i, 348, 353. Professor Donaldson suggests that Durham of Grange also joined Moray: *All the Queen's Men*, p.73. Unfortunately he gives no authority for this, and the probability remains that the laird of Grange referred to in *Knox's History*, ii, pp.158, 161 was Kirkcaldy. The only 'Grange' to receive a remission in 1566 for his part in the Chaseabout Raid was Kirkcaldy: *RSS*, v, 2698, 2699, 2700, 2701.
7. *Knox's History*, ii, p.161; *RSS*, v, 2678.
8. *CSP(F) Eliz. 1564-5*, no. 1510; *Knox's History*, ii, p.156.
9. *Knox's History*, ii, p.158.
10. *RMS*, ii, 494; WRH, The Haigh Inventory, i, p.88; I. Flett, 'The Geneva of Scotland', p.76.
11. I. Flett, 'The Geneva of Scotland', p.71.
12. *RPC*, i, 380-1.
13. G. Donaldson, *All the Queen's Men*, pp.74-5.
14. NLS, ms.5407 f.2; *RPC* i 132.
15. SRO, Benholm and Hedderwick mss., GD 4.30; Reg.Deeds, RD 1.1 f.154v.
16. *RPC*, i, 386.
17. *RSS*, ii, 1226, 1227, 1233, 1235, 1272, 1335, 1372, 1435.
18. F.D. Bardgett, 'Faith, families and factions', ii, appendix B under 'Lindsay'.
19. WRH, The Haigh Inventory, i, p.105: charter of 3 July 1559.
20. See Ch. 1, n. 50. J. Wormald, 'Princes' and the regions in the Scottish Reformation', *Church, Politics and Society*, ed. Macdougall, p.65f. discusses the 'contractual' nature of magnate power.
21. *RSS*, v, 2229.
22. F.D. Bardgett, 'Faith, families and factions', ii, appendix A.b no. 081.
23. F.D. Bardgett, 'Faith, families and factions', ii, appendix A.b no. 069.
24. F.D. Bardgett, 'Faith, families and factions', ii, appendix A.b no. 015.
25. SRO, Bk. Assumpt. E 48.1.1 f.348r. By 1568, the whole of the temporality of Brechin seems to have been feued, under Argyll's instructions.
26. Crawford had resigned the office to Gray in 1532 under reversion for £550. The eleventh earl attempted to regain the office by tendering the sum in 1595. WRH, The Haigh Inventory, i, 108.
27. See Ch. 4, n.99; the competition against Ruthven: *RPC*, i, 64, 68.
28. WRH, NRA(S) 217, 369; inventory of Kinfauns Muniments, vol. 1, no. 5; SRO, Reg.Deeds RD 1.2 f.39r.

29. *Scots Peerage*, iv, pp.280-25.

30. SRO, Reg.Deeds RD 1.6 f.41v.

31. SRO, Reg.Deeds RD 1.9 f.162r.

32. Strathmore writs, NRA(S) 885 box 134 bund. 7.

33. Strathmore writs, NRA(S) 885 box 134 bund. 7

34. Sir F. Mudie and others, *Broughty Castle* (Abertay Historical Society pub.15, 1970), pp.32-3.

35. JRL, The Craw. mss., box E ii; SRO, Acts and Decs., CS 7.29 f.106r.

36. WRH, The Haigh Inventory, i, p.90; ii, pp.82, 83, 84: actions continued from 1558 to February 1562/3.

37. See Ch. 1, n.34.

38. *RPC*, i, 218.

39. JRL, The Crawford mss., 81.1.11: 'Ordour of geneology of lords of Glenesk 1623'.

40. See Ch. 1, n.56. JRL, The Crawford mss., 81.1.2; WRH, The Haigh Inventory, ii, 199; *Spald.Misc.*, ii, p.203; The Haigh Inventory, ii, p.52; SRO, The Airlie mss., GD 16.44.5.

41. WRH, The Haigh Inventory, ii, p.87, 86.

42. WRH, The Haigh Inventory, ii, p.78: contract 6 June 1559.

43. *RMS*, iii, 3219; SRO, The Dalhousie mss., GD 45.16.646; Reg. Deeds RD 1.4 f.307r; WRH, The Haigh Inventory, ii, p.89.

44. Hannay, 'Some Papal Bulls': *SHR*, xxii, p.37.

45. *RSS*, vi, 2558 and F.D. Bardgett, 'Faith, families and factions',ii, appendix A.b no.059.

46. F.D. Bardgett, 'Faith, families and factions', ii, appendix A.a no.163; JRL, The Crawford mss., 3.2.4,5,12; also, Lord Lindsay, *Lives*, i, pp.329-333; also article by Dr. J. Durkan cited in n.47.

47. J. Durkan, 'Commentary', *Northern Scotland*, v (1984-5), p.105.

48. Cf. M. Lynch, *Edinburgh*, p.29.

49. F.D. Bardgett, 'Faith, families and factions', ii, appendix A.2 (linkages of parishes) and A.c no.194.

50. G. Donaldson, *Scotland, James V — James VII* (Edinburgh 1978), pp.157-166 gives a clear and thoughtful summary of events.

51. *CSP(S)*, ii, 650; see G. Donaldson, *All the Queen's Men*, pp.91-116.

52. *CSP(S)*, ii, 618.

53. SRO, Ogilvy of Inverquharity mss., GD 205 box 1 no.7. Prof. G. Donaldson incorrectly modernises Inverquharity as Inverarity: *All the Queen's Men*, p.110.

54. His appointment was confirmed by Morton in 1562: SRO, Inverquharity mss. GD 205 box 1 no.30.

55. SRO, Inverquharity mss. GD 205 box 1 no. 9.

56. *CSP(S)*, ii, 752; Pitcairn, *Criminal Trials*, i, p.75.

57. SRO, Justiciary courts, JC 26.1.62. Andrew Naiff in Carsebank also took part in conflict at the Haugh of Meikleour: *RSS*, vi, 681.

58. *RSS*, vii, 1062.

59. *RPC*, i, 655, *RSS*, vii, 1062.

60. *RPC*, i, 645.

61. Strathmore mss., NRA(S) 885 box 235 bund. 3 no.16.

62. *RPC*, i, 646. First Mr James Haliburton, provost of Dundee, and then Lord Glamis was instructed to take possession of Kinnaird castle: *RPC*, i, 647; *RPC*, xiv, p.64; Strathmore mss. box 235 bund. 3 no.13.

63. *RPC*, 654, 622, 633f.

64. See Ch. 4, *passim*.

65. Fraser, *Douglas Book*, iii, p.265 no.212.

66. *Scots Peerage*, iii, p.570; WRH, Inventory of Errol Charters NRA(S) 0925 and SRO GD 175, no.775.

67. *CPS(S)*, iii, 221.

68. *Publications of the Clan Lindsay Society,* ed. J.Lindsay, vol. iii, no.9 (Edinburgh 1924), 'Lindsays of Evelick', p.3; *RSS,* vi, 276.

69. Ordered to ward in Edinburgh as a condition of his surrender in May 1569, Crawford found as his cautioners the catholic Sir David Graham of Fintry and the insubstantial Fenton of Ogil. They were forfeit £5,000 when Crawford left ward in September, of which £2,000 was given to the provost of Dundee: *RSS,* vi, 755.

70. *CSP(S),* ii, 502, 515, 632.

71. *RPC,* i, 655.

72. *RPC,* ii, 2, 3.

73. JRL, The Crawford mss., 3.2.7: 13 August (blank) — possibly 1570.

74. Calderwood, *History,* iii, 153.

75. Kinnaird, Southesk Charters, box 1 bund. 19 no.9; box 6 nos. 1,2; SRO, Airlie mss., GD 16.52.1; 16.24.67,68; Acts and Decs., CS 7.68 f.385v; JRL, The Craw. mss., 3.2.1.

76. SRO, Airlie mss GD 16.24.64.

77. G. Donaldson, *All the Queen's Men,* pp.85-6. Maule of Panmure and the constable of Dundee were also part of the somewhat select company at the coronation.

78. T.A. Kerr, 'John Craig 1512 ?-1600' (Edinburgh Ph.D. 1954), pp.98-103.

79. *Satirical Poems,* i, p.230 lines 99-101.

80. *CSP(S),* iii, 123; *Satirical Poems,* i, p.231 lines 128, 130.

81. *Satirical Poems,* i, p.235 lines 279-288.

82. *RPC,* i, 633f., and ii, p.9.

83. *RPC,* xiv, pp.32, 42.

84. *CSP(S),* iii, 221.

85. G. Donaldson, *All the Queen's Men,* p.119.

86. APL, ms. court book 1563-75 fs. 48v, 50r; *RSS,* vi, 415; SRO, Airlie mss. GD 47.2.

87. SRO, Airlie mss., GD 16.47.13.

88. SRO, Airlie mss., GD 16.52.1.

89. Kinnaird Castle, Southesk muniments, Log Book of Royal Letters.

90. APL, ms. Arbroath court book 1563-75 f.54v; *APS,* iii, 233.

91. *CSP(S),* iii, 386.

92. *CSP(S),* iii, 386.

93. *RPC,* xiv, 15, 64, 67-72; *CSP(S),* iii, 290, 386, 389, 399, 402, 404, 406, 410, 429, 431; *RSS,* vi, 981, 1003.

94. *Diurnal,* p.190.

95. *CSP(S),* iii, 426.

96. *CSP(S),* iii, 386.

97. APL, ms. Arbroath court book 1563-75 f.55v; Pitcairn, *Criminal Trials,* i/ii, p.15.

98. *CSP(S),* iii, 464.

99. JRL, The Crawford mss., 4.1.83 and WRH, The Haigh Inventory, i, 99 (box C).

100. *CSP(S),* ii, 895. The defeat of Crawford and Ogilvy by Glamis' coalition of Angus lairds is reminiscent of Killigrew's now famous comment of 1572: 'Methinks I see the noblemen's great credit decay . . . and the barons, burghs and such-like take more upon them'. See M. Lynch, *Edinburgh,* p.164, citing *CSP(S),* iv, 476.

101. The Adam Gordon raid was a highly successful military operation. Attacking by surprise on Sunday 6 July, he drove Glamis, Crawford, Buchan and Gray from Brechin. Montrose was ransomed for £2,000 and two tuns of wine: the house of Dun was sacked. Arbroath and Forfar were occupied: worship at Monifieth was abandoned, the kirk register recording, 'the q[uhil]k day wes nathing gatherit . . . uprior w[a]t wes in ye cuntry for Adam Gour[doun]'. Mar and Morton swiftly diverted forces, and had expelled the raiders by the sixteenth. OPR 310/1 f.19r; *CSP(S),* iv, 3834; *RPC,* ii, 143, 156.

102. F.D. Bardgett, 'Faith, families and factions', ii, appendix B. no. 139.

103. SRO, Airlie mss., GD 16.48.19: draft contract in name of Lord Ogilvy, now in France, dated (blank) 1572. He was present in Angus in 1573: *CSP(S)*, iv, 605, but again abroad in 1574 and 1575 and was warded by Morton on his return: SRO, Reg.Deeds RD 1.14 f.201r; *RPC*, ii, 427.

104. BL, Egerton ms.1819 f.77.

105. BL, Egerton ms.1819 fs.78,79.

106. *CSP(S)*, iv, 250.

107. *CSP(S)*, iv, 384.

108. *RSS*, vi, 2292; vii, 2669.

109. *RPC*, ii, 188. This dispute dated back to 1536 when the Grays attacked the then Henry Lovell of Ballumbie, claiming his fishings. In 1547 the English took possession of Broughty's fishings. When they left, the French garrison replaced them. In 1551, the Lovells of Ballumbie and the Grays continued their dispute both at law and by violence. Pitcairn, *Trials*, i/i, 177*; SRO, Acts and Decs., CS 7.24 f.39v (14 May 1562); CS 7.55 f.277r. (4 Mar. 1573/4).

110. F.D. Bardgett, 'Faith, families and factions', ii, appendix A.2 sections 1 and 2. Some readers were deposed: see Appendix A.c nos. 233, 036; also cf. A.c no.162.

111. F.D. Bardgett, 'Faith, families and factions', ii, appendix A.c nos.032, 143.

112. F.D. Bardgett, 'Faith, families and factions', ii, appendix A.c no. 124.

113. OPR 310/1 f.9v-f.10r covers the jump. Unfortunately the register is no longer in its original binding (some folios are bound in reverse chronological order), so it is impossible to determine whether entries ceased during this period or if they were removed.

114. OPR 310/1 f.11v, 12r, for example.

115. OPR 310/1 fs.13v, 17v.

116. OPR 310/1 fs.19v-24v.

117. APL, court book 1563-1575 f67r; *CSP(S)*, iv, 699.

118. APL, court book 1563-1575 f34v: 7 April 1567: 'The q[uhi]lk day W[illl[ia]m Storok apellit fra ye Jugme[n]t of ye elderis and deconis anent ye wordis of iunuris gyffin to hy[m] be Jhone Lyne and Besse Hunter his spous ye said Jhon Lyne offerit hy[m] rady to fulfill yair dekreit in all pointis for his part and his said spous and askit act and iust remeid y[air] upoun.' See also: APL, court book 1563-1575 f35r: 18 April 1567: 'The sa[m]in day it is decernit be ye bailzeis minister elderis and deconis y[a]t gyf Jhon Ra[m]say wobster missa[y] Jonat Lain his moder w[i]t wordis of iuniuris he sall tyn his fredu[m] and com[m]on landis ye first tym and ye secund tym to be banist ye town and gyf ye said Jonat his moder misparsun ye said Jhon and beis co[n]vyt y[air] intill sche sall tyn hir lyfrent of hir said com[m]on landis ye first tym and ye secund tym to be banist ye toun.' It must be admitted that these entries are the only examples of their kind, but they parallel the relationship between the council and eldership of Dundee: Maxwell, *Old Dundee*, pp.72-3.

119. APL, court book 1563-1575, f67v.

120. APL, court book 1563-1575, f68r: 27 Oct 1573: 'The q[uhi]lk day ye bailzeis and haill nyboris concludit y[a]t yair be ane maister of gram[m]er schwell prouidit and to mak by yame zeirly viii s. of ilk barn w[i]tin ye toun and twenty pundis to be maid to hy[m] of O[u]r Lady benifes or derygeis a[n]wellis w[i]t his chalm[er] maill fre and Dauid Nycholl is rasault y[air] to for yis zeir quha hes promisit to enter y[air]to at New Zeir Day nyxt to cum.'

121. APL, court book 1563-1575, f72r: 8 Oct 1574.

122. In lending occasional support to the regents and in (re-)adopting the reformed order in 1574, Arbroath's civil war career paralleled that of Aberdeen — which nevertheless retained a basically conservative religious preference. A. White, 'Religion, Politics and Society', pp.274-5.

123. G. Hewitt, *Scotland under Morton*, pp.13-5.

124. G. Hewitt, *Scotland under Morton,* pp.83-116; G. Donaldson, *Reformation,* p.93; F. Bardgett, 'Four parische kirkis to ane preicheir', *RSCHS,* xxii, 195f.

125. SRO, Ogilvy of Inverquharity mss., GD 205 box 6 bund. 11: NLS ms. 25.9.6; SRO, GD 205 box 1 bund. 30, NLS ms. 5308 no. 1262.

126. SRO, GD 205 box 1 bund. 11: NLS ms. 5308 no. 1259.

127. SRO, Airlie mss GD 16.48.25, 26 for tacks of 14 Feb. 1576/7. SRO, Ogilvy of Inverquharity mss. GD 205 box 1 no. 16 for Morton's letter of 2 Mar. 1576/7 to Adamson.

128. SRO, Ogilvy of Inverquharity mss. GD 205 box 1 no. 17.

129. Morton's early years may have been spent at Glenbervie: Hewitt, *Morton,* p.2.

130. SRO, Reg.Deeds RD 1.5 f.22r: Glamis' curators were Morton and Bellenden of Auchnoule on 27 December 1561 when he bought out Atholl's rights to his ward and marriage.

131. *CSP(S),* ii, 327, 502, 616, 632; *ibid.,* ii, 84, 119, 122, 227, 231, 363.

132. *CSP(S),* v, 1-3, 284.

133. G. Donaldson, *Scottish Church History,* p.120f.

134. Strathmore mss., NRA(S) 885 box 235.3 no. 9.

135. *CSP(S),* v, 284.

136. *CSP(S),* v, 326: Randolph to (Killigrew): 'All the divels in hell are sturringe and in greate rage in this countrye. The Regent is discharged, the country broken, the Chancellor slain by the Earl of Crawford'.

137. *Knox's History,* i, 121.

138. *Knox's History,* i, 201, 231-2, 261-2, 264, 275, 344.

139. *Satirical Poems,* i, p.231 line 136.

140. SRO, Mar and Kellie mss., GD 124 10.37 and GD 124.10.40. SRO, Mar and Kellie mss., GD 124 3.10. Douglas of Lochleven had already married regent Mar's sister Margaret: *Scots Peerage,* vi, p.369.

141. *CSP(S),* iv, 590; see J.G.B. Young, 'Scottish Political Parties 1573-1603' (Edinburgh Ph.D. thesis 1976), pp.38-9.

142. MTH, Montrose mss. M/WK/16: signet letter discharging burgesses of Montrose from an array following their provost's presence at parliament 'with others of the most able and honest inhabitants '.

143. *RPC,* ii, 98.

144. *RPC,* ii, 112-3.

145. T. Crockett, 'Life of John Erskine of Dun', p.195.

146. T. Crockett, 'Life of John Erskine of Dun', pp.195-7.

CHAPTER 7

The Reformation Endures

To estimate the influence of religion in society by counting heads has long been recognised as fallacious. The Scottish Reformation may not have resulted from — or itself engineered — any 'magical mass conversion',[1] but what it did achieve was in the long run more decisive. The parochial reformation introduced a new and dynamic energy of evangelism and education into Scottish culture: kirk discipline. From the beginning, the support of the 'gentlemen of Angus and the Mearns' ensured that the new kirk enjoyed acceptance and sponsorship by men who controlled institutions of government in these two east-coast shires. Despite its original minority status, the reformed religion won for itself an enduring place in Scottish national life by effective control of the agencies of local cultural life and institutions.[2] However, even theology based on divine revelation has to be both developed and implemented in the world as it is by men and women whose thoughts, motives and emotions relate not only to God but to their manifold social, economic and political environments. In the rapidly changing society of James VI's Scotland the patterns of church life that developed in Angus and the Mearns owed their forms not just to the ideals and programmes of the reformed theologians: the more conservative traditions and aspirations of those who held power in the shires also played their part.

The failure of the pre-Reformation church had been primarily an institutional failure: entrenched personal, legal and economic privileges had thwarted that effective internal reform of acknowledged abuses which alone could have prevented criticism of the clergy by the faithful from flowing into protestant channels.[3] It has been suggested that the 1550s saw a limited but significant switch from traditional to reformist values, if not necessarily from catholic to protestant. The evidence for this is, it must be admitted, somewhat tenuous. The vicar of Dundee's opinions were considered significant; so too were the changing personnel of the chapter of Brechin, and the secularisation of various chaplaincies and altarages.[4] Unfortunately no surviving testamental evidence relates to Angus and the Mearns from the pre-Reformation period, so this route to assessing doctrinal attitudes remains closed. Nevertheless, one volume of minor testaments from the St Andrews' deanery of Fife does exist and its contents tend to support a thesis of growing doctrinal change in the 1550s. Initial prefaces to wills in 1549 uniformly follow the classic traditional Marian format.[5] By 1551, however, an alternative form was at least as frequent in which reference to the Virgin and the Saints was omitted,[6] although as payments to the chaplains 'on the day of my burial' remained, this second formula ought to be categorised as 'mixed traditional/reformist' according to canons of English testamental morphology.[7] Traditional Catholic orthodoxy was under fire from several quarters in the 1550s. It is a commonplace that the weakest time for a regime is when it seeks to introduce long-overdue reform; the existing institutions of the church failed to cope with the challenge of increasingly dissident faith.[8]

Within limits, the lairds of Angus and the Mearns were able to determine their own priority-ranking of the various claims made upon them.[9] A sufficient number placed their obedience to their perception of the claims of God sufficiently high on their lists to spark the Reformation crisis — even if their faith was little more than simple piety.[10] In the quarter-century that followed, some appear to have come to a deeper understanding of reformed doctrine; the majority were content to die sustained by a conventional, though protestant, faith.

To assess the extent of individual belief in the protestant faith, a survey of registers of testaments produced the discovery of twenty-seven testaments testamentary made by lairds of Angus or the Mearns, or by their wives.[11] Research by historians of England suggests that evidence from testaments cannot be made the object of statistical precision, for their religious preambles owed their wording not just to the deceased's wishes, but also to the notary he employed, to traditional formulae and (possibly) form-books. Nevertheless, authorities are convinced that testaments do convey a reliable doctrinal climate of opinion;[12] this sample of lairds' wills is small (by English standards) but informative, being selected on the basis of names and careers already known. Of the wills with religious preambles, by far the greatest number were phrased neutrally, omitting equally clauses explicitly catholic and overtly protestant. Archibald Douglas of Glenbervie, for example,

> co[m]ittit his soule unto ye father omnipotent ye creat[ou]r of all and committit his gudis and geir . . . (to William his son as executor with James earl of Morton and Falconer of Haulkerton as overmen) as they sall answer befoir God at ye day of judgment.

Six further examples of this wording were found,[13] all made by lairds (or ladies) who, while accepting the Reformation, were not among its devotees. These preambles followed closely in the traditions of the pre-Reformation non-Marian formulae used in St Andrews testaments, which had also concluded with an admonition concerning the Last Judgment.

Five further wills were explicitly protestant. William Durham of Grange left £100 to the poor of the parish of Monifieth, and appointed his friend John Erskine of Dun as overman to his executors. He specified that, in so bestowing gifts on the poor, 'I no[ch]t suppois yat ony mereit is obtenit be bestowing of yame bot my mereit is in ye faith of Jesus Christ onlie'. His will had commenced with a preamble similarly expressive of trust in the remission of sin promised by Christ, and reminiscent of contemporary English formulae.[14] The laird of Grange's known associations and career, together with his eldership in Monifieth kirk, leave no doubt that the protestantism expressed in his will was sincere. Similarly, both Sir John Wishart of Pittarrow and Jonet Falconer his wife expressed their faith in salvation through the merits of Jesus Christ alone; Sir John also left a legacy of £100 for the poor 'in my awin landis as weill husbandmen as cotteris'.[15] Less certainly personal were the wills of Sir Robert Carnegy of Kinnaird and Robert Durham of Grange. Whereas both William Durham and John Wishart had authorised wills written in the first person, Sir Robert Carnegy's final will, which left 'his saule in the mercie of God throwcht Jesus Chris[t] ouer onlie Sauiowr', was in the third person and may well have owed its protestant terminology to the fact that it was heard and written by John Ure, minister of Leuchars and canon of St Andrews priory. Sir Robert's first will, written by himself, had been religiously neutral.[16] Finally, Robert Durham of Grange's will had a preamble which was an exact copy of his elder brother's, made fifteen years earlier; it is hence unclear whether the wording originated in fraternal piety or protestant faith, or whether it was due to the influence of Andrew Auchinleck, minister of Monifieth under both lairds and a witness to both their wills. Robert Durham, however, left nothing to the poor. His 'second-generation' faith does appear to have been cooler than that of his brother.[17] Thus of the known wills of lairds of Angus and the Mearns, only two were explicitly protestant — according to criteria modelled by comparison with English standards.

The attitudes of the Scots reformers to death were, however, much more radical than those of the southern kingdom. The first Book of Discipline had recommended only a minimal religious content at funerals, to counter prevailing superstition.[18] That eleven of the lairds' testaments contained no religious terminology at all by way of committing or bequeathing the soul may well reflect reformed instruction as well as those with explicitly protestant wording. The likelihood that Scottish testamentary practice was more radical than the English is enhanced by consideration of the careers of the people who thus left untraditional wills. The list includes John Lord Glamis, the chancellor of Scotland; Alexander Whitelaw of Newgrange

F

(John Knox's agent in 1559); William Fullerton of Craigo (John Erskine of Dun's agent and sub-collector of the third in Angus); Robert Graham of Morphie; Alexander Lindsay of Vane, Alexander Guthrie of Haulkerton (iconoclast and Bible publisher); and Jonet Anderson, widow of Hercules Guthrie of Lunan and probably sister of Mr Thomas Anderson, minister of Montrose.[19] These people were no less adherents of the reformed faith than Wishart of Pttarrow or Durham of Grange.

Of these twenty-seven wills, only one was explicitly catholic. William Graham, earl of Montrose, gave in his testament on 22 May 1570, dying a year later. A decade after the Reformation, he left '. . . my saule to my God omnipotent and to ye glorious Virgin Marie his moyer and to all and haill ye spreittis in heuin . . .' The Graham, however, though he took his title from his small barony of Old Montrose (to the south-east of the Montrose Basin), had his main house and residence at Kincardine, by Alloa between Stirling and Perth.[20] His religious conservatism had more in common with that of central Scotland than with the protestantism of Angus and the Mearns. Finally, three testaments may be described as 'reformist': expressed in traditional formulae modified according to reformed principles. Thus Richard Melville of Baldovie, minister of Maryton, left '. . . and recom[m]endis my saule to ye lord Jesus Christ and my body to ye erthe quhairfra it came to be bureit w[i]t my foirbaires in ye kirk of Maritoun . . .' In thus seeking burial with his kin in their church, the minister proved more loyal to tradition than to the Book of Discipline, which held it unsuitable for a place of preaching and communion also to be used for burials. The altered bequeathing clause, however, reveals his reformed allegiance. Euphame Durham and Christine Arbuthnott, ladies respectively of Claypotts and Balzeordie, used the traditional non-Marian formula altered in one respect. Where their predecessors had declared themselves 'sick in body but whole in mind' (or 'in spirit'), the former's will ran 'haill in saule' and the latter's 'haill and p[er]fyt in soule', thus reflecting greater protestant assurance of salvation.[21] Whereas in England legacies for requiems and other modes of posthumous expiation continued only somewhat abated until the reign of Elizabeth, the known testaments of the lairds and ladies of Angus and the Mearns, with one exception, therefore reflect various modes of the protestant faith.[22]

The sons of Dame Katherine Campbell serve as excellent examples of the differing degrees of individual religiosity to be found among those brought up as the first generation in reformed Scotland. Both David Lindsay of Glenesk and Mr John Lindsay, parson of Menmuir, had been educated abroad in France and England during the 1560s under the tutorship of David Lawson.[23] Mr John became a noted lawyer at court: he had a pension of £100 granted by archbishop Patrick Adamson, and was made a lord of session by the patronage of Esmé Stewart, duke of Lennox. Well-informed though critical comments on the second Book of Discipline were probably drafted by him, and demonstrate knowledge of Calvin's *Institutes*.[24] He retained his links with the more radical section of the kirk, however, being married to Marion Guthrie, daughter of Alexander Guthrie, the town clerk of Edinburgh. Mr James Lawson's wife was Jonet Guthrie; John Lindsay was thus kin by marriage to one of the most militant ministers of the Kirk. Both Edzell and Menmuir on different occasions stood as witnesses at baptisms of Lawson's children, and Menmuir had licence to be one of Lawson's executors despite the minister's death in exile during the Black Acts crisis. In the Crawford and Balcarres papers are preserved John Lindsay's list of the baptismal dates of Lawson's children, as also is John Cairns' certificate of the baptisms of John Lindsay's own children at St Giles' while he was an elder there. The list of witnesses chosen for Mr John Lindsay's children is impressively reformed, including ministers John Durie, Walter Balcanquhal, James Lawson and Robert Bruce, the English ambassador Robert Bowes, and Alexander Guthrie (son of 'King Guthrie'), Edinburgh's town clerk.[25] In 1587/8, Menmuir was chosen as one of Edinburgh's commissioners to the General Assembly.[26] Though he was associated with King James VI's court, rising to be one of the Octavians, Lord Menmuir's essential protestantism seems to have been in no doubt. Though hardly a Melvillian presbyterian, he was an active member and office bearer in the kirk.[27]

David Lindsay of Edzell also served the reformed kirk in a manner appropriate to his status as lord of a major barony. The minister of Fern, Mr Alexander Norie, looked to him for support in raising a tax from his tenants to repair the church, and in his quest for a full glebe.[28] Edzell sought and obtained a special commission of justiciary, dated 1 February 1587/8, to apprehend, try and execute a 'vagabond', Robert Murray, for witchcraft. The records of the trial are still extant in the Crawford papers at Manchester: Murray was convicted.[29] When Edzell required a certificate of his illness and inability to compear at court in 1588, his minister, Mr James Fullerton, together with Mr Andrew Leitch, minister of Maryton, and David Straiton at the Mill of Dalbog, an elder of Edzell kirk, drew up and witnessed the document.[30] The extent to which Edzell's view of the word corresponded to that of the reformed kirk can also be measured by the sculptured panels that adorned the formal garden or 'pleasance' that he had constructed at Edzell. Inset into the wall were carvings representing the Seven Cardinal Virtues, including *Fides,* with a Cross and a Chalice in her hands. The presence of the Seven Liberal Arts and the Seven Planetary

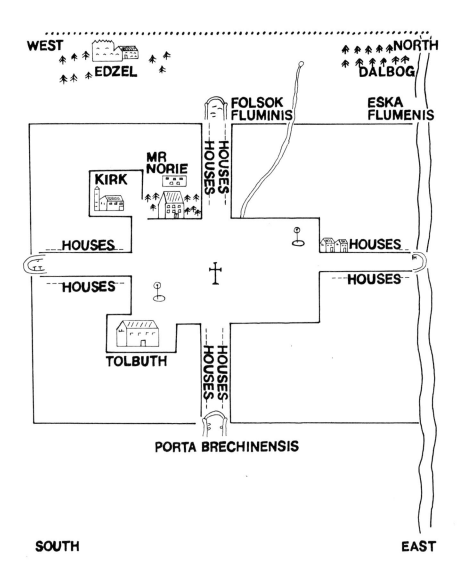

Diagram 7.1. 'Pourtraicte of ye new citie of Edzel, 4 Septeb. 1592: idea.' Redrawn from a ms. in the Crawford and Balcarres muniments at the John Rylands University Library of Manchester: 4.1.97. In this diagram of 'Ideal Edzell' buildings drawn on the original are represented by the word 'HOUSES'. All other words and drawings occur on the original.

Deities serves to remind the visitor that David Lindsay of Edzell inherited traditions stemming both from the Reformation and the Renaissance.[31]

Finally, the fundamentally feudal and mediaeval aspects of David Lindsay's mind should be noted. He secured the erection of Edzell as a burgh of barony in 1588; a contemporary plan by him of a rebuilt burgh entitled 'pourtraicte of ye new citie of Edzel' shows a walled burgh whose dominant features are the kirk and manse, tolbooth and trons, and at the very centre, the mercat cross.[32] Christian institutions and symbolism were inescapably part of the world of the laird of Edzell; he was patron of his own parish church, he held several tacks of teinds from his ministers, and he enforced the rights and law of the kirk within his jurisdictions.[33] His library included Bibles, New Testaments, and at least one work by that European advocate of church discipline, Oecolampadius.[34] This protestant Christian gentleman was also involved in the feud — the laird of Edzell participated in the murder of his mother's kinsman Campbell of Lundie in 1582, in support of his brother-in-law and chief, the earl of Crawford. John Lindsay wrote admonishingly to his brother, warning that nothing but trouble would ensue from such an act:[35]

> The ground of all thir matters proceeds of your rash consenting to assist the Earl of Crawford to do ane manifest wrang, . . . Consider how troublesome is the warld, how easily ony man who is stronger nor ye at ane time may do you ane wrang, and how little justice there is in the country for repairing thereof. Therefore I wald desire you above all things to travail to live in peace and concord with all men, otherways your life and pairt of the warld shall be very unpleasant, ever in fear, danger and trouble . . .

Though Mr John Lindsay, elder of the kirk and lord of session, was trained to value the king's peace, his brother the laird of Edzell found it possible to combine the Christian values of his pleasance with the cause of the honour of his kin; even in his youth, David Lawson had found it difficult to train the son of the ninth earl of Crawford in humility.[36]

Three other of Dame Katherine's sons deserve mention. Mr James Lindsay became a minister of the reformed kirk, holding the valuable parsonage of Fettercairn from 1576 to 1579. The young man was to die an early death at Geneva, to which he had travelled seeking a cure for 'ane naturall diseis to quhilk I am subject and havelie vext'. Andrew Melville wrote a Latin elegy in his memory. In his will, 'being uncertane quhen and quhere it sall pleis God to call me . . .', Lindsay commended 'my saule to ye grete god omnipotent my creato[u]r and saviour my body to ye erth . . .'[37] The will, written in the first person, reads as a document written in haste, leaving it to Mr Walter of the Haugh, his brother and executor, to provide tokens of his affection for 'my haill bru[th]eris and sisteris'.[38] Whereas Mr

James Lindsay thus had the closest association of any of his immediate kin with the reformed kirk, his chosen executor, Mr Walter, was (as Lindsay of Balgavies) one of Scotland's most noted recusant catholics, together with Dame Katherine's eldest son, James Lord Ogilvy of Airlie.[39] Buried in 1606 according to the rites of the old church, Lord Ogilvy left behind for his heir a letter of direction, containing both spiritual and practical advice. It contains some of the most purely Christian sentiments to be found in the literature of the period of the Reformation in Angus and the Mearns.[40]

Dame Katherine's sons exhibit a marked personal religiosity; the character and direction of their faith was in large measure determined by themselves, and influenced by their respective educations and political and social circles. Her Lindsay sons thus maintained the tradition of their house and of their father, who had added an aisle to his parish church in the earlier sixteenth century. Before and after the Reformation, lairds in the relatively wealthy, stable and settled shires of Angus and the Mearns were aware of inheriting a Christian faith and its responsibilities; and they had sufficient means and leisure to develop these for themselves. During the 1540s and 1550s, this religious frame of mind had been fertile ground for the teaching of the protestant preachers; sufficient men of authority had been committed to the protestant cause to see it to victory in 1559/60. Angus and the Mearns are thus to be clearly distinguished from other regions of Scotland. In the less settled Borders, for example, 'the mass of people did not feel strongly enough about any religion to risk their lives for it'.[41] In Dumfriesshire, 'There appears to have been little demand for reform before 1560'.[42] The faith of men like Sir David Lindsay of Edzell, Lord Edzell, was not necessarily theologically profound: indeed, it was patently mixed with values stemming from very different traditions. It was, however, deeply held and sincere. If it is possible to presume that the son was not unlike the father, some insight into the support gained in the previous generation by men like George Wishart is possible.

If the Reformation is explained at least in part as an expression of personal faith, the institutions and customs it created also served to encourage and revive faith. The kirk emphasised its role in interpreting and maintaining the rites of passage; though the number of sacraments recognised had been reduced, greater weight was placed on baptism, and on preparation for death. From being a private occasion, capable of being validly performed by midwives, baptism became (in the main) part of public worship and was restricted to the ministry — initially to ministers and readers; by the later 1570s, to ministers only. The role of godparent was continued under the form of witnesses, often men bearing the same Christian name as that of the child.[43] The suitability of this ceremony to name-conscious Scottish society is clear. Baptismal occasions were opportunities for expressing kinship or the patron-client relationship, or simply friendship, as was thought appropriate. Mr John Lindsay, parson of Menmuir, endorsed the baptismal certificate of his children, 'Extract be John Cairnes reidar at Edinburch of . . . special days of ye baptising of my bairns'.[44] It can be seen that, as with the Durhams of Grange, Lord Menmuir's sons were named after at least one of the witnesses to their baptism and the day was considered 'special' thereafter by their father. In linking the congregational and kinship aspects of baptism by the device of the witness, the Scottish kirk differed from the practice of both Geneva and England, where the nuclear family was increasingly valued.[45]

The deathbed held a special place in the custom of the reformed kirk. It could be the occasion *par excellence* for giving confession of the faith. John Knox, for example, recounted the pre-Reformation dying profession of faith by Elizabeth Adamson, who 'suffered most grievous torment of her body, yet out of her mouth was heard nothing but praising of God'.[46] Her death followed the singing of Psalm 103, and was '. . . no small comfort of those that saw her blessed departing. This we could not omit of this worthy woman, who gave so notable a confession . . .' Knox's own death was to be held in similar esteem.[47] As the kirk had virtually banned funeral ceremony, visitation of the sick and pre-death counselling gained greater weight, featuring in the *Book of Common Order*.[45] Whereas before the Reformation, lairds had given their confession (of sins) and made their will before their chaplain or chosen confessor,[49] after 1560 both readers and ministers took on this function. Seventy-seven wills (testaments testamentary) have been discovered witnessed by a total of twenty-nine ministers and readers. Many do not include the date of death of the testator, but of the thirty-six that do, twenty-seven were made within a month of death in the presence of the parish minister, or his reader.[50] Thus George Symmer of Balzeordie made his will on the day of his death before Mr Andrew Elder, notary and reader at Menmuir. William Elder at the Stone of Benholm made his testament on 13 October 1573 in the presence of Mr John Elder his brother, Mr William Elder, reader at Benholm, and Mr Andrew Elder, and died the same month. James Davidson, burgess of Montrose, made his will 'with his own mouth' on 23 November 1579 before both his minister and reader, Mr Thomas Anderson and John Baty, and died the next day. Archibald Douglas of Glenbervie similarly made his will the day before his death in the presence of John Christison, parson and minister of Glenbervie.[51] All levels of propertied society thus summoned reformed clergy to their deathbeds.

This, then, like baptism, was an occasion for reformed instruction that merged with an event of importance in Scots society. Death and inheritance were crucial in Scottish patriarchal society; the appointment of executors and giving of bequests required the presence of a dying man's kin. When Sir Robert Carnegy made his second and last will at Leuchars, 'beinge in his bed deidly seik in bodie', three of his sons were present: John the eldest, together with Mr David of Panbride and Mr Robert, parson of Kinnoull. That his minister, John Ure, used the opportunity to emphasise the uniqueness of Christ as 'ouer onely Sauiowr' has already been suggested.[52] A fuller 'confession' was made by Mr David Balward, parson and minister of St Madoes in his manse on 1 December 1590:[53]

> gaif ye confessioun of his fayt y[a]t his salvation consistis onlie in ye deith and passioun of Jesus Christ tro[ch]t ye fre mercie of eternall lord o[ur]e God hoiping assurtlie to be resaiffit y[air]to thro[ch]t and be no uy[er] meanis.

Similar testamental preambles occur among those longer wills registered at Edinburgh. On 22 December 1573, Elizabeth Nevay, spouse of James Wichthand in the mill of Inverarity, began her will in this fashion:[54]

> Ye said Elizabeth being seik and infirme in bodie bot zit of gud rem[em]brance left and disponit her saule to ye eternal God, Father, Sone and Hailie Gaist to be participand of yat eternall glorie q[uhi]lk o[ur]e savio[u]r Jesus Christ hes purchasit to hir and all faithful be ye schedding of his precious blude and ordains hir body to be bureit in yr paroche kirk of Inneraritie yair amang ye faithfull . . .

The influence of a minister may well be behind such a doctrinal statement, and is surely obvious in the will of sir Richard Smart — made thus under his style as a pre-Reformation priest on 15 August 1582. The legacy section was subscribed in the name of John Fullerton, minister of Inverkeilor, and ran:[55]

> I ye said . . . haill in spreit and mynd albeit weik and febill in body levis my soule to God thro[ch]t Jesus Christ my saviou[r] my onlie redemer . . .

Smart's executors were his wife Helen Leslie and his eldest son, William, so the trust in Christ expressed in his will may have been his own sentiments as well as those of his minister. Fullerton's name and style with the words 'sit.sub.' are recorded at the foot of Richard Smart's testament, indicating that it was written by the minister. Occasionally, this is elaborated with an explanation that the testator could not write.[56] Whereas epistolary skills were increasingly common in England, so that the dying could exercise some choice in the selection of his scribe, they seem less so in Scotland; the Scots reformed ministry therefore maintained a tighter (though certainly not exclusive) grip on the deathbeds of their flock.[57]

The endurance of the Reformation, then, can be ascribed not only to the individual religiosity of lairds (and others) in Angus and the Mearns, but to the longer-lasting union of reformed practice with Scottish culture. The Reformation revived a religious frame of mind that was not only integrated with society at large, but in many respects fundamental to it. The significant moments of individual life — birth, marriage and death — were interpreted by its ceremonies and ministry in ways that were appropriate to the kin-based nature of Scotland.[58] Reformed theological emphasis on the communal and congregational nature of baptism harmonised with the traditions in Angus of Christian names being handed down from generation to generation.[59] Teaching on a Christian's duties to die a responsible and godly death and to be charitable to the poor suited a society which valued good lordship.[60] John Erskine of Dun's theology of conflict and its practical application in the witch-hunt was not confined to himself: others associated with such commissions of justiciary were Lord Ogilvy (before his conversion to catholicism), Ogilvy of Inverquarity and Lindsay of Edzell. Patrick Collinson suggests that the union of magistrate and minister was at least in part a response to an unstable society; lords in England and lairds in Scotland found in reformed teaching an ideology which supported social control and conservatism in combating sin and the wiles of the adversary.[61] That David Lindsay of Edzell and John Erskine of Dun both studied Oecolampadius is not coincidental.[62] Society in Angus before and after the Reformation was certainly unusually disturbed.[63] The reformed kirk's parochial customs had much to offer the sixteenth-century Scottish lairdly culture that had given it birth.

At an institutional level, the new kirk was not only integrated with society, but also integrative of it. By the mid-sixteenth century, the process of sub-infeudation was well developed. The feuing of church and crown lands, and the wadsetting of baronial lands, had resulted in most lairds of any substance holding lands from several superiors — and hence finding themselves subject to several, possibly competing, jurisdictions.[64] The re-creation of the parish as the dominant unit of local society was the product of the Reformation, and appears to have met a desire to belong that neither kindred nor baron court could entirely fulfil. In the confusion of loyalties of 1559/60, the myth of the Congregation had offered its devotees both ideological and practical support. Subsequently, the parish assembly could prove a suitable court in which local lairds might co-operate in establishing parochial discipline and even attempt such delicate matters as arbitration between opposing factions.[65] At Monifieth, for example, the eldership linked together tenants-in-chief, tenants of the regality of Kirriemuir, and subtenants holding lands in the regality from the earl of Crawford. The procedures of the kirk's courts were those of the familiar baron court, which all free tenants had a duty to attend. That baron courts were held in the name of a sole superior may find an echo in the dominant position of Durham of Grange at Monifieth and Graham of Morphie at Ecclesgreig. Decisions, however, ran in the name of the 'haill court' (i.e. all the suitors present) or of its jury in the feudal arena, and of the 'haill assemblie' or its eldership in the ecclesiastical.[66] The reign of James VI saw a period when 'many of the familiar landmarks' of feudal Scotland were in decay;[67] at a local level, the new institution of the reformed parish and its eldership both harmonised with the Scottish experience and created new social and administrative units, more rational than the baronies.[68] Culturally and institutionally, the parochial reformation harmonised with Scottish rural society — and thereby became a means by which faith might be cultivated and life experienced within a Christian framework.[69]

How far was protestantism in Angus and the Mearns confined to the propertied classes? Because of the shortage of kirk session registers, there is virtually no means of answering this question. Testamentary evidence is of little help, for the surviving register of testaments for Brechin is of small or minor testaments — a large proportion of which were dative. Those which were not were worded almost without exception from various combinations of four standard formulae.[70] Two tentative conclusions may be drawn. First, that radical protestantism made little headway until the 1590s; only at that period do the obviously protestant preambles studied earlier from the Edinburgh-registered larger testaments make their appearance at this level. Neither, however, was there any indication of recusancy. Out of fifty-four testaments testamentary registered at Brechin between 1576 and 1584, only one included a legacy for 13/4d., 'to be spendit at yir die of my burial', thus harking back to a common feature of pre-1560 catholic testamentary practice.[71] Protestantism, though in a traditional and diluted form, had come to stay.

One interesting piece of evidence suggesting a wider reception of the Reformation can be found in the Monifieth kirk register, on those occasions where the clerk recorded the number attending the annual communion.[72] Because of the solemn and climactic nature of the annual Lord's Supper, these figures represent church attendance at its maximum. By April of 1576, approximately 600 people took communion; this figure was to remain fairly stable for some years, and at its peak of 780 represented a ministry that reached a high proportion of the population.[73] Comparison of figures for communion collections for the poor with the normal weekly offering demonstrates clearly the exceptional nature of this attendance. Whereas at communions in the early 1580s total gifts of three to four hundred pence were regular, the weekly average for 1582 was only thirty pence.[74] Study of

PENCE

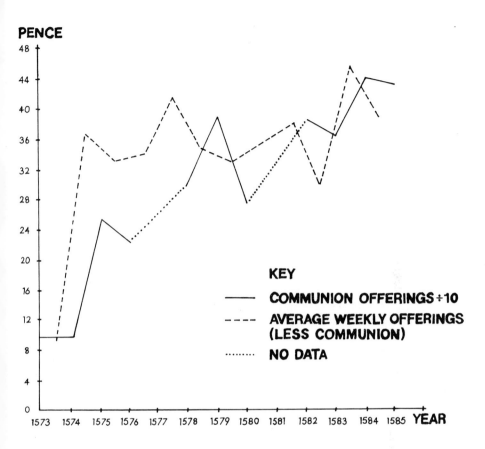

Diagram 7.2. Correspondence of weekly and communion giving at Monifieth. The weekly average offerings shown have been calculated from the quarterly medians; hence this excludes erratic occurrences such as nil collections due to snow or the unusually large offerings of a wedding. The communion offerings are compared with the weekly average by dividing the former by 10.

the normal and communion offering totals suggests further conclusions regarding church attendance at Monifieth: first, that weekly attendance was roughly ten per cent of that at communions, and second that attendances whether annual or weekly improved in the early 1580s.[75] The sacramental and rites-of-passage aspects of the reformed kirk appear to have been more acceptable to the bulk of parishioners than the weekly diet of worship and preaching at Monifieth. As this parish appears to have been in some respects a model reformed rural parish, there must have been many where the lairds were less devout than William Durham of Grange and where the kirk was less well received.[76]

The problems experienced at Monifieth in obtaining regular church attendance may have been due to the fact that the integration of kirk and society at a local level was at the same time a source of both strength and weakness. Though William Durham of Grange and Alexander Lauder of Omachie supported the kirk and led the session, Henry Ramsay of Laws and Ninian Guthrie of Kingennie were at odds with the leading elders, Laws being prosecuted for adultery by the kirk. This dispute probably had its origin in secular matters and had a further context in the wider divisions of Angus society. The mother of Durham of Grange had been a Ramsay: William Durham entertained a claim, possibly inherited from his father, to half the estate of Laws. If relations between the neighbouring houses of the Grange and Laws were therefore sour, so too were those between Omachie and Kingennie: Alexander Lauder of Omachie had slain Ninian Guthrie's heir.[77] When the contract of assythment was subscribed in 1562, it was witnessed for Lauder by the earl of Morton as tutor of Omachie's superior the earl of Angus, whereas Kingennie's main 'friend' was Patrick Lord Gray whom he served as deputy-sheriff.[78] The Grays were involved in disputes with other lairds who supported the Monifieth establishment: Gilbert Auchinleck of that ilk and John Lovell, fiar of Ballumbie.[79] Given the event of 1562 and Kingennie's association with the Grays, it is hardly surprising that his part in the affairs of his parish kirk was limited.[80]

The longest-running feud to affect Monifieth was that between the Lovells of Ballumbie and the house of Gray: a quarrel which originated with a dispute over who had the right to control the fishing off Broughty. Dating back to at least 1536, this dispute was deepened by the occupation of Broughty by first English and then French troops, and during the 1560s by conflict between Henry, liferenter of Ballumbie and his son John, the fiar of the estate. Even after Henry Lovell's death, the effects of the long conflict continued. When John eventually gained full possession of Ballumbie, he found the estates seriously embarrassed. In 1579, John Lovell was forced to raise money by selling lands of Ballumbie to the master of Glamis; in 1581, he was escheated twice for non-payment of debts. The gifts of the escheats were granted to Andrew Gray, son of Patrick Lord Gray.[81] While Lovell had been in ward in Edinburgh, the Grays took the opportunity to raid Ballumbie's lands with a force of 200 men.[82] Patrick Lord Gray received a further gift of an escheat of John Lovell in September 1584. It appears to have been a characteristic of the Grays never to forget an injury. By 1591, William Lovell of Ballumbie, John's heir, was still being forced to raise money: in his case, a loan of 12,000 merks against the security of lands in Monifieth.[83]

A feud of this magnitude, continued for so long, could not fail to have had a detrimental impact on the development of the kirk in Monifieth. The Lovells were an important element of the population. The lairds of Ballumbie held sections of Monifieth itself; other Lovells possessed lands in Balmossie, Linlathen and Barnhill. John, fiar of Ballumbie, and Henry Lovell in Barnhill were elders in 1573 and 1579 respectively. Another Henry Lovell was a deacon in 1579.[84] When John Lovell's wife, Barbara Ogilvy, sister of Gilbert Ogilvy of that ilk, died in July 1579, she was buried in the kirk.[85] When Henry Lovell in Barnhill had his son Alexander baptised, one of the witnesses was Robert Durham of Grange.[86] The long-serving reader of the kirk was James Lovell, brother to Thomas in Linlathen.[87] The lairds of Ballumbie could have been a major source of support for the kirk in Monifieth, especially as their own parish kirk at Ballumbie was provided with no reformed services of its own.[88] John Lovell was missing from the elders lists of 1575 and 1579, however, having been second-named after William Durham of Grange in 1573. A laird with such considerable family, financial and factional troubles must have proved a liability rather than an asset to the eldership.[89]

The troubles of John Lovell of Ballumbie illustrate both the strengths and weaknesses of the congregation of Monifieth. The kirk was rooted in the local population. Within its register can be found the spectrum of local society: the major lairds, the chief tenants, the brew-house keeper, the prostitutes, the 'gangarell puir'. All three ministers and the reader during the Reformation period were of local kin. The leaders in the kirk were the natural leaders of Monifieth parish society. In an age when loyalties could be divided, the parish kirk offered a familiar society where men and women had their allotted places within a corporate fellowship. Its institutions provided a link between the normal events of birth, marriage and death, and the eternal. In all these factors, the local roots of the kirk were its great strength. On the other hand, weakness could also flow from the kirk's closeness to local society. It was impossible to separate the religious duties of the lairds from their factional disputes. Monifieth was controlled by the

Durhams of Grange; to a lesser extent by the lairds of Omachie. From this establishment, the Guthries of Kingennie were excluded. Further, the reformed system worked best when the natural leaders of society were also men of firm personal faith. This had been true of William Durham of Grange: his heir, Robert, though he heads the elders' lists in 1575 and 1579, played a less active role. He appears in connection with baptisms, but not as a cautioner for future obedience. His part in day-to-day kirk discipline must therefore be open to question, and his younger son Alexander was actually brought to repentance for fornication in August 1585.[90] Problems were also experienced with Alexander Lauder of Omachie, who succeeded his father in 1580.[91] An unknown woman was summoned in the spring of 1585 for fornication with the young laird: both were ordered to show repentance. Alexander Lauder younger seems also to have had difficulty with his financial affairs. There is a letter from the earl of Angus, his superior, to the baron-bailie Ogilvy of Inverquharity ordering the apprising of Omachie's goods to repay a cautioner who had been fined when Lauder failed to meet a debt. For those with retentive memories of the godly early days of the congregation, Lauder's election to the session of 1596 must have lacked credibility.[92] Dependence on local leadership could be a tremendous asset to the kirk: it could also be a liability.

Just as the divisions of parochial society weakened the congregation of Monifieth, so the wider feuds and factional strife of Forfarshire affected the development of the reformed kirk throughout the province. The 1570s and 1580s were marked by a series of violent clashes between the major groupings of the shire: clashes which also merged into the general political turmoil of those years. A note for James VI on feuds between the great families of Scotland listed that between the neighbouring central Angus families, the Guthries and the Gardynes, as one of eight begun since the king's assumption of the government.[93] Patrick Gardyne of that ilk was murdered on 10 May 1578 by William, son of Guthrie of that ilk. Various actions for lawburrows were raised between the two sides through the Privy Council during 1578 and 1580; nevertheless, Alexander Guthrie of that ilk was slain on 5 October 1587 by the Gardynes.[94] This was a dispute between two former king's men; during the 1570s both had been clients of John Lord Glamis, the chancellor. The causes of the feud are now forgotten, but the fact that only a few miles separated the houses of the two sides must have rendered the dispute the more bitter.[95]

The main political effect of the Guthrie/Gardyne feud was to weaken the party of Mr Thomas Lyon, master of Glamis, who with his responsibilities for the house of Glamis after the chancellor's death took over the feud between his kin and the earl of Crawford. The latter, who persisted in proclaiming his innocence, found general support from his kin in Angus: among his cautioners were the Lindsays of Edzell, Evelick and Kinnettles.[96] Although a prosecution against him was begun, the earl had licence to go abroad in 1580,[97] returning in August 1581. Further bonds of caution were required of the master of Glamis and the earl in February 1581/2.[98] During the crises of the early 1580s, the master of Glamis and the eleventh earl of Crawford were invariably on opposite sides. Whereas Crawford supported Lennox, the master was a leading light of the Ruthven Raid that captured King James and banished Lennox.[99] Mr Thomas Lyon took the opportunity of the Raiders' success to renew his prosecution of Crawford; but the earl was among the faction that rallied to the king in the summer of 1583, being rewarded with the provostry of Dundee,[100] and of lands in the regality of Scone forfeit to the crown after the fall of Gowrie.[101] The master, meanwhile, was driven into exile in 1583 and 1584/5.[102] By the autumn of 1585, the fall of Arran brought Mr Thomas Lyon back to power and Crawford was warded. The dispute continued between the two men and their factions into the next century.[103]

The support granted by David Lindsay of Edzell to his brother-in-law the eleventh earl of Crawford in the aftermath of the 1578 killing of Lord Glamis has already been noted as extending to his participation in the murder of Campbell of Lundie in 1582.[104] One consequence of this support was the enmity of the Lyons and their friends. On 13 October 1581, the master together with a formidable gathering of over 230 men, 'bodin with jakis, speiris, steilbonettis, lang gunnis', attacked and captured Edzell's brother Robert, wounding him and killing members of his party. Major lairds who assisted the Lyons in this fray were Scrymgeour of Dudhope, Ogilvy of Inverquharity, Lauder of Omachie, Wishart of Logie, Lyall of Murthill, Thornton of that ilk and Gray of Dunninald with Gilbert Gray, son of Patrick Lord Gray. All these families had supported the king's regents during the civil wars and been clients of the chancellor,[105] though the faction was by no means as comprehensively representative of the shire as the 1568 bond had been.

The master of Glamis and his faction had a respite for these murders in October 1582; in addition, Ogilvy of Inverquharity and his sons were also respited for their prior killing of Alexander Lindsay of Blairyfeddon. This occurred during a violent clash on 4 July 1581 during which John Lindsay, Alexander's successor, also killed John Ogilvy, fiar of Inverquharity.[106] Inverquharity's support for Glamis' conflict with the Angus Lindsays not only cost him a son. His association with Morton and Glamis during the civil wars had led him into opposition to James Lord Ogilvy, at whose expense Morton had rewarded him.[107] Ogilvy, however, with Crawford, was in favour with the court, dominated by Lennox until August 1582. With the fall of Angus earlier in 1581, the master of Ogilvy had been appointed by the crown to Inverquharity's previous office as justiciar and bailie of the regality of Kirriemuir.[108] In September 1581, Inverquharity was accused of the murder of Alexander Lindsay; his castle was forfeit, his goods escheated and gifted to the master of Ogilvy. With this gift as his bargaining counter, Ogilvy persuaded Inverquharity to renounce the tacks of teinds Morton had engineered for him.[109] Inverquharity was understandably a supporter of the Ruthven Raid, and was warded in Blackness by July 1585 — when the keeper complained that the old laird, his wife and their servants had refused to pay their expenses.[110] Inverquharity, who had been one of the first members of the Congregation in Angus, had died by October 1587; his successor and grandson made peace with Lord Ogilvy by subscribing a band of manrent in 1591.[111]

The defeat and exile of the master of Glamis after the failure of the Ruthven Raid had the effect of rendering more acute the isolation of the house of Dun in Angus. John Erskine opposed the actions of the retrenched Arran regime against the church in 1583:[112]

> The laird of Dunne, father of the religious and well affected in Scotland, has written earnestly to the King to persuade him to stay his violent course, and chiefly against the church, concluding that otherwise he will be the last of his name that shall reign in that realme.

Erskine's Knoxian admonitions were ignored, however. With Dame Katherine Campbell dead, her son Lindsay of Edzell supporting Crawford, and Ogilvy of Inverquharity escheated, Dun had fewer friends willing to support his views of the spiritual independence of the kirk than perhaps at any time in his career. His son Robert and his grandson John of Logie had supported John, earl of Mar, in his *coup* of 1578 when the earl had seized Stirling Castle;[113] In view of the Ruthven Raiders' appeal to Dun for assistance,[114] it would not be surprising if at least one of the younger members of the house was not compromised by his presence soon after the capture of the king. Robert was in fact a cautioner for Adam Erskine, commendator of Cambuskenneth, and was fined £2,500 when his principal was forfeited in August 1584.[115] With Crawford and Ogilvy triumphant in Angus, the laird of Dun did not seek to resist the Black Acts. He was named, in fact, in November and December 1583, together with the aged John Wishart of Pittarrow, David Carnegy of Colluthie, the laird of Braid and David Lindsay, minister of Leith, as arbiters to attempt to secure the surrender and return of the Ruthven Raiders.[116]

In some respects, 1583-4 saw a reversal of the victory of the Angus king's party of 1568-70: Glamis' faction had, however, considerably shrunk from its original size. With James VI's assumption of the government, however nominally, older Angus traditions had reasserted themselves. The lairds of the shire, mainly men of small names and fortunes, looked to preserve their independence by service to the crown. Certainly they traditionally resisted outside interference, and looked askance at the aspirations and poor lordship of the house of Finavon. In the late 1570s and 1580s, however, there was again an adult king to be served — even if that meant co-operation with Ogilvy and Crawford. Thus Mr John Lindsay and Sir David of Edzell, John Carnegy of that ilk, Mr Peter Young of Seaton and Alexander Fullerton younger of Craigo all in their own ways supported the dominant court factions during the early 1580s.[117] Even Mr Thomas Lyon, master of Glamis, should be seen in this perspective. Forced into opposition by his inherited feud against Crawford, he early won the respect of the king — who appears to have protected the master as far as he was able.[118] James, like his predecessors, appears to have appreciated the loyalty of men from Angus: no fewer than three, Menmuir, Colluthy and Young, were to be Octavians. John Erskine of Dun's service, too, was not unrecognised.[119] Loyal service to James VI and his governments was welcomed, and could be profitable.[120]

Angus and the Mearns have been described as part of the 'conservative north' of Scotland during the sixteenth century.[121] From such facts as the submission of the northern ministers to the Black Acts and their later episcopalian tendencies, Professor Donaldson seeks to demonstrate that John Erskine of Dun's 'diocese' fits his thesis of the ecclesiastical conservatism of the provinces north of the Tay. The facts can hardly be disputed;[122] undoubtedly these shires, among the first to accept reformed doctrines, had lost their radicalism within two decades of 1560. It is, however, questionable whether the explanation for this trend ought to be found wholly in ecclesiastical and theological developments.[123]

Instead of looking primarily to the religious sphere to explain the increasing conservatism of the church in Angus and the Mearns, a broader explanation should be sought that refers to more general social trends,[124] as well as to the personalities involved. Although the province had been one of those showing the 'greatest fervency' for the Reformation before 1558, it has been argued that John Erskine of Dun's circle of Mearns lairds were more committed than many of those further south in Angus; that the Reformation was rather more accepted than welcomed in the southern of these two shires.[125] Further, among the motives that led to lairds accepting the new kirk were ones that were inherently conservative: approval of the new religion of 'discipline' or social control,[126] and of an anticlericalism that

G

promised to restore to them a measure of control over the economic resources devoted to the church by their predecessors.[127] The new kirk succeeded best where its principles meshed with those of the shires; where they did not, for example regarding burying within churches, they were ignored. If spiritual purity was thus compromised, a broader acceptance was achieved. The pragmatism of John Erskine of Dun's exercise of his superintendency in favour of local interests has been noted.[128] Many factors apart from the theological weighed with the gentry, whose sponsorship was critical both in the establishment of the reformed kirk and in prescribing the general direction of its development.

If a certain degree of conservatism was inherent in the Reformation in Angus from the beginning, political events conspired to enhance this trend. The circumstances of the crisis of 1559-60 were unique, enabling the reformers to lay claim to a patriotic zeal in both the religious and political aspects of their programme. Support for the Congregation in 1560 and support for the regents after 1567 could plausibly be represented as support for 'the authority', and hence not out of step with the traditions of the Angus gentry. Once the king assumed the government, not only did he attract loyalty to his policies as well as to his person, but the very existence of a royal court gave new weight to the magnates like Crawford and Ogilvy who composed it. They were therefore vastly less easy to ignore, as the queen's lords had been ignored between 1568 and 1573. As the nobility, whether of Angus (the tenth earl of Crawford and lords Ogilvy and Gray) or of the Mearns (the earl Marischal), had been less than enthusiastic for the Reformation throughout the 1560s, King James's support for Lennox and his Angus clients, the eleventh earl of Crawford, Ogilvy, Carnegy and Edzell, had added significance.[129] The defeat of the Ruthven Raiders and their Angus supporters, the master of Glamis and Ogilvy of Inverquharity, confirmed the increasingly conservative tone north of the Tay.

Moreover, it is difficult to find among the second generation of the kirk's lay supporters in Angus or the Mearns men quite as devoted to the spiritual aspects of the cause as John Erskine of Dun, John Wishart of Pittarrow or Mr James Haliburton. Mr Thomas Lyon, master of Glamis, leader of the Angus factions opposed to the catholic lords, was a hard and resolute man — but hardly an especially spiritual one. His protestantism may have been genuine, but its importance to him appears to have been its political appeal.[130] It is noteworthy that Glamis retained the older form of linked ministry longer than the rest of Angus; the master can hardly have made it a priority to obtain the sole services of a minister.[131] The problems of leadership observed in microcosm at Monifieth were replicated on the larger scale of the shire itself. Increasingly it fell to the ministers to assert the spiritual priorities of the kirk, for which they could incur the wrath of local magnates. Mr Andrew Milne, minister of Fetteresso, was said to have become so obnoxious to William Douglas, catholic heir of the laird of Glenbervie, that the latter threatened his life.[132] Protestant leaders like the master of Glamis, however, could equally fall victim to the kirk's hostility to the feud when they sought to maintain the honour of their kin.[133] The shrunken influence of the house of Dun by the 1580s may well have been due to the laird's decision to opt out, as far as possible, from the more violent forms of political involvement.[134] The difficulty John Erskine experienced in riding both secular and ecclesiastical horses at once cannot have encouraged others to do likewise once the initial impetus of Reformation zeal had dwindled. Besides, by the 1580s a full four-fifths of the lairds active in 1540 had died. The new generation had priorities and horizons of its own.[135]

Nevertheless, despite difficulties and the necessity to compromise, the Reformation endured and the reformed kirk secured a lasting place in the society of Angus and the Mearns. If the aspirations of the more godly were disappointed, the interaction of the kirk's ministry and institutions with those of the shires was thorough; the kirk's parochial discipline and polity was harmonised with traditional Scottish cultural patterns. In time, the processes of education, preaching and social control initiated at the Reformation were to spread the Christian faith in its protestant form to an ever-broader social spectrum. The lives of martyrs like David Straiton and George Wishart had not been given in vain. At the end of his life, John Erskine of Dun could look back with some satisfaction at the financial and institutional integrity and security that had been obtained for the kirk in his province. Many obstacles had been overcome and challengers — both religious and political — thwarted. His conclusion might well have been that of the minister and historian John Row:[136]

> The Lord God, that workes his workes marvelouslie, wrought his worke of Reformation of Religion in Scotland aboue men's expectation, considering the instruments whom God used in the same, and the power and authoritie that wer against them.

NOTES

1. M. Lynch, *International Calvinism*, ed. Prestwich, p.233.
2. The interaction of religion with other sectors of society is discussed conceptually by sociologists of religion. R. Robertson's *The sociological interpretation of religion* (London 1970), pp. 56-7 emphasises the importance of cultural and institutional aspects in addition to

assessing degrees of individual belief: 'Social-structural and cultural aspects of religiosity are notoriously difficult to isolate and assess. But there is no denying their great independent significance. It is indeed quite clear that, ... the religiosity of a society cannot be represented simply as the summation of the religiosity of individuals'. R. Gill insists that 'theology acts at times as both a dependent and an independent variable within society': *Theology and Social Structure* (London 1977), p.18. T.F.O'Dea, in his summary of the discipline, *The Sociology of Religion* (London 1983, 1966), accepts both a tripartite description of 'culture, social system and personality' for studying human behaviour (p.4) and agrees that 'religion is both affected by, and affects, social conditions. It is both cause and effect' (p.95).

3. See pages 14-22.

4. See pages 42-44, 69.

5. SRO, St Andrews testaments CC 20.4.1, see fs.1-10 and, for example, f.24r: testament testamentary of Helen Redpath, 27 Nov. 1549. 'Et ego prodicta Helena [int]egra corp[or]e sana tame[n] me[n]te condo testame[n]tum meu[m] in hunc modum do et lego a[n]i[m]am mea[m] deo o[mn]ipotenti b[ea]te Marie semp[er] virgini et o[mn]ibus sanct[is] corp[or]is meu[m] sepuliendum in eccl[es]ia Sancti Lawrenti. Do et lego in die sepulturea mea p[res]b[et]ris et aliis minist[ris] eccl[es]ia vi s. viii d. ...' All testaments cited hereafter are at the SRO.

6. St A. tests., CC 20.4.1 f. 118v: Alison Alexander, (x) Jun. 1550: 'Cum nihil sit cert[i]us morte nec in[cer]t[i]us hora mortis hinc est q[uod] ego Alisona Alex[ande]r [int]egro corp[or]e sana tam[en] me[nt]e condo testame[n]tum meu[m] in hunc modum. Do et lego a[n]i[m]am mea[m] deo o[mni]potenti corpus meu[m] sepuliend[um] in eccl[es]ia mea p[er]ro[c]hi an[it]a. Item lego cap[ellanis] in die sepulture mea et aliis necessariis vi s. ...'

7. G.L. Meyhew, 'The progress of the Reformation in East Sussex', *Southern History* v (1983), pp. 58-61.

8. Professor A.G. Dickens' conclusions with regard to mid-Tudor England may usefully be compared with the 1550s in Scotland: 'It (mid-Tudor heresy) was so often fragmentary, fleeting, and elusive: it involved a climate of opinion rather than a number of specific heretics, each with an integrated theology and under the guidance of educated leaders'. *Lollards and Protestants in the Diocese of York* (London 1959), p. 243. The 'old order', however, had been effectively disturbed: at least in parts of Angus and the Mearns, belief in purgatory and 'the usefulness of veneration of saints' was no longer 'part of the air people breathed' by 1560. Cf. J.J. Scarisbrick, *The Reformation and the English People* (London 1984), p. 12.

9. See pages 9, 13-14.

10. See page 68, for example.

11. Registers from Edinburgh (CC 8.8.1f.), Brechin (CC 3.3.1) and St Andrews (CC 20.4.1) and their indices were surveyed. Testaments dative were registered by court-appointed executors; testaments testamentary by those appointed by the deceased personally. Only the latter type contain a legacy section (called the 'lattirwill') by which the testator bequeathed his property (and soul) and named executors. Testaments aimed to value moveables and debts.

12. A.G. Dickens, *Lollards and Protestants*, pp. 171-2, 215-7, 220-1; M. Spufford, 'The scribes of villagers' wills', *Local Population Studies,* vii (1971), pp. 28-41; C. Cross, 'The development of protestantism in Leeds and Hull: the evidence from wills', *Northern History,* xviii (1982), pp. 230-8; G.L. Mayhew, 'The progress of the Reformation in East Sussex — the evidence from wills', *Southern History,* v (1983), pp. 38-61; J.J. Scarisbrick, *The Reformation and the English People* (London 1984), pp. 2-12; P. Collinson, *The Religion of Protestants* (Oxford 1984), pp. 196-7.

13. Edin. tests. CC 8.8.4 f.178r (Glenbervie); CC 8.8.5 f.60v (George Symmer of Balzeordie); CC 8.8.5 f. 18 (James Keith of Drumlithie); CC 8.8.5 f. 206r (John Mortimer of Flemington); CC 8.8.8. f.195r (Robert Arbuthnott of that ilk); CC 8.8.7 fs.60r, 148v (Dame Katherine Campbell, countess of Crawford); CC 8.8.19 f.347v (Alexander Guthrie of that ilk).

14. Edin. tests. CC 8.8.3 fs. 172v-5r; more of the will is transcribed on page 100. The preamble is similar to one of G.L. Mayhew's types: 'The Reformation in East Sussex', p. 60.

15. Edin. tests. CC 8.8.12 f. 297r: Janet Falconer 'recom[m]endis hir soule to ye m[er]cies of God through Jesus Christ hir saviou[r] hir body to ye erth to ye generall resurrectioun'. In CC 8.8.15 f. 231r her husband 'co[m]ittis my soule to God to be ressavit to his glory be his mercy on Jesus Christ and threw his mereittis'.

16. Kinnaird, Southesk Misc. box 3 bund. no. 32; Fraser, *Southesk*, i, 51. For Kinnaird's first will, page 59.

17. Edin. tests. CC 8.8.22 f. 203v.

18. *First Book*, pp. 199-201. J.K. Cameron discusses the implementation of these recommendations in footnotes to these pages.

19. Edin. tests. CC 8.8.6 f. 150r (Glamis); CC 8.8.4 f. 248r (Whitelaw); CC 8.8.9 f. 69r (Fullerton); CC 8.8.13 f. 172r (Graham); CC 8.8.19 f. 288r (Lindsay); CC 8.8.6 f. 27v (Guthrie); CC 8.8.11 f. 310v (Anderson). Whitelaw: *CSP (F) Eliz.*, i, 888, in which Throckmorton described him as 'very religious' and advised that he should be kept as far as possible from seeing sin in England. For Guthrie, *RSS*, iv, 1919 (remission for iconoclasm) and *RPC*, ii, 544 (surety for Bassinden's licence to print an edition of the Bible, 1576). For Fullerton, SRO, Reg. Deeds RD 1.9 226r (appointment as collector) and F.D. Bardgett, 'Faith, families and factions', ii, appendix A.c. no. 003. Other non-traditional wills were made by: John Wishart of that ilk/of Logie (CC 8.8.3 f. 249v); John Baldovie of that ilk (CC 8.8.6 f. 248v); David Garden of Leys (CC 8.8.9 f. 274r); John Scrymgeour of Dudhope, constable of Dundee (CC 8.8.21 f. 228r). Such wills either proceeded directly to the appointment of executors or beginning with the traditional formula 'Sick in body but whole in mind/ spirit', then jumped to nominating executors.

20. Edin. tests. CC 8.8.4 f. 178r; *Estimate of the Scottish Nobility during the minority of James the sixth*, ed. C. Rogers (Grampian Club 1873), p. 11; *pace* J.R. Todd, 'The Reformation in the diocese of Dunblane' (Edinburgh Ph.D. thesis 1973), p. 40 who held that the earl of Montrose's history lay outwith the diocese of Dunblane in 'the north country'.

21. Edin. tests. CC 8.8.5 f. 140r, see F.D. Bardgett, 'Faith, families and factions', ii, appendix A.c no. 146, *First Book*, p. 210; CC 8.8.10 f. 6r, CC 8.8.12 f. 96v. Euphame Durham was sister to William and Robert, lairds of Grange; her testament was witnessed by both William Christison and William Kyd, minister and reader of Dundee and hence had a good reformed pedigree. Christine Arbuthnott's will was drawn up by Mr Andrew Elder, John Erskine of Dun's resident notary during the 1560s: see appendix A.a no. 097.

22. J.J. Scarisbrick, *The Reformation*, p. 4; C. Cross, 'Protestantism in Leeds and Hull', pp. 231-2.

23. F.D. Bardgett, 'Faith, families and factions', ii, appendix A.b no. 059 for most of what follows on John Lindsay.

24. *Second Book*, pp. 254-7.

25. For 'King' Alexander Guthrie, whose radicalism declined in later life, see M. Lynch, *Edinburgh*, pp. 282, 331-2, 369.

26. *Second Book*, p. 287.

27. J. Kirk notes Menmuir defending the doctrine of the ordination of elders for life, though with polemical intent: *Second Book*, p. 94.

28. See pages 105-6, 107.

29. JRL, The Crawford mss., box Fii and 4/1/96.

30. JRL, The Crawford mss., 4/1/95.

31. *Edzell Castle* by W. Douglas Simpson, revised R. Fawcett (HMSO 1982), pp. 9-12. See also the wooden carving of a crucifixion at Edzell.

32. See diagram 7.1, as redrawn from the ms. at JRL, The Crawford mss. 4/1/97.*RMS*, v, 1579 for Edzell's erection as a burgh.

33. His right of patronage: WRH, The Haigh Inventory, ii, 122, 123. Tacks of teinds, ibid., ii, 122: 19 Feb. 1581/2, Edzell for 19 years; ibid., ii, 135: Fern, and ii, 145: Newdosk.

34. JRL, The Crawford mss. 4/1/103.

35. Lord Lindsay, *Lives,* i, pp.339-42 prints the entire letter. *RMS,* v, 602, 27 Aug. 1583, contains the remission. Sir David Lindsay of Edzell, knight, had been accompanied by his youngest brother Robert of Balhall, William Fullerton of Craigo, Lindsay of Keithock, John Forbes of Towie, three Straitons, a Symmer and others to a total of twenty besides himself.

36. K.M. Brown, *Bloodfeud in Scotland 1573-1625* (Edinburgh 1986), pp.184-207 considers the tensions between the Christian faith and contemporary violence. E.J. Cowan considers the events of 1582 in the context of the Lyon/Lindsay feud and the Campbell/Ogilvy feud: 'The Angus Campbells', p.33. Lawson's letter from London to Dame Katherine of 11 Nov. 1567 wrote that David Lindsay was 'not so obedient to my counsel *for keeping of modestie* as I wald wish . . .': JRL, The Crawford mss. 3/2/4 and Lindsay, *Lives,* i, 332 — which omits the words in italics above.

37. Edin. tests. CC 8.8.8 f.283r.

38. F.D. Bardgett, 'Faith, families and factions', ii, appendix A.c no. 126.

39. Lindsay, *Lives,* i, p.327.

40. R. Wilson, *The House of Airlie* (London 1924), pp.162-4.

41. S. Keeling, 'The Reformation in the Anglo-Scottish Border Counties', *Northern History,* xv (1979), p.41.

42. I. Cowan, 'The Reformation in Dumfriesshire', *Transactions of the Dumfriesshire and Galloway Natural History and Antiquarian Society,* 3rd series, vol. lxi (1981), p.90.

43. See pages 99, 151; also, *First Book,* pp.91, 192-3.

44. F.D. Bardgett, 'Faith, families and factions', ii, appendix A.b no.059.

45. J. Bossy, 'Godparenthood', p.199-220; see I. Cowan, *Reformation,* p.150-152 for further discussion of baptism after 1560.

46. *Knox's History,* i, 119-20.

47. *Memorials of transactions in Scotland by Richard Bannatyne,* ed. R. Pitcairn (Bannatyne Club 1836), pp.283-5.

48. *First Book,* pp.199-201; I.B. Cowan, *Reformation,* p.155; *BCO ad loc.*

49. *Formulare,* i, no.177: Alexander earl of Crawford made his last will in his own hand in the presence of a friar, his chosen confessor.

50. These figures were compiled during a complete search of the first extant volume of Brechin testaments, CC 3.3.1 (c.1576-c.1584), and a search of the Edinburgh testaments, CC 8.8.1f., for entries obviously derived from Angus and the Mearns. The vast majority of Brechin entries contain standard formulae only.

51. CC 8.8.5 f.60v; CC 8.8.5 f.83r; CC 3.3.1 f.19v; CC 8.8.12 f.34v.

52. Kinnaird, Southesk Misc. box 3 bund. 32; and see n.16 above.

53. CC 8.8.23 f.224v.

54. CC 8.8.5 f.198v.

55. F.D. Bardgett, 'Faith, families and factions', ii, appendix A.a 320.

56. CC 8.8.8 f.275r: Thomas Lovell in Linlathen's will was written by 'my darrest and best belouit eldest germane broder James Lovell reidar w[i]tin my paroche kirk of Monyfurth' — 31 Dec. 1577. Christine Spens, wife of Alexander Ramsay burgess of Dundee, required 'ane vigilant pastour in Christ William Cristisoun minister in Dundee and Thomas Ireland notare public to subscrive this my latterwill . . .': CC 8.8.5 f.238r-26 June 1571.

57. M. Spufford, 'The scribes of villagers', p.41. James Lindsay, notary public, was a reasonably common choice for drawing up wills registered at Brechin: CC 3.3.1 fs.3r, 27v, 29r, 34v. His formulae differ little from those used by ministers and readers.

58. For marriage, see pages 13-14, 102-103, 124-5; *First Book,* pp.191-8.

59. See page 4.

60. See page 149, and above, nn. 14-5.

61. P. Collinson, *The Religion of Protestants* (Oxford 1984), pp.181-7.

62. See n.34.

63. See Ch. 1, *passim.*

64. See pages 9, 99.

65. NRH, OPR 310/1 f.57v: two men gave surety by 'vphaldng y[air] handis tyll stand at yir decreit of Andro Duncan [and others] of all debittis betwixt y[aim]'. K. Brown suggests that arbitration was 'the best society had to offer' to prevent violence: *Bloodfeud,* p.59.

66. *The Court Book of the Barony of Carnwath, 1523-42* (SHS 1937), ed. W.C. Dickinson provides a printed court book to compare with the Monifieth kirk assembly register; Dickinson's introduction, pp.lxxv, lxxxii and xciii for the points made above. See Ch. 5 nn. 76, 84 for the elders. Sir William Douglas of Glenbervie, earl of Angus, wrote on 14 June 1589 to Sir John Ogilvy of Inverquharity announcing his intention to hold a regality court in person at Kirriemuir, requested his bailie to summon the tenants and promised to continue his favour towards him: Fraser, *Douglas Book,* iv, no.228.

67. *The Early Modern Town in Scotland* (London 1987), p.74, ed. M. Lynch; his chapter, 'The Crown and the Burghs'.

68. G. Donaldson, *Scottish Church History,* pp.225-9 on the importance of the parish as a focus of the local community.

69. The functions of religion in maintaining social cohesion in certain societies has long been recognised: B. Wilson, *Religion in sociological perspective* (Oxford 1982), p.33.

70. These were: a) 'Since nothing is more certain than death and more uncertain than the hour of death'; b) 'sick in body but whole in mind' (with variants); c) 'bequeaths his soul to almighty God and his body to be buried'; d) 'instructs his executors to act as they will answer to God on the day of judgment'. These clauses can all be found in a Latin form in the St Andrews testaments registered 1549-1551: CC 20.4.1. The Marian clauses, however, and reference to the company of the Saints, are wholly missing, together with any legacies for burial-day requiems (but see n.71 below).

71. CC 3.3.1 f.29r, 26 December 1580; cf. CC 20.4.1 — St.A. tests.

72. OPR 310/1: f31v, 23 Apr. 1576: 'ye communion wes ministratit to sex h(undre)t persounis'. Summaries of subsequent entries follow:

f37v 27 Apr. 1578: 600.	f51v (—) May 1582: 700.
f41v 26 Apr. 1579: 700.	f54v 14 Apr. 1583: 700 '& odds'.
f45r 17 Apr. 1580: 600.	f57v 12 Apr. 1584: 780.

The entry for 1584 was written in careful Gothic-style script distinguishing it from the surrounding entries. Subsequent entries, however, fail to give numbers, that for 1586 being relegated to the margin and much abbreviated — 10 April, f.63r.

73. Population statistics are notoriously difficult for Scotland in this period. J. Malcolm, *The parish of Monifieth* (Edinburgh 1910), p.245 cites Dr Webster's report of 1755 for a total then of 1421. *The Statistical Account* (1794) gave 1218. The 1801 census gave 1407. The sixteenth-century total may have been as much as 1400, as the number of baptisms recorded around 1580 was similar to those c.1755 — an average of 38 p.a. and 39 p.a. respectively: see, Malcolm *Monifieth,* p.245. G. Donaldson, however, calculates 700 as the average population of non-burghal parishes: *Scottish Church History,* p.220. The proportion of the population whose baptisms were recorded may have altered between 1580 and 1755.

74. Based on the medians for the quarters of 1582. See diagram 7.2, which is derived from charting the weekly collections registered in OPR 310/1, *passim.*

75. See diagram 7.1.

76. Two accounts for cash expended for bread and wine for communion exist from Angus in this period. On 24 May 1582, 42s. were deducted from Lord Ogilvy's dues for Lintrathen — not a large sum. On 24 Feb. 1594, £12 was required for communion at Kirriemuir, suggesting a larger gathering: SRO, The Airlie mss, GD 16.47.1 and 16.47.23.

77. See Ch.5, nn.63, 92.

78. SRO, Scrymgeour-Wedderburn mss., GD 137.639 and Reg.Deeds RD 1.5.384.

79. *RPC,* i, p.655: Gilbert Auchinleck of that ilk raised letters against Patrick Lord Gray and others for their protection of those who slew James Ramsay, tutor of the Laws, in which quarrel Auchinleck's brother Alexander lost an arm: 19 April 1569.

80. Kingennie did stand caution for the learning of 'ye .3.' on 24 November 1577: OPR 310/1 f.35v. His heir, William Guthrie, had his marriage to Elspeth (blank) proclaimed on 21 August 1580: f.46r.

81. F.D. Bardgett, 'Faith, families and factions', ii, appendix B nos. 157-161 for the succession in Ballumbie. The conflicts involving the Lovells of Ballumbie often surface in the Register of the Privy Council: *RPC*, i, p.460, p.555, p.685; *RPC*, ii, p.138, p.335, p.429. See also: *RSS*, vii, 474; *RMS*, iv, 2874; *RSS*, viii, 476, 535; SRO, Reg.Deeds RD 1.9 f.162r.

82. *RPC*, iii, pp.436-7.

83. NLS ch.4772.

84. See Table 5.2.

85. OPR 310/1 f.42v, 30 July 1579.

86. OPR 310/1 f.42r, 12 May 1579.

87. F.D. Bardgett, 'Faith, families and factions', ii, appendix A.c no.131; Edin.tests. CC 8.8.8 f.375r.

88. 'Ballumbie neidis na reidar': the parish was linked to Dundee, see appendix A.2. Its rental had not been given up in 1561, so that the 'superplus' was available as a gift to John's heir William in 1579: *RSS*, vii, 2042.

89. The laird of Ballumbie was in fact prosecuted for fornication with Kristen Kay in 1582, three years after his wife died: OPR 310/1 f.52r.

90. OPR 310/1 f.61r, 29 Aug. 1585.

91. *RSS*, vii, 2651.

92. OPR 310/1 f.60r, 11 Apr 1585; Fraser, *Douglas Book*, iv, no.221; OPR 310/1 f.87v, 30 Mar. 1596.

93. BL, Add. mss. 33,531 f.263.

94. *RPC*, ii, p.701; iii, pp.92, 118, 249, 266; Edin.tests CC 8.8.19 f.347.

95. See pages 128-9. Though this feud is not mentioned in K. Brown, *Bloodfeud*, it is a good illustration of his thesis on the local feud: pp.65-80.

96. WRH, The Haigh Inventory, i, 111 and JRL, The Crawford mss. box E; on 9 May 1578 Crawford wrote to Lord Ross seeking his support at a trial summoned for 3 November: 'as God knawis I am most innocent and as all yat sawe and knawis ye circumstances of yat unhappy accident vnerstandis and hes beine ewer sensyne villing to hawe had ye mater tryit . . .' Bands of caution for the earl: *RPC*, ii, 705; *ibid.*, iii, 233, 288, 245.

97. *RPC*, xiv, 349; Pitcairn, *Trials*, i/ii, 85.

98. *CSP(S)*, vi, 51; *RPC*, iii, 500-1. Scrymgeour of Dudhope, two Rollocks and Lyon of Cossins were sureties for the master; the Lindsays of Edzell, Vane and Evelick and Mr Walter Lindsay for the earl.

99. Pitcairn, *Trials*, i/iii, p.119; *CSP(S)*, vi, 121, 154, 156, 177, 179.

100. *CSP(S)*, vi, 549, 580, 608, 654. Dundee protested this imposition of Crawford in place of 'their old provost': Flett, 'Geneva of Scotland', pp.104-5; M. Lynch, *The Early Modern Town in Scotland*, ed. by him (London 1987), pp.56-8, 63.

101. *RMS*, v, 772.

102. *CSP(S)*, vi, 617; *Hamilton Papers*, ii, p.697: the master was reckoned by the English Council to be of the best judgment of all the exiled lords.

103. K. Brown, *Bloodfeud*, pp.124-127 traces the national politics involved in this feud.

104. See above, page 153.

105. *RSS*, viii, 965; also pages 128-9.

106. *RSS*, viii, 1466.

107. See pages 138-9.

108. SRO, Airlie mss., GD 16.25.87.

109. SRO, Airlie mss., GD 16.41.53-4, *RSS*, viii, 464-5; GD 16.41.60, 79; Airlie mss., GD 16.48.26; GD 16.11.6-8 — whereby the murdered fiar of Inverquharity's lands were adjudged to have fallen to the crown with the Angus forfeiture and were gifted to the master of Ogilvy. The marriage of John, apparent of Inverquharity, was also gifted to the master.

110. *RSS*, viii, 1713: remission for participation in the Ruthven Raid; *RPC*, iii, p.756.

111. NLS ms. 593.2038; SRO, Airlie mss. GD 16.25.9 for the bond which is listed by J. Brown, 'Bonds of manrent in Scotland', no. 512.

112. *CSP(S)*, vi, 721: 29 Dec. 1583.

113. *RPC*, iii, 688-692; Band of the Friends of Mar.

114. NLS ms. 2208 f5r.

115. T. Crockett, 'Life of Erskine of Dun', p.254.

116. *CSP(S)*, vi, 611, 698, 700, 714.

117. Fullerton was granted Scone from the Ruthven forfeiture and had assisted with Strachan of Brigton at the murder of Campbell of Lundie: *RMS*, v, 695; *RSS*, viii, 1476.

118. *CSP(S)*, vi, 492: on May 1583 it was reported that James had sought the master's assistance in freeing himself from the Raiders. James also sought to reconcile Crawford and Thomas Lyon: *CSP(S)*, vi, 583. See also K. Brown, *Bloodfeud*, p.225.

119. T. Crockett, 'Life of John Erskine of Dun', p.270 suggests that Dun contemplated a simoniacal bargain with Ludovic duke of Lennox in 1586 whereby Lennox and Blantyre his tutor were granted by Dun a pension of 500 merks annually and Dun had his stipend as superintendent restored to its former level. Certainly Dun's stipend did remain high after 1586: *ibid*.

120. K. Brown, *Bloodfeud*, p.234. Brown also emphasises the importance of the court in Jacobean Scotland before 1603: pp.117-123.

121. G. Donaldson, 'Scotland's Conservative North in the Sixteenth and Seventeenth Centuries', in *Scottish Church History*, pp.191-203; and especially p.201: 'Angus and Kincardine, though south of the Mounth, are quite distinctly part of the conservative north'.

122. J. Kirk, 'The Melvillian Movement', i, p.391 suggests that Angus and the Mearns were among the areas 'particularly receptive' to presbyterianism. But besides the Melvilles, only five of its long-term ministers appear in his lists of Melvillians: Andrew Milne, James Balfour, Henry Duncan, Patrick Galloway and William Christison, together with John Durie after his banishment from Edinburgh.

123. Besides, John Erskine of Dun cannot safely be described as 'emphatically' in favour of episcopacy — unless of the sort advocated by archbishop Grindal of Canterbury. It has already been argued that Dun's tradition was that of the Helvetian Confession — rather than that of any earlier Lutheranism. G. Donaldson, 'Conservative North', pp.200-1. For Grindal, P. Collinson, *The Elizabethan Puritan Movement* (London 1967), p.191f; *The remains of Edmund Grindal*, ed. W. Nicholson (London 1843), p.382.

124. The value of such studies as C. Haws, 'Continuity and change: the reformation in the diocese of Moray 1560-1574', *Northern Scotland*, v (1983), similarly limited to ecclesiastical factors, must be restricted.

125. See pages 81-2.

126. See above, pages 157-8.

127. See pages 21-2, 105.

128. See pages 91-5.

129. J. Wormald, ' "Princes" and the regions in the Scottish Reformation', *Church, politics and society*, ed. Macdougall, p.65f. demonstrates the difficulty caused to magnates by the kirk's demands upon them.

130. J.G.B. Young, 'Scottish political parties', pp.90, 355.

131. F.D. Bardgett, 'Faith, families and factions', ii, appendix A.2.

132. F.D. Bardgett, 'Faith, families and factions', ii, appendix A.c no.152.

133. K. Brown, *Bloodfeud*, p.192.

134. K. Brown, *Bloodfeud*, p.80: 'aggressive competition was necessary if power was to be

held onto'. John Erskine of Dun, however, obtained exemption from attendance at sheriff courts while superintendent: R. Woodrow, *Collections upon the lives of the Reformers* (Maitland Club 1834), appendix v. p.62.

135. Of the 300 lairds surveyed for this study, 112 were active in 1540. This number shrank decade by decade as follows: 1550: 73; 1560: 56; 1570: 37; 1580: 21; 1590: 6. John Erskine of Dun's longevity was exceptional; see F.D. Bardgett, 'Faith, families and factions', ii, appendix B.

136. J. Row, *Historie of the Kirk of Scotland* (Maitland Club 1842), pt. i, p.1.

Bibliography

PRIMARY SOURCES:
MANUSCRIPT, INCLUDING UNPUBLISHED INVENTORIES

ABERDEEN

Aberdeen University Library Department of Special Collections
The Arbuthnott manuscripts (ms. 2764)
  including ms. volume 'Originis et incrementi Arbuthnoticae familiae descriptio historicae', Alexander Arbuthnott (principal of King's College, Aberdeen), translated by Mr William Morrison, parson of Benholm kirk, s.d.

ARBROATH

Arbroath Public Library
Court book of the burgh of Arbroath, 1563-1575.

DUNDEE

The City of Dundee District Archive and Records Centre
Burgh protocol books:
  3: Thomas Ireland, 1534-1572
  4: Thomas Ireland, 1566/7-1575
  6: Herbert Gledstanes, 1562/3-1567
  7: Alex Wedderburn's 1st book, 1554-1565
  8: Alex Wedderburn's 2nd book, 1565-1570
  10: Alex Wedderburn's 3rd book, 1570-1577
  13: Alex Wedderburn's 5th book, 1581-1582
  21: Alex Wedderburn II's 1st book, 1583-1587

Burgh council minute books:
  1. 1553 to 1558
  2. 1587 to 1603   with typed transcripts

Burgh and head court books:
  1-12; nos. 1-4 with typed transcripts

University of Dundee: The Department of Private Law
Sacra Romana Rota: manualia
  (Scottish materials from the Vatican Archives, available as photocopies: derived from Ross Fund research)

University of Dundee: The University Library
  (acting for Strathmore Estates (Holdings) Ltd.)
The Strathmore muniments

EDINBURGH

National Library of Scotland
Charters:
  968   (Maule of Panmure/Carnegy of Panbride)
  3802   (Presentation to parsonage of Ballumbie)

4772	(Lovell of Ballumbie)
5407	(John Erskine of Dun)
5773	(Ogilvy of Inverquharity)
5869	(Gilbert Ogilvy of that ilk)
5871	(Guthrie of that ilk)

National Library of Scotland
Manuscripts:

17.1.3	Chartulary Priories of Pittenweem and Sanctandrois
17.1.4	The register of assignations and modifications of stipends — 1574
25.9.6	(Collection of bonds to the House of Angus)
29.2.5	Balcarres papers
31.1.1	Perth Kirk Session Register vol.1, 1577-1620
75.28	(Erskine of Dun/earl of Buchan)
76.15	Morton muniments
592.1916	(Ogilvy of Inverquharity)
592.1960	(Ogilvy of Inverquharity)
593.2038	(Ogilvy of Inverquharity)
2208	(Laird of Dun)
2933	(Proclamation by Superintendents)
5308	(Ogilvy of Inverquharity)
5407	(Alexander master of Crawford)

New Register House

| OPR 310/1 | The kirk assembly register of Monifieth |

Scottish Record Office

B 4.1.1	Protocol book David Lyell (Arbroath), 1575-1588
B 22.1.67	John Hay's fifth protocol book
B 51.1.1,2	Protocol books Richard and James Guthrie (Montrose): 1574-1583, 1585-95
B 51.10.2	Court book of Montrose, 1586-7
B 51.10.3	Court book of Montrose, 1603-6
B 51.15	Misc. documents from Montrose
CC 1.1a	Extract register of the General Assembly
CC 3.1.1	Brechin Commissary court act book, 9 Mar. 1579 to 30 Jun. 1582
CC 3.3.1-6	Brechin testaments, 14 Mar 1576/7 to 17 Mar 1602/3, 1 June 1584 to 25 Aug 1593, and through to 1666
CC 8.2.1	Edinburgh Commissary acts and decreets
CC 8.8.1-34	Edinburgh Commissary court registers of testaments
CC 8.9.1	Edinburgh Commissary court testament minute book
CC 20.4.1,5.	St Andrews Commissary court registers of testaments
CH 4.1.2	Register of Presentations to Benefices
CH 6.6.1,2	Register of charters by abbots and commendators of Jedburgh
CS 1.3	Books of Sederunt
CS 7.	Acts and Decreets
DI 90.1	Perth hornings
DI 91.1	Perth inhibitions
E 2.	Signatures in the office of the Comptroller
E 45.	Compt of Collectors-General of Thirds
E 46.3,4,9	Compt of subcollectors of the thirds of benefices: Fife, Forfar and Kincardine, Perth

E 47.1 to .10	Register of assignations and modifications of stipends (1576-1615)
E 48.1.1	The Book of Assumption
E 48.2	Register of Ministers and Readers, 1567-1572
GD 1.47	(Documents from Miss Low)
GD 1.1039	(Tacks by Balmerino Commendators)
GD 4	The Benholm and Hedderwick writs
GD 16	The Airlie muniments
GD 45	The Dalhousie muniments
GD 49	The Barclay-Allardice muniments
GD 70	The Scott of Brotherton muniments
GD 79	James VI Hospital Perth muniments
GD 83.1092	The Bamff Charters: protocol style book sir Alexander Ramsay
GD 86	Inventory of Fraser Charters
GD 121	The Murthly Castle muniments (handlist only)
GD 123	The Erskine of Dun muniments
GD 124	The Mar and Kellie muniments
GD 130	The Earl of Northesk muniments
GD 137	The Scrymgeour-Wedderburn muniments
GD 175	The Erroll charters
GD 205	The Ogilvy of Inverquharity muniments
GD 212	Maitland Thomson notebooks: no. 6, Foulis-Easter Charters; no.23, Moray writs
JC 1.6,7	Justiciary Court records: court books
JC 26 box 1	Justiciary Court: loose papers
NP 1.16	Protocol book of Duncan Gray, 1554-1572
NP 1.33	Protocol book of George Fyffe, 1573-1587
NP 1.36	Protocol book of Thomas Auchinlek, 1576-1615
NP 1.43	Protocol book of Ronald Brown, 1584-1607
NP 2.1	Register of admissions
PS 1.	Register of the privy seal of Scotland
RD 1.1 etc	The Register of Deeds
RH 1.2.373	(Letters by two Brechin canons)
RH 2.1.20	Transcript of protocol book of James Harlaw
RH 2.1.22	Transcript of protocol book of sir Duncan Gray
RH 6.	Calendar of Register House Charters
RS 48	Perth Sasines secretaries' register
SP 13.68	(State Papers)

West Register House

RH 4.96	Microfilm of protocol book of William Pettilok
RHP 9280	Sketch of the royal burgh of Inverbervie
RHP 35213/14	Plans of Brechin Castle
NRA(S) 5	Inventory of writings belonging to the Right Hon. John Viscount of Arbuthnott, Lord Inverbervie
NRA(S) 124	Inventory of Jackson of Kirkbuddo writs
NRA(S) 224	Inventory of writs of Carnegy of Lour
NRA(S) 237	Inventory of Scottish muniments at Haigh
NRA(S) 217,369	Inventories of Kinfauns movements
NRA(S) 885	The Strathmore Writs
NRA(S) 0925	Inventory of Erroll Charters

GLASGOW

Glasgow University: Department of Scottish History
Draft calendars of materials in the Vatican archives: derived from Ross Fund materials
      Acta Sancti Paenitentiarae Apostolicae
      Resignationes et Consensus
      Lateran Register
      Register of Supplications
      Armarium
      Libri annatarum

KINNAIRD CASTLE, ANGUS

The Southesk private family muniments

LONDON

British Library
Add. mss 33,531   State papers (Scotland)
Add. mss 38,747   State papers (Scotland)
Egerton ms 1818   State papers (Scotland)
Egerton ms 1819   State papers (Scotland)

Public Record Office
SP 50.3   State papers (Scotland)
E 351/213   Accounts relative to Broughty Craig
E 351/3327   Accounts relative to Broughty Craig

MANCHESTER

The John Rylands University Library of Manchester
The Crawford muniments

MONTROSE

The Town House, Montrose
Montrose burgh muniments

PERTH

The Sandeman Library Archives Department
B 59/8/13   Protocol book of Malcolm Bower, 1572/3-78

ST ANDREWS

St Andrews University Library, Department of Manuscripts
Ms. index to graduates of St Andrews

PRIMARY SOURCES: PRINTED

Accounts of the Collectors of Thirds of Benefices, ed. G. Donaldson (SHS Edinburgh 1949).

Accounts of the Lord High Treasurer of Scotland, ed. T. Dickson/Sir J. Balfour Paul (Edinburgh 1877-1916).

Acta Facultatis Artium Universitatis Sanctiandree, 1413-1588, ed. A.I. Dunlop (SHS 1964).

Acts of the lords of council in public affairs, 1501-1554, ed. R.K. Hannay (Edinburgh 1932).

Acts of the parliaments of Scotland, ed. T. Thomson (1814).

Anderson, James, *The Winter Night* (Glasgow 1713).

Ane account of the familie of Innes (Spalding Club 1864).

Ane Resonyng by William Lamb, ed. Roderick J. Lyall (Aberdeen 1985).

Autobiography and diary of Mr James Melvill (Woodrow Society, Edinburgh 1842).

Ayr Burgh Accounts, ed. G.S. Pryde (SHS 1937).

Banff Charters, ed. J.H. Ramsay (Oxford 1915).

Beaugue, Jean de, *Histoire de la guerre d'Ecosse* (Maitland Club 1830).

Black Kalendar of Scotland, ed. A.H. Millar (Edinburgh 1884).

Book of Common Order (Knox's Liturgy), ed. G.W. Sprott (Edinburgh and London 1901).

Book of the Universall Kirk; Acts and Proceedings of the General Assemblies of the Kirk of Scotland, 1560-1618, ed. T. Thomson, (Bannatyne and Maitland Clubs, Edinburgh 1839-45).

Buik of the kirk of the Canagait, 1564-1567, ed. Alma B. Calderwood (SRS 1961).

Calderwood's History of the Kirk of Scotland, ed. T. Thomson (Wodrow Society, Edinburgh 1842-49).

Calendar of Laing charters, ed. J. Anderson (Edinburgh 1899).

Calendar of State Papers, foreign series, of the reign of King Edward VI, ed. W.B. Turnbull (London 1861).

Calendar of State Papers, foreign series, of the reign of Mary, ed. W.B. Turnbull (London 1861).

Calendar of State Papers, foreign series, of the reign of Queen Elizabeth: 1558-9, ed. J. Stevenson (London 1863) and further vols.

Calendar of State Papers relating to Scotland and Mary Queen of Scots, 1547-1603, vols i 1547-1563 to vi 1581-1583, ed. Joseph Bain and others (Edinburgh 1898-1910).

Calendar of writs at Yester House (SRS 1830).

Calvin: Institutes of the Christian Religion, ed. John T. McNeill (London 1961).

Catholic Tractates of the Sixteenth Century, 1573-1600, ed. T.G. Law (STS Edinburgh and London 1901), 'The Refutation of an ansver made be schir Iohne Knox to ane letter send by Iames Tyrie', Paris 1573.

Charters of the Abbey of Coupar Angus, ed. D.E. Easson (SHS xl + xli, 1947).

Charters, writs and public documents of the royal burgh of Dundee, 1292-1880, ed. William Hay (Dundee 1880).

Chronicles of the Frasers by Mr James Fraser, ed. W. Mackay (SHS 1905).

Clan Campbell: abstracts relating to Campbells in the books of council and session, ed. Rev Henry Paton (Edinburgh 1922).

Commissariot record of Brechin: register of testaments, 1576-1800, ed. Francis J. Grant (SRS Edinburgh 1902).

Complaynt of Scotland (c.1550) by Mr Robert Wedderburn, ed. A.M. Stewart (STS Edinburgh 1979).

Compt buik of David Wedderburn merchant of Dundee, 1587-1630, ed. A.H. Millar (SHS Edinburgh 1898).

Copiale Prioratus Sanctiandree, ed. J.H. Baxter (Oxford 1930).

Correspondance de Theodore de Beze, ed. H. Aubert (Geneva, 12 vols. 1960x1986).

Court Book of the Barony of Carnwath, 1523-42, ed. W.C. Dickinson, (SHS 1937).

Decades of Henry Bullinger, ed. Rev. Thomas Harding (Parker Society, Cambridge, vol. iv, 1851; vol. v, 1852).

Diurnal of remarkable occurrents in Scotland (Bannatyne Club 1833).

Douglas Book, ed. William C.B. Fraser (Edinburgh 1885).

Early records of the University of St Andrews, ed. J.M. Anderson (SHS 1926).

Estimate of the Scottish nobility during the minority of James the sixth, ed. Rev. Charles Rogers (The Grampian Club, London 1873).

Exchequer rolls of Scotland, ed. George Powell McNeill, vols. xvi 1529-36 to xxi 1580-88 (Edinburgh 1897-1901).

First Book of Discipline, ed. J.K. Cameron (Edinburgh 1972).

Geneva Bible, a facsimile of the 1560 edition (University of Wisconsin 1969).

Gude and Godlie Ballatis, ed. A.F. Mitchell (STS 1897).

Hamilton Papers: letters and papers illustrating the political relations of England and Scotland in the XVIth century, ed. J. Bain (Edinburgh 1890-92).

Historic Manuscripts Commission: appendix to Fifth Report (HMSO 1876).

History of the Reformation in Scotland by John Knox, ed. W.C. Dickinson (Edinburgh 1949).

Hume, David, *History of the House and Race of Douglas and Angus* (London 1820).

Inquisitionum ad capellam dominum regis retornatarum . . . abbreviatio, ed. Thomas Thomson (1811 by command).

Inventory of documents relating to the Scrymgeour family estates, 1611, ed. J. Maitland Thomson (SRS, Edinburgh 1912).

Letters and papers foreign and domestic of the reign of Henry VIII, ed. J. Gairdner and R.H. Brodie (HMSO 1901).

Letters and papers of Patrick, master of Gray (Bannatyne Club 1835).

Letters of James the fourth, 1505-13, ed. R.K. Hannay and R. Mackie (SHS 1953).

Letters of James Vth., ed. Denys Hay (Edinburgh 1954).

Liber ecclesiae de Scone (Bannatyne and Maitland Clubs 1843).

Liber S. Thome de Aberbrothoc 1329-1536 (Bannatyne Club 1856).

Melanchthon and Bucer, ed. Wilhelm Pauck (London 1969): 'De Regno Christi' (Bucer).

Memorials of transactions in Scotland, by Richard Bannatyne, ed. R. Pitcairn (Bannatyne Club 1836).

Narratives of Scottish Catholics under Mary Stuart and James VI, ed. William Forbes Leith (London 1889): 'Letter of Fr John Hay'.

New Testament in Scots; Purvey's revision of Wycliffe's version turned into Scots by Murdoch Nisbet c.1520, ed. T.G. Law (STS, 1901).

New Testament Octapla, ed. Luther A. Weigle (New York, 1962):
'The Tyndale Bible, 1534'
'The Great Bible, 1540'
'The Geneva Bible, 1560'.

Papers from the collection of Sir William Fraser, ed. J.R.N. Macphail (SHS 1924):
'Excerpts from the mss. of Mr John Napier'
'Ancestry of the family of Barclay of Mathers and Urie 1110 to 1610 AD.'
'Writs relative to the Hays of Urie'.

Petrie, A., *A compendious history of the Catholick Church (600-1600)* (The Hague 1662).

Pitcairn, R., *Ancient Criminal Trials in Scotland (1488-1624)* (Bannatyne and Maitland Clubs 1833).

Protocol book of dom. Thomas Johnstoun (SRS Edinburgh 1920).

Protocol book of Gilbert Grote (SRS Edinburgh 1914).

Protocol book of Nicol Thounis (SRS Edinburgh 1927).

Protocol book of sir John Cristisone, 1518-1551, ed. R.H. Lindsay (SRS, Edinburgh 1928).

Records of the Convention of the Royal Burghs of Scotland, 1295-1597 (Edinburgh 1866).

Register of Ministers, Exhorters and Readers, and of their stipends after the period of Reformation (Maitland Club 1830).

Register of the Great Seal of Scotland: Registrum Magni Sigilli Regum Scotorum, vols. 1513-46, 1546-80, 1580-93, ed. James Balfour Paul, J.M. Thomson and others (Edinburgh 1883-88).

Register of the Ministers, Elders and Deacons of St Andrews, 1559-1600, ed. D.H. Fleming (SHS Edinburgh 1889-90).

Register of the Privy Council of Scotland, ed. J.H. Burton and D. Masson, 1st ser., 14 vols. (Edinburgh 1877-1898).

Register of the Privy Seal of Scotland: Registrum Secreti Sigilli Regum Scotorum, vols. ii 1529-42 to viii 1581-84, ed. D.H. Fleming and others (Edinburgh 1921-1982).

Registrum de Panmure (Edinburgh 1874 privately).

Registrum domus de Soltre necnon ecclesie collegiate S. Trinitatis proper Edinburgh (Bannatyne Club 1861).

Registrum Episcopatus Brechinensis, ed. J.I. Chalmers (Aberdeen 1856).

Remains of Edmund Grindal, ed. W. Nicholson (London 1843).

Rentale Book of the Cistercian Abbey of Cupar-Angus, ed. Rev. Charles Rogers (The Grampian Club, London): vol i 1897, vol ii 1880.

Rentale Sancti Andree, 1538-46, ed. R.K. Hannay (SHS 1913).

St Andrews Formulare 1514-1546, ed. G. Donaldson and C. Macrae (Stair Soc. 1942, 1944).

Satirical poems of the time of the Reformation, ed. James Cranstoun (STS, Edinburgh 1843).

Scots Confession of 1560, ed. G.D. Henderson, trans. James Bulloch (Edinburgh 1960).

Scottish Correspondence of Mary of Lorraine, ed. A.I. Cameron (SHS, Edinburgh 1927).

Second Book of Discipline, ed. James Kirk (Edinburgh 1980).

Spalding Club Miscellany, vol. ii (Aberdeen 1842):
'The chronicle of Aberdeen'
'The Arbuthnott Papers'
'The Pittodrie Papers'
'The Errol Papers'.

Spalding Club Miscellany, vol. iv (Aberdeen 1849):
'Ane letter wrettin to the Queinis grace and regent, be the professouris of Christis ewangell, in the realme of Scotland'
'Ane epistill wrettin to any faythfull brother, be Johne Erskyne of Dwne' ('Of the Kirk of God')
'Ane sermon vpone the ix. chapter of Mathew, at the 37 and 38 verses'
'Ane sermon vpone the seventh chapter of Luke from the 36th verse'.

(Third) Spalding Club Miscellany, vol. ii (Aberdeen 1940):
'A genealogie of the barons of the Mearns'.

Tracts by David Fergusson (Bannatyne Club 1860).

Two Books of Common Prayer . . . in the reign of King Edward the Sixth (Oxford 1838).

Wodrow Miscellany, vol. i (Edinburgh 1844):

'A Historie of the Estate of Scotland'
'Ane Compendius Tractive etc . . . be Maister Quintine Kennedy' (1558)
'The forme and maner of buriall used in the kirk of Montrois'.
Wodrow, Rev. Robert, *Collections upon the lives of the Reformers,* ed. W.J. Duncan (Maitland Club, Glasgow 1834).
Works of John Knox, ed. D. Laing (Wodrow Society, Edinburgh 1846-64).
Zwingli and Bullinger, ed. Rev. G. Bromiley (London 1953):
'Of the Holy Catholic Church' (Bullinger).

REFERENCE WORKS

Adams, David G., *Celtic and mediaeval religious houses in Angus* (Brechin 1984).
Burghs of Scotland by George Smith Pryde, ed. A.A.M. Duncan (Oxford 1965).
Cowan, I.B., *Parishes of medieval Scotland* (SRS, 1967).
Cowan, I.B. and Easson, D.E., *Medieval Religious Houses of Scotland* (London 1976).
Craven, Neil, *A bibliography of the county of Angus* (Forfar 1975).
Dictionary of National Biography.
Fasti Ecclesiae Scoticanae, ed. Hew Scott (new ed. 1915-50).
Ferguson, Joan P.S., *Scottish Family Histories* (Edinburgh 1986).
Haws, C.H. *Scottish parish clergy at the Reformation* (SRS, 1972).
MacGibbon, D. and Ross T., *The castellated and domestic architecture of Scotland from the 12th to the 18th centuries* (Edinburgh 1887).
Matheson, Glenis A. and Taylor, F., *Handlist of personal papers from the muniments of the earl of Crawford and Balcarres, deposited in the John Rylands University Library of Manchester* (Manchester 1976).
New Statistical Account, vol. xi (Edinburgh 1845).
Scots Peerage, ed. Sir James Balfour Paul (Edinburgh 1910-1914).
Watt, D.E.R., *Fasti Ecclesiae Scoticanae Medii Aevi ad annum 1638* (SRS, 1969).

SECONDARY SOURCES

Apocalypse in English Renaissance thought and literature, ed. C.A. Patrides and Joseph Wittreich (Machester 1984).
Arbuthnot, Mrs P.S.-M., *Memoires of the Arbuthnots of Kincardineshire and Aberdeenshire* (London 1920).
Avis, Paul D.L., *The Church in the Theology of the Reformers* (London 1981).
Bauckham, Richard, *Tudor Apocalypse* (Oxford 1978).
Black, David Dakers, *Brechin* (Alexander Black 1839).
Blair-Imrie, William, *A record of Lunan, its transmission from 1189 to 1849* (privately, 1902).
Brown, Jennifer M., *Scottish society in the Fifteenth Century* (London 1977).
Brown, K.M., *Bloodfeud in Scotland, 1573-1625* (Edinburgh 1986).
Bryce, W.M., *The Scottish Grey Friars* (Edinburgh 1909).
Buchan, P., *An account of the ancient and noble family of Keith* (Peterhead 1820).
Chadwick, Owen, *The Reformation* (London 1972).
Church, Politics and Society, ed. Norman Macdougall (Edinburgh 1983).
Collinson, P., *The Elizabethan Puritan Movement* (London 1967).
Collinson, P., *The religion of Protestants* (Oxford 1984).
Cowan, Ian B., *The Scottish Reformation* (London 1982).

Dickens, A.G., *Lollards and Protestants in the Diocese of York* (London 1959).

Donaldson, Gordon, *All the Queen's Men* (London 1983).

Donaldson, Gordon, *James V to James VII* (Edinburgh 1978).

Donaldson, Gordon, *Mary Queen of Scots* (London 1974).

Donaldson, Gordon, *Scottish Church History* (Edinburgh 1985).

Donaldson, Gordon, *The Scottish Reformation* (Cambridge 1960).

Dundee and District, ed. S.J. Jones (The British Association 1968).

Durkan, John and Ross, Anthony, *Early Scottish Libraries* (Glasgow 1961).

Early Modern Town in Scotland, ed. M. Lynch (London 1987).

Elton, G.R., *Reformation Europe* (London 1963).

Fairweather A., *Memorandum on the Fairweathers of Menmuir parish, Forfarshire* (London 1898).

Fathers of the Kirk, ed. Ronald Selby Wright (Oxford 1960).

Firth, Katherine, *The Apocalyptic tradition in Reformation Britain* (Oxford 1979).

Forbes-Leith, W.S., *Pre-Reformation scholars in Scotland in the XVIth century* (Glasgow 1915).

Fraser, William, *History of the Carnegies, earls of Southesk* (Edinburgh 1867, privately).

Gilbert, Alan D., *The making of post-Christian Britain* (London 1980).

Gill, R., *Theology and Social Structure* (London 1977).

Grant, I.F., *The social and economic development of Scotland before 1603* (Edinburgh 1930).

Greaves, Richard L., *Theology and revolution in the Scottish Reformation* (Washington 1980).

Greeley, Andrew M., *The persistence of religion* (London 1973).

Guthrie, D.C., *The Guthrie family* (privately, 1906).

Haldane, A.R.B., *The Drove Roads of Scotland* (Edinburgh 1960).

Haller, William, *Foxe's Book of Martyrs and the Elect Nation* (London, 1963).

Hay, George, *History of Arbroath to the present time* (Arbroath 1876 and 1899).

Henderson, George A., *The kirk of St. Ternan, Arbuthnott* (Edinburgh 1962).

Hewitt, George R., *Scotland under Morton, 1572-1580* (Edinburgh 1982).

History of the King's Works, vol. iv: 1485-1666, pt. ii, ed. H.M. Colvin and others (HMSO, London 1982).

International Calvinism, 1541-1715, ed. Menna Prestwich (Oxford 1985).

Jacob, Violet, *The lairds of Dun* (London 1931).

Jervise, Andrew, *Memorials of Angus and Mearns,* revised by James Gammack (Edinburgh 1885).

Jones, N., *Faith by Statute* (London 1982).

Kyle, Richard G., *The mind of John Knox* (Kansas 1984).

Lamont, William, *Godly Rule* (London 1969).

Larner, Christina, *Enemies of God* (Oxford 1983).

Larner, Christina, *Witchcraft and Religion* (Oxford 1984).

Lee, M.jr., *Government by Pen* (London 1980).

Lindsay, Lord, *Lives of the Lindsays* (London 1849).

Locher, G.W., *Zwingli's Thought: New Perspectives* (Brill 1981).

Low, James G., *Edzell Castle past and present* (Montrose 1900).

Low, James G., *Galraw, home of the Foullartons* (Montrose 1937).

Low, James G., *Memorials of the Church of St John the Evangelist* (Montrose 1891).

Lynch, Michael, *Edinburgh and the Reformation* (Edinburgh 1981).

Lythe, S.G.E., *The economy of Scotland in its European setting* (Edinburgh 1960).

McCrie, T., *Life of Andrew Melville* (Edinburgh 1824).

McEwen, James S., *The Faith of John Knox* (London 1961).

Makey, W., *The Church of the Covenant, 1637-1651* (Edinburgh 1979).

Malcolm, J., *The parish of Monifieth in ancient and modern times* (Edinburgh 1910).

Martin, David, *The religious and the secular* (London 1969).

Maxwell, Alexander, *The history of old Dundee* (Edinburgh/Dundee 1884).

Medieval church of St Andrews, ed. David McRoberts (Glasgow 1976).

Miller, David, *Arbroath and its abbey* (Edinburgh 1860).

Mitchison, Rosalind, *Life in Scotland* (London 1978).

Mullan, David George, *Episcopacy in Scotland* (Edinburgh 1986).

Munro, R.W. and Munro, Jean, *The Scrymgeours and their chiefs* (Edinburgh 1980).

New perspectives on the politics and culture of early modern Scotland, ed. J. Dwyer and others (Edinburgh 1982).

O'Day, Rosemary, *The debate on the English Reformation* (London 1986).

O'Dea, Thomas F. and Aviad, Janet O'Dea, *The sociology of religion* (London 1983).

Olsen, V. Norskov, *John Foxe and the Elizabethan Church* (Berkeley 1973).

Percy, Lord E., *John Knox* (London 1937).

Reid, Alan, *The royal burgh of Forfar, a local history* (Forfar 1902).

Reid, Alan, *The regality of Kirriemuir* (Edinburgh 1909).

Reid, W. Stanford, *Trumpeter of God* (Michigan 1974).

Religion and Society in early modern Europe, ed. Kaspar von Greyerz (London 1984).

Renaissance and Reformation in Scotland, essays in honour of Gordon Donaldson, ed. Ian B. Cowan and Duncan Shaw (Edinburgh 1983).

Ridley, J., *John Knox* (Oxford 1968).

Robertson, R., *The sociological interpretation of religion* (London 1970).

Rogers, Rev. C., *Life of George Wishart, the Scottish martyr* (Grampian Club 1876).

Rogers, Rev. C., *Memorials of the Scottish families of Strachan and Wise* (Grampian Club 1877).

Rose, D.M., *Allardice of that ilk* (xerox, Edinburgh Central Library).

Ross, A., *The Lyons of Cossins and Wester Ogil* (Edinburgh 1901).

Row, J., *Histoire of the Kirk of Scotland* (Maitland Club 1842), pt. i.

Rupp, Gordon, *Patterns of Reformation* (London 1969).

Sanderson, Margaret B., *Cardinal of Scotland: David Beaton, 1494-1546* (Edinburgh 1986).

Sanderson, Margaret B., *Scottish rural society in the 16th century* (Edinburgh 1982).

Scarisbrick, J.J., *The Reformation and the English People* (Oxford 1984).

Scott, Rev. James, *A history of the lives of the Protestant reformers in Scotland* (Edinburgh 1810).

Scott, J.M., *Martyrs of Angus and Mearns* (Arbroath 1885).

Scottish Nation, ed. Gordon Menzies (London 1972).

Shaw, D., *The General Assemblies of the Church of Scotland, 1560-1600* (Edinburgh 1975).

Source Book of Scottish Witchcraft, ed. C. Larner, C. Lee and H. McLachlan (Glasgow 1977).

Studies in Church History, ed. D. Baker (Oxford 1979).

Studies in the history of worship in Scotland, ed. Duncan Forrester and Douglas Murray (Edinburgh 1984).

Thomas, Keith, *Religion and the decline of magic* (London 1971).

Thoms, David Boath, *The council of Brechin: a study in local government* (The Society of Friends of Brechin Cathedral 1971).

Thornton-Kemsley, Colin, *Bonnet Lairds* (Montrose 1972).

Tyrie, A., *The Tyries of Drumkilbo, Dunnideer and Lunan* (Glasgow 1893).

Warden, Alexander J., *Angus or Forfarshire* (Dundee 1880-1885).

Warden, Alexander J., *History of the Scrymgeours* (Dundee 1886).

Wedderburn, A., *The Wedderburn Book* (1898 privately).

Wendel, Francois, *Calvin* (London 1980).

Williamson, Arthur, *Scottish National Consciousness in the age of James VI* (Edinburgh 1979).

Wilson, B., *Religion in sociological perspective* (Oxford 1982).

Wilson, R., *The House of Airlie* (London 1924).

Wishart, D. *Genealogical history of the Wisharts of Pitarrow and Logie-Wishart* (Perth 1914).

Wormald, Jenny, *Court, Kirk and Community: Scotland, 1470-1625* (London 1981).

PUBLISHED ARTICLES

Adams, David G., 'Maidlin Chapel' *SFBC* (1984).

Anderson, W.J., 'Two documents of the Scottish Reformation' *IR* x (1959).

Apted, M.R. and Robertson, W. Norman, 'Late fifteenth century church paintings from Guthrie and Fowlis Easter' *Proceedings of the society of antiquaries of Scotland* (1961-62).

Arbroath Abbey, ed. R. Fawcett and others (HMSO 1982).

Bardgett. F.D., 'Four parische kirkis to ane preicheir' *RSCHS* xxii (1986).

Brown, Keith M., 'The nobility of Jacobean Scotland, 1567-1625' *History Today* xxxiiii (December 1984).

Burleigh, J.H.S., 'The Scottish Reforming Councils, 1549-1559' *RSCHS* xi (1955).

Burrell, S.A., 'The Apocalyptic vision of the early covenanters' *SHR* xliii (1964).

Cameron, James K., 'Aspects of the Lutheran contribution to the Scottish Reformation' *RSCHS* xxii pt. 1 (1984).

Cameron, James K., 'The Cologne reformation and the Church of Scotland' *JEH* xxx no. 1 (January 1979).

Christensen, Thorkild Lyby, 'Scots in Denmark in the sixteenth century' *SHR* xlix (1970).

Cowan, E.J., 'The Angus Campbells: origins of the Campbell/Ogilvy feud' *Scottish Studies* xxv (1981).

Cowan, I.B., 'The Reformation in Dumfriesshire' *Transactions of the Dumfriesshire and Galloway Natural History and Antiquarian Society* 3rd series lxi (1981).

Cowan, I.B., 'Some aspects of the appropriation of parish churches in medieval Scotland' *RSCHS* xiii (1959).

Cowan, I.B., 'Vicarages and the cure of souls in Medieval Scotland' *RSCHS* xvi (1969).

Cross, C., 'The development of protestantism in Leeds and Hull: the evidence from wills' *Northern History* xviii (1982).

Devine, T.M. and Lythe, S.G.E., 'The economy of Scotland under James VI, a revision article' *SHR* l (1971).

Dilworth, Mark, 'Monks and Ministers after 1560' *RSCHS* xviii (1974).

Donaldson, Gordon, 'The parish clergy and the Scottish Reformation' *IR* x (1959).

Donaldson, Gordon, 'Scottish parish clergy at the Reformation by Charles H. Haws, a review article' *SHR* liii (1974).

Donaldson, Gordon, 'The Second Book of Discipline edited by James Kirk, a review article' *SHR* lxi (1982).

Doughty, D.W., 'The Library of James Stewart, earl of Moray' *IR* xxi-ii (1970-1).

Duncan, A.A.M., 'Hector Bruce and the medieval tradition' *Scots antiquaries and historians* (Abertay Historical Society, Dundee, no. 16).

Durkan, John, 'Chaplains in Late Medieval Scotland' *RSCHS* xx (1980).

Durkan, John, 'Commentary' *Northern Scotland* v (1984-5).

Durkan, John, 'Henry Scrymgeour, Renaissance Bookman' *Edinburgh Bibliographical Society Transactions* v pt. 1 (1978).

Durkan, John, 'James, Third Earl of Arran: the Hidden Years' *SHR* lxv (1986).

Edzell Castle, ed. R. Fawcett (HMSO 1982).

Fergusson, James, 'On the fringes of fame: Thomas Maule of Panmure' *Scots Magazine* ns.xxix (1938).

Hannay, R.K., 'Some Papal Bulls among the Hamilton Papers' *SHR* xxii (1925).

Haws, C.H., 'Continuity and change: the reformation in the diocese of Moray, 1560-1574' *Northern Scotland* v (1983).

Haws, C.H., 'The diocese of St Andrews at the Reformation' *RSCHS* xviii (1974).

Haws, C.H., 'Scottish religious orders at the Reformation' *RSCHS* xvi (1969).

Keeling, S., 'The Reformation in the Anglo-Scottish Border Counties' *Northern History* xv (1979).

Kirk, J., 'The influence of Calvinism on the Scottish Reformation' *RSCHS* xviii (1972-74).

Kirk, J., 'The Kirk and the Highlands' *Northern Scotland* vi (1986).

Kyle, R., 'The Nature of the Church in the thought of John Knox' *SJT* xxxvii (1985).

Lake, Peter, 'The Significance of the Elizabethan identification of the Pope as Antichrist' *JEH* xxxi (1980).

Lenman, Bruce, 'Alexander Warden and the local history of Dundee and Angus', *Scots Antiquaries* (Abertay Historical Society no. 16).

Lindsay, J., 'The Lindsays of Evelick' *Publications of the Clan Lindsay Society* vol. iii no. 9 (1925).

Lindsay, J., 'The Lindsays of Kinnettles' *Publications of the Clan Lindsay Society* vol. iii no. 11 (1928).

Lindsay, J., 'The Lindsays of Pitairlie' *Publications of the Clan Lindsay Society* vol. iii no. 10 (1926).

McKay, Denis, 'Parish Life in Scotland, 1500-1560' *IR* x (1959).

McNeill, John T., 'The Church in Reformed Theology' *The Journal of Religion* xxii (1942).

McNeill, W.A., 'Scottish entries in the Acta Rectoria Universitatis Parisiensis' *SHR* xliii (1964).

Mahoney, M., 'The Scottish hierarchy, 1513-1565' *IR* x (1959).

Merriman, M.H., 'The assured Scots: Scottish collaborators with England during the rough wooing' *SHR* xlvii (1968).

Meyhew, G.L. 'The progress of the Reformation in East Sussex — the evidence from wills' *Southern History* v (1983).

Mitchison, Rosalind, 'The Making of the Old Scottish Poor Law' *Past and Present* lxiii (May 1974).

Mudie, Sir R.F. and Walker, D.M., *Mains Castle and the Grahams of Fintry* (Abertay Historical Society Publication no. 8, 1964).

Mudie, Sir R.F., Walker, D.M. and MacIvor, I., *Broughty Castle* (Abertay Historical Society Publication no. 15, 1970).

Muller, G., 'Protestant theology in Scotland and Germany in the early days of the Reformation' *RSCHS* xxii pt. ii (1985).

Ramsay, Sir James Henry of Bamff, 'Ogilvies of Auchterhouse, Ogilvies of Airlie, Ogilvies of Inverquharity, Ogilvies of Clova' *The Genealogist* xxxv (1919).

Reid, W. Stanford, 'Clerical taxation: the Scottish alternative to dissolution of the monasteries, 1530-1560' *Catholic Historical Review* xxxv pt.2 (1948).

Sanderson, M.H.B., 'Catholic Recusancy in Scotland in the Sixteenth century' *IR* xxi (1970).

Sanderson, M.H.B., 'Manse and Glebe in the Sixteenth Century' *RSCHS* xi (1974).

Shaw, D., 'Zwinglian Influences on the Scottish Reformation' *RSCHS* xxii pt.11 (1985).

Spufford, M., 'The scribes of villagers' wills' *Local Population Studies* vii (1971).

Taylor, M., 'The conflicting doctrines of the Scottish Reformation' *IR* x (1959).

Thoms, David Boath, 'The Cathedral Kirk of Brechin' *SFBC* xi (1958).

Thoms, David Boath, 'The chanonry of Brechin' *SFBC* xxvii (1978).

Thoms, David Boath, 'Maisondieu' *SFBC* xiv (1962).

Thoms, David Boath, 'The College of Brechin' *SFBC* iii (1950).

Thoms, David Boath, 'Church and school in Brechin' 1560-1872' *SFBC* ix (1956).

Torrance, Iain R., 'Patrick Hamilton and John Knox: a study in the doctrine of Justification by Faith' *Archiv für Reformationsgeschichte* lxv (1974).

Wallace, D. D. jnr., 'Puritan propaganda and popular religion in Elizabethan England' *Sixteenth Century Journal* ix no.1 (1978).

Watt, Donald E.R., 'The organisation of the medieval diocese of Brechin' *SFBC* xix (1970).

Wiedermann, Gotthelf, 'Alexander Alesius' lectures on the psalms at Cambridge, 1536' *JEH* xxxvii no.1 (1986).

Wiedermann, G., 'Martin Luther versus John Fisher: the debate on Lutheran Theology at St Andrews' *RSCHS* xxii pt.i (1984).

Yellowlees, Michael J., 'The ecclesiastical establishment of the diocese of Dunkeld at the Reformation' *IR* xxxvi no.2 (1985).

Zupko, Ronald Edward, 'The weights and measures of Scotland before the union' *SHR* lvi (1977).

UNPUBLISHED THESES and other works

Bardgett, F.D., 'Faith, families and factions: the Scottish Reformation in Angus and the Mearns' (Edinburgh Ph.D. 1987).

Brown, Keith M., 'The extent and nature of feuding in Scotland 1573-1625' (Glasgow Ph.D. 1983).

Bush, M.L., 'The rise to power of Edward Seymour, Protector Somerset' (Cambridge Ph.D. 1964).

Crockett, Thomas, 'The Life of John Erskine of Dun' (Edinburgh D.Litt. 1924).

Demura, Akira, 'Church discipline according to Joannes Oecolampadius in the setting of his life and thought' (Princeton Th.D. 1964).

Flett, Iain E.F., 'The conflict of the reformation and democracy in the Geneva of Scotland' 1443-1610' (St Andrews M.Phil. 1981).

Haws, Charles H., 'Scottish parish clergy at the Reformation' (Glasgow Ph.D. 1969).

Kelley, M.G.R., 'The Douglas earls of Angus: a study in the social and political bases of power' (Edinburgh Ph.D. 1973).

Kerr, T.A., 'John Craig 1512?-1600' (Edinburgh Ph.D. 1954).

Kirk, James, 'The development of the Melvillian movement in late sixteenth century Scotland' (Edinburgh Ph.D. 1972).

Low, James G., 'The ancient hospital of Montrose' (ms lecture 1942; Montrose public library 58.362.5).

McLennan, Bruce, 'Presbyterianism challenged, a study of catholicism in the north-east of Scotland 1560-1650' (Aberdeen Ph.D. 1977).

Mason, R.S., 'Kingship and commonweal: political thought and ideology in Reformation Scotland' (Edinburgh Ph.D. 1983).

Merriman, M.H., 'The struggle for the marriage of Mary, queen of Scots' (London Ph.D. 1975).

Murray, Athol L., 'The exchequer and crown revenues of Scotland' (Edinburgh Ph.D. 1961).

Sanderson, M.H.B., 'The social and economic implications of the feuing of ecclesiastical property in Scotland in the late 15th and 16th centuries' (Edinburgh Ph.D. 1972).

Todd, John R., 'The Reformation in the diocese of Dunblane' (Edinburgh Ph.D. 1973).

White, A.J., 'Religion, Politics and Society in Aberdeen' (Edinburgh Ph.D. 1985).

Young, John G.B., 'Scottish political parties, 1573-1603' (Edinburgh Ph.D. 1976).

Index

SELECT INDEX OF PLACES AND SUBJECTS

Arbroath 4, 133, 134, 136, 137-8.
Arbroath, abbey of 13, 28, 51, 58, 78, 92, 133
'Assured' Lairds 29-33, 36-7

'Beggars' Summons' (1559) 69-70
Bonds of Manrent 35, 53, 54, 72, 76-7, 78, 80, 138, 140
Books of Discipline 82, 87, 94, 96, 102-4, 108-9, 111, 149
Brechin 1, 7, 59, 74-6, 106, 107, 122, 134
Broughty Castle 29, 31-3, 54, 99, 123, 133, 134-6

Churches, repair of 106-7
Complaynt of Scotland, by Mr Robert Wedderburn 42-4
Coupar Abbey 36, 53, 73, 78, 122, 124, 126

Dundee 4, 7, 20, 25, 28-9, 35, 45-6, 69, 70, 110, 120-21

Elders 95-102, 151-3, 157-8, 159-162

Farnell 122-3, 131, 133
Feuds 128, 131, 134, 140, 159-61, 162-4, 165
Finavon, spulzie of 8-9, 11-13, 26

Gude and Godlie Ballatis 45

Iconoclasm 28-9

King's Men Bonds 128-30, 139

Lamentation of Lady Scotland (1572) 106-7, 132, 140

Manse and Glebe 104-6
Marriage, contracts of 11-2, 13-4, 80, 121, 123, 124, 140
Monifieth 30-1, 96-100, 102-4, 106, 136-7, 157-62, 166
Montrose 7, 34, 35, 70, 121

Privy Kirks 46-8, 53, 61, 95

Reformation Parliament (1560) 78-81
Register of Assignation and Modification of Stipends 90, 97-8, 107-9, 110

Wills (testament evidence of) 52, 59, 100, 147-50, 153-4, 155-7, 158.

SELECT INDEX OF PERSONS

NOTE: this index includes dates and/or brief descriptions of the persons listed as a guide to their identity. Apart from normal works of reference, the main source for dates is F. Bardgett, 'Faith, families and factions', ii appendix B (Lairds and Magnates). Dates are given new style.

Listing is by family surname in all cases in order to group earls with lairds of their name.

Key
b. = born this year.
c. = around (normally, before this date).
d. = died during this year/s.
f. = flourished (known to be alive at date given).
s. = succeeded to title/lands.

Abercromby, sir Robert 75-6
Airlie, Lords Ogilvy of: see under Ogilvy
Alane, Alexander 40 n.54.
Allardice, John of that Ilk *(s.1540; d.1547)* 33.
Allardice, John of that Ilk *(s.1547)* 50, 79.
Airlie, Lord: see Keith, Mr Robert
Anderson, James in the North Ferry 31, 97, 99.
Anderson, Mr Thomas 69, 93, 95, 117 n.84, n.98, 150, 155.

Angus, Earl of: see under Douglas
Arbroath, abbots and commendator of: see Beaton, David; Douglas, George; Hamilton, Lord John; Stewart, Esmé
Arbuthnott, Mr Alexander 51
Arbuthnott, Andrew of that Ilk *(s.1579)* 79
Arbuthnott, David of that ilk *(d.1522)* 51.
Arbuthnott, Robert of that ilk *(s.1522: d.1579)* 50 n.9, 17 n .56, 24, 26-7, 51, 79.

DATE DUE

HIGHSMITH   # 45220